Insight & outlook:

A COLLECTION OF SHORT STORIES

Okanagan Regional Correspondence School
P.O. Bag 4700
Merritt, B.C.
V0K 2B0
378-4245
1-800-662-3536

Insight & outlook:

CARSON McCULLERS
RUTH SUCKOW
LANGSTON HUGHES
NATHANIEL BENCHLEY
MONTY CULVER
MARY LAVIN
ISAAC ASIMOV
ANNA GUEST
BORDEN DEAL
WILLIAM IVERSEN
HUGH PENTECOST
J. F. POWERS
SHIRLEY JACKSON
ENRY GREGOR FELSEN
PATRICK McCALLUM
DOROTHY WEST

Insight & outlook:

A COLLECTION OF SHORT STORIES

Edited by
MURRAY ROCKOWITZ

 GLOBE BOOK COMPANY, Inc. NEW YORK 10010

About the Editor

MURRAY ROCKOWITZ has served as a department chairman and principal in the New York City School System. As chairman of English, he innovated reading programs for high school students of varying abilities. A member of the Board of Examiners of the New York City Board of Education, Dr. Rockowitz is a specialist in reading problems and holds the degree of Ph.D. from New York University.

SECOND EDITION 1975. Copyright © 1970 by Globe Book Company, Inc. 50 West 23rd Street, New York, N.Y. 10010

This edition may be used with all other editions, in the same classroom, without conflict of any kind.

Third Edition 1987

ISBN: 0-87065-150-1

Published simultaneously in Canada by Globe/Modern Curriculum Press. Copyright © 1970 by Globe Book Company, Inc., 190 Sylvan Avenue, Englewood Cliffs, New Jersey 07632. All rights reserved. No part of this book may be kept in an information storage or retrieval system, transmitted or reproduced in any form or by any means without the prior written permission of the publisher.

Printed in the United States of America.

30   29   28   27   26   25   24   23   22   21   20

Contents

Introduction

The stories in this collection were chosen primarily for you to enjoy. But in addition to bringing you pleasure, these stories present problems for the mature student, problems that can be profitably discussed in class and, if properly thought through, lead to a deeper, more adult, understanding of yourself and the world.

After reading the stories in this collection, you will want to continue to read short stories on your own. Good short stories can be found in magazines, such as *The New Yorker* and the *Atlantic,* in other books by the authors you will meet, and in annual collections of the best short stories.

READING THE SHORT STORY

"Have you heard this one?" "Listen to this!" "Tell me a story." These requests indicate man's interest in stories from the beginning of time. For many thousands of years, stories were passed from generation to generation orally either in words or in song. These stories were religious or national in character. Stories that attempt to explain natural happenings are called *myths.* *Epics,* stories told in verse, tend to glorify national heroes. Animal tales with moral lessons added have come down to us from Greece and India with Aesop the most famous writer of these *fables.* The Bible is full of stories: Ruth, Esther, Jonah, and Daniel are among many in the Old Testament; there are many *parables* in the New Testament. In the Middle Ages *A Thousand and One Nights,* Boccaccio's *Decameron,* Chaucer's *Canterbury Tales,* and other verse collections testify to the popularity of story-telling.

In the four hundred years after Chaucer's death in 1400, literature in England excelled both in poetry and prose, but story-telling was mainly in the form of long novels. In nineteenth-century America, the short story came into its own. Most important in its development were three writers: Washington Irving, Edgar Allan Poe, and Nathaniel Hawthorne. It has been said that "Irving . . . discovered the short story and introduced a form which has become the most characteristic product of American literature." His *Sketch Book* contains "Rip Van Winkle" and "The Legend of Sleepy Hollow." It was Poe who defined the short story in his "Philosophy of Composition" and left us such masterpieces as "The Gold Bug," "The Pit and the Pendulum," and "The Murders in the Rue Morgue." Hawthorne's *Twice Told Tales, Mosses from an Old Manse,* and *The Snow Image and Other Twice Told Tales* are three collections of classic short stories. These led the way for such writers as Bret Harte and O. Henry. It was O. Henry who led off the short story explosion in 1904 with his *Cabbages and Kings.* It has made the twentieth century in America the century of the short story.

The short story seems to be well suited to the American reader. It is brief. (It can be finished in a single sitting, in most cases.) It is concentrated. (The characters are few in number and the action is limited.) Only the short story brings so much pleasure for such a small investment in time and effort.

You will not go wrong if you ask yourself these three questions about any story you read: What is happening? To whom? Why?

If this were all you asked, however, you would miss out on many of the less obvious aspects of the short story. The fact that the story is short forces the reader to fill in many of the details himself. Sometimes the point of the story has to be gathered by the reader from the tone of the story and the nature of the characters in it. Many writers in recent years have been content with creating a mood, getting the reader interested, and then leaving him to wonder about the outcome.

The *Guide to Reading the Short Story* that follows will help in your reading. Not all the questions included in the guide will apply to every story, but many will. You need not use the guide for all the stories in this book. Too much analysis may destroy the fun of just reading them. Sensible analysis, however, will provide you not only with an appreciation of the short story as a form of literature but also with an understanding of the meaning of the stories you read.

GUIDE TO READING THE SHORT STORY

Setting

Place. Where does the action of the story take place? How do you know? (By description? By the action? By the dialogue?) What effect, if any, does the setting have on the action in the story?

Time. When does the action of the story take place? Past? Present? Future? At what time of year (or at what time of day) does the action take place? How is this made clear to the reader? How long does the action take? Are there any flashbacks? What effect does time have on the action?

Point of View

From whose point of view is the story told? Does the main character tell his own version of the action? Or does an observer who takes part in the action describe what takes place? (Both of these points of view are *first person* accounts of the action.)

Is the story told by an observer-author who reports the action objectively and relates what is said without interpretation, but who does not tell the thoughts and feelings of the characters? Or is it told by an omniscient (all-knowing) author who can enter into and analyze the thought of one or more of the characters and who can also explain their feelings? (Both of these points of view are *third person* accounts of the action.) Is the action seen through the eyes of only one character?

Characters

Who is involved in the story? How are they identified? (By their words? By their thoughts? By their actions? By the words and actions of others?) How do they happen to come together at the place and time of the action?

What relationships exist among the characters? Do these change in the course of the story? Why do the characters act as they do? Do the characters themselves change in the course of the story? Do their actions come about as a natural result of their personal qualities?

Conflict

What kind of conflict takes place in the story? Is it physical? (Between man and man or man and nature?) Is it a conflict of ideas? Is it a conflict of emotions? Is it a conflict within a single character? Or is it between two characters or groups of characters? (Note: More than one conflict may take place in a single story.)

Development

Is the story a single incident or a series of actions? Do the actions follow naturally from one another? Do they build up suspensefully to a climax, the high point in the action? Do they build up to a moment of truth where the meaning of the action is made known?

Conclusion

How is the conflict resolved? (Does one side triumph?) Does the conclusion result naturally from the setting, the characters, and the series of actions which led up to it? Is the conclusion true to life? Is it satisfying to you, the reader?

Theme

What is the meaning of the story? What point was the author trying to get across? Why do you think he wrote the story? What meaning is suggested, if it is not stated? How universal are the characters or objects in the story? (To what degree are they symbols?)

The Story As a Whole

Unity. Is the story unified? Is it told from a single point of view? Do the actions within the story add to the total effect or do they take away from it?

Tone. Is the author's attitude toward the action and the characters (and you, the reader) consistent throughout? Is the author detached or involved? Is the tone serious and sober or light and humorous? Does it accept things as they are or poke fun at them?

Style. Is the diction (vocabulary) suited to the characters and to the action? Is the dialogue realistic and convincing? Are the descriptions vivid and accurate?

Compression. Are important items chosen to create a single effect? Is the selection honest? Is too much included or is too much left out?

Effect

Does the story get me involved as the reader? Does it make me think? Does it capture my emotions? Do I share in the characters' difficulties, or am I repelled by them? Do I accept the theme of the story, or do I reject it? Does the story satisfy my purpose in reading it? Does it entertain? Does it add to my knowledge?

FACING
LIFE'S
PROBLEMS

Y OU'LL never forget some moments in your life: the first date you ever had, the first dollar you earned, the first trip you ever took away from home.

The stories you are about to read show important moments in people's lives—that first job, the decision to leave home, the unforgettable quarrel with a friend. These are the ways people grow toward maturity—at times through bitter experience, at times through sheer determination.

These stories, while they depict very ordinary crises of day-to-day life, are works of art. They get you involved emotionally. You feel Daisy Switzer's loneliness. You share Nancy Lee's disappointment. You understand Pete's rejection of his cousin.

Don't look for the "and they lived happily ever after" of the world of the fairy tale in these stories. As in life, sometimes the crisis is happily resolved. But more often, the moment of crisis lingers on, leaving you and the characters in the story wondering when, if ever, there will be a genuine conclusion.

The stories often focus on how people react to events rather than on the events themselves. A young girl spends her first day away from home. A high school girl thinks about an acceptance speech, only to find that she hasn't won the prize. But because of the skill with which the authors create the characters in these stories and make you a party to their feelings, you begin to know all people just a bit better. Indeed, you will gain new understanding of that most elusive character of all—yourself.

Sucker

CARSON McCULLERS

Approaching the Story . . .

HAVE you ever had a younger relative look up to you and make you feel like the most important person in the world? How did you treat him in return? Were you generous, or did you make him feel small and unimportant? In this story, you will meet Pete and Sucker who are more than just cousins. Most brothers and almost all teen-agers have experienced their moods and their problems. After you've read the story, you'll put the book down and wonder: "Have I ever been like either of these two?"

Carson McCullers was one of the most talented modern writers. Novelist, short-story writer and playwright, she had a special knack for understanding the way teen-agers think and act. Carson McCullers wrote in 1963 about "Sucker," "I think it was my first short story; at least it was the first story I was proud to read to my family. I wrote it when I was seventeen, and my daddy had just given me my first typewriter. I remember writing the story in longhand, and then painfully typing it out. I liked it then, and like it now . . ."

...And Keep
in Mind

"SUCKER" is a story of the changing relationship
between two cousins, one aged sixteen, the other
twelve. Try to determine the nature of their relationship at the start and then trace the changes
in it. Maybelle, Pete's girl, plays an important
role in Pete's feelings towards Sucker. Judge for
yourself just what her role is. As you read, put
yourself, in turn, in the place of Pete and of
Sucker. React to their conversations with one
another. Then realize why Pete tells us, "More
than anything I want to be easy in my mind
again."

You'll come away from "Sucker" with an understanding of the terrible power of the word
spoken in anger. You may begin to consider the
importance of being sensitive to the feelings of
others.

IT WAS ALWAYS LIKE
I had a room to myself. Sucker slept in my bed with me but
that didn't interfere with anything. The room was mine and
I used it as I wanted to. Once I remember sawing a trap door
in the floor. Last year when I was a sophomore in high school
I tacked on my wall some pictures of girls from magazines
and one of them was just in her underwear. My mother never
bothered me because she had the younger kids to look after.
And Sucker thought anything I did was always swell.

Whenever I would bring any of my friends back to my
room all I had to do was just glance once at Sucker and he
would get up from whatever he was busy with and maybe

half smile at me, and leave without saying a word. He never brought kids back there. He's twelve, four years younger than I am, and he always knew without me even telling him that I didn't want kids that age meddling with my things.

Half the time I used to forget that Sucker isn't my brother. He's my first cousin but practically ever since I remember he's been in our family. You see his folks were killed in a wreck when he was a baby. To me and my kid sisters he was like our brother.

Sucker used to always remember and believe every word I said. That's how he got his nickname. Once a couple of years ago I told him that if he'd jump off our garage with an umbrella it would act as a parachute and he wouldn't fall hard. He did it and busted his knee. That's just one instance. And the funny thing was that no matter how many times he got fooled he would still believe me. Not that he was dumb in other ways—it was just the way he acted with me. He would look at everything I did and quietly take it in.

There is one thing I have learned, but it makes me feel guilty and is hard to figure out. If a person admires you a lot you despise him and don't care—and it is the person who doesn't notice you that you are apt to admire. This is not easy to realize. Maybelle Watts, this senior at school, acted like she was the Queen of Sheba [1] and even humiliated me. Yet at this same time I would have done anything in the world to get her attentions. All I could think about day and night was Maybelle until I was nearly crazy. When Sucker was a little kid and on up until the time he was twelve I guess I treated him as bad as Maybelle did me.

Now that Sucker has changed so much it is a little hard to remember him as he used to be. I never imagined anything would suddenly happen that would make us both very differ-

[1] *Queen of Sheba:* beautiful Yemenite Queen of the tenth century B.C., mentioned in the Bible.

ent. I never knew that in order to get what has happened straight in my mind I would want to think back on him as he used to be and compare and try to get things settled. If I could have seen ahead maybe I would have acted different.

I never noticed him much or thought about him and when you consider how long we have had the same room together it is funny the few things I remember. He used to talk to himself a lot when he'd think he was alone—all about him fighting gangsters and being on ranches and that sort of kids' stuff. He'd get in the bathroom and stay as long as an hour and sometimes his voice would go up high and excited and you could hear him all over the house. Usually, though, he was very quiet. He didn't have many boys in the neighborhood to buddy with and his face had the look of a kid who is watching a game and waiting to be asked to play. He didn't mind wearing the sweaters and coats that I outgrew, even if the sleeves did flop down too big and make his wrists look as thin and white as a little girl's. That is how I remember him— getting a little bigger every year but still being the same. That was Sucker up until a few months ago when all this trouble began.

Maybelle was somehow mixed up in what happened so I guess I ought to start with her. Until I knew her I hadn't given much time to girls. Last fall she sat next to me in General Science class and that was when I first began to notice her. Her hair is the brightest yellow I ever saw and occasionally she will wear it set into curls with some sort of gluey stuff. Her fingernails are pointed and manicured and painted a shiny red. All during class I used to watch Maybelle, nearly all the time except when I thought she was going to look my way or when the teacher called on me. I couldn't keep my eyes off her hands, for one thing. They are very little and white except for that red stuff, and when she would turn the pages of her book she always licked her thumb and held out her little finger and turned very slowly. It is impossible to describe Maybelle. All the boys are crazy about her but she didn't even notice me. For one thing she's almost two years older than I am. Between periods I used to try and pass very close to her in the halls but she would hardly ever smile at me. All I could do was sit and look at her in class—and sometimes it was like the whole room could hear my heart beating and I wanted to holler or light out and run for Hell.

At night, in bed, I would imagine about Maybelle. Often this would keep me from sleeping until as late as one or two o'clock. Sometimes Sucker would wake up and ask me why I couldn't get settled and I'd tell him to hush his mouth. I suppose I was mean to him lots of times. I guess I wanted to ignore somebody like Maybelle did me. You could always tell by Sucker's face when his feelings were hurt. I don't remember all the ugly remarks I must have made because even when I was saying them my mind was on Maybelle.

That went on for nearly three months and then somehow she began to change. In the halls she would speak to me and every morning she copied my homework. At lunch time once I danced with her in the gym. One afternoon I got up nerve and went around her house with a carton of cigarettes. I knew ᵥshe smoked in the girls' basement and sometimes outside of school—and I didn't want to take her candy because I think that's been run into the ground. She was very nice and it seemed to me everything was going to change.

It was that night when this trouble really started. I had come into my room late and Sucker was already asleep. I felt too happy and keyed up to get in a comfortable position and I was awake thinking about Maybelle a long time. Then I dreamed about her and it seemed I kissed her. It was a surprise to wake up and see the dark. I lay still and a little while passed before I could come to and understand where I was. The house was quiet and it was a very dark night.

Sucker's voice was a shock to me. "Pete? . . ."

I didn't answer anything or even move.

"You do like me as much as if I was your own brother, don't you Pete?"

I couldn't get over the surprise of everything and it was like this was the real dream instead of the other.

"You have liked me all the time like I was your own brother, haven't you?"

"Sure," I said.

Then I got up for a few minutes. It was cold and I was glad to come back to bed. Sucker hung on to my back. He felt little and warm and I could feel his warm breathing on my shoulder.

"No matter what you did I always knew you liked me."

I was wide awake and my mind seemed mixed up in a strange way. There was this happiness about Maybelle and all that—but at the same time something about Sucker and his voice when he said these things made me take notice. Anyway I guess you understand people better when you are happy than when something is worrying you. It was like I had never really thought about Sucker until then. I felt I had always been mean to him. One night a few weeks before I had heard him crying in the dark. He said he had lost a boy's beebee gun and was scared to let anybody know. He wanted me to tell him what to do. I was sleepy and tried to make him hush and when he wouldn't I kicked at him. That was just one of the things I remembered. It seemed to me he had always been a lonesome kid. I felt bad.

There is something about a dark cold night that makes you feel close to someone you're sleeping with. When you talk together it is like you are the only people awake in the town.

"You're a swell kid, Sucker," I said.

It seemed to me suddenly that I did like him more than anybody else I knew—more than any other boy, more than my sisters, more in a certain way even than Maybelle. I felt good all over and it was like when they play sad music in the movies. I wanted to show Sucker how much I really thought of him and make up for the way I had always treated him. We talked for a good while that night. His voice was fast and it was like he had been saving up these things to tell me for a long time. He mentioned that he was going to try to build a canoe and that the kids down the block wouldn't let him in on their football team and I don't know what all. I talked some too and it was a good feeling to think of him taking in everything I said so seriously. I even spoke of Maybelle a little, only I made out like it was her who had been running after me all this time. He asked questions about high school and so forth. His voice was excited and he kept on talking fast like he could never get the words out in time. When I went to sleep he was still talking and I could still feel his breathing on my shoulder, warm and close.

During the next couple of weeks I saw a lot of Maybelle. She acted as though she really cared for me a little. Half the time I felt so good I hardly knew what to do with myself.

But I didn't forget about Sucker. There were a lot of old things in my bureau drawer I'd been saving—boxing gloves and Tom Swift [2] books and second rate fishing tackle. All this I turned over to him. We had some more talks together and it was really like I was knowing him for the first time. When there was a long cut on his cheek I knew he had been monkeying around with this new first razor set of mine, but I didn't say anything. His face seemed different now. He used to look timid and sort of like he was afraid of a whack over the head. That expression was gone. His face, with those wide-open eyes and his ears sticking out and his mouth

[2] Tom Swift *books:* series of adventure novels for boys by Edward Stratemeyer.

never quite shut, had the look of a person who is surprised and expecting something swell.

Once I started to point him out to Maybelle and tell her he was my kid brother. It was an afternoon when a murder mystery was on at the movie. I had earned a dollar working for my Dad and I gave Sucker a quarter to go and get candy and so forth. With the rest I took Maybelle. We were sitting near the back and I saw Sucker come in. He began to stare at the screen the minute he stepped past the ticket man and he stumbled down the aisle without noticing where he was going. I started to punch Maybelle but couldn't quite make up my mind. Sucker looked a little silly—walking like a drunk with his eyes glued to the movie. He was wiping his reading glasses on his shirt tail and his knickers flopped down. He went on until he got to the first few rows where the kids usually sit. I never did punch Maybelle. But I got to thinking it was good to have both of them at the movie with the money I earned.

I guess things went on like this for about a month or six weeks. I felt so good I couldn't settle down to study or put my mind on anything. I wanted to be friendly with everybody. There were times when I just had to talk to some person. And usually that would be Sucker. He felt as good as I did. Once he said: "Pete, I am gladder that you are like my brother than anything else in the world."

Then something happened between Maybelle and me. I never have figured out just what it was. Girls like her are hard to understand. She began to act different toward me. At first I wouldn't let myself believe this and tried to think it was just my imagination. She didn't act glad to see me any more. Often she went out riding with this fellow on the football team who owns this yellow roadster. The car was the color of her hair and after school she would ride off with him, laughing and looking into his face. I couldn't think of anything to do about it and she was on my mind all day and night. When I did get a chance to go out with her she was snippy and didn't seem to notice me. This made me feel like something was the matter—I would worry about my shoes clopping too loud on the floor, or the fly of my pants, or the bumps on my chin. Sometimes when Maybelle was around, a devil would get into me and I'd hold my face stiff and call grown men by their last names without the Mister and say rough things. In the night I would wonder what made me do all this until I was too tired for sleep.

At first I was so worried I just forgot about Sucker. Then later he began to get on my nerves. He was always hanging around until I would get back from high school, always looking like he had something to say to me or wanted me to tell him. He made me a magazine rack in his Manual Training [3] class and one week he saved his lunch money and bought me three packs of cigarettes. He couldn't seem to take it in that I had things on my mind and didn't want to fool with him. Every afternoon it would be the same—him in my room with this waiting expression on his face. Then I wouldn't say anything or I'd maybe answer him rough-like and he would finally go on out.

I can't divide that time up and say this happened one day and that the next. For one thing I was so mixed up the weeks just slid along into each other and I felt like hell and didn't care. Nothing definite was said or done. Maybelle still rode around with this fellow in his yellow roadster and sometimes she would smile at me and sometimes not. Every afternoon I went from one place to another where I thought she would be. Either she would act almost nice and I would begin thinking how things would finally clear up and she would care for me—or else she'd behave so that if she hadn't been a girl

[3] *Manual Training class:* class in industrial arts, such as woodworking.

I'd have wanted to grab her by that white little neck and choke her. The more ashamed I felt for making a fool of myself the more I ran after her.

Sucker kept getting on my nerves more and more. He would look at me as though he sort of blamed me for something, but at the same time knew that it wouldn't last long. He was growing fast and for some reason began to stutter when he talked. Sometimes he had nightmares or would throw up his breakfast. Mom got him a bottle of cod liver oil.

Then the finish came between Maybelle and me. I met her going to the drug store and asked for a date. When she said no I remarked something sarcastic. She told me she was sick and tired of my being around and that she had never cared a rap about me. She said all that. I just stood there and didn't answer anything. I walked home very slowly.

For several afternoons I stayed in my room by myself. I didn't want to go anywhere or talk to anyone. When Sucker would come in and look at me sort of funny I'd yell at him to get out. I didn't want to think of Maybelle and I sat at my desk reading *Popular Mechanics* or whittling at a toothbrush rack I was making. It seemed to me I was putting that girl out of my mind pretty well.

But you can't help what happens to you at night. That is what made things how they are now.

You see a few nights after Maybelle said those words to me I dreamed about her again. It was like that first time and I was squeezing Sucker's arm so tight I woke him up. He reached for my hand.

"Pete, what's the matter with you?"

All of a sudden I felt so mad my throat choked—at myself and the dream and Maybelle and Sucker and every single person I knew. I remembered all the times Maybelle had humiliated me and everything bad that had ever happened. It seemed to me for a second that nobody would ever like me but a sap like Sucker.

"Why is it we aren't buddies like we were before? Why—?"

"Shut your damn trap!" I threw off the cover and got up and turned on the light. He sat in the middle of the bed, his eyes blinking and scared.

There was something in me and I couldn't help myself. I don't think anybody ever gets that mad but once. Words came without me knowing what they would be. It was only afterward that I could remember each thing I said and see it all in a clear way.

"Why aren't we buddies? Because you're the dumbest slob I ever saw! Nobody cares anything about you! And just because I felt sorry for you sometimes and tried to act decent don't think I give a damn about a dumb-bunny like you!"

If I'd talked loud or hit him it wouldn't have been so bad. But my voice was slow and like I was very calm. Sucker's mouth was part way open and he looked as though he'd knocked his funny bone. His face was white and sweat came out on his forehead. He wiped it away with the back of his hand and for a minute his arm stayed raised that way as though he was holding something away from him.

"Don't you know a single thing? Haven't you ever been around at all? Why don't you get a girl friend instead of me? What kind of a sissy do you want to grow up to be anyway?"

I didn't know what was coming next. I couldn't help myself or think.

Sucker didn't move. He had on one of my pajama jackets and his neck stuck out skinny and small. His hair was damp on his forehead.

"Why do you always hang around me? Don't you know when you're not wanted?"

Afterward I could remember the change in Sucker's face. Slowly the blank look went way and he closed his mouth. His eyes got narrow and his fists shut. There had never been such a look on him before. It was like every second he was getting older. There was a hard look to his eyes you don't see usually in a kid. A drop of sweat rolled down his chin and he didn't notice. He just sat there with those eyes on me and he didn't speak and his face was hard and didn't move.

"No you don't know when you're not wanted. You're too dumb. Just like your name—a dumb Sucker."

It was like something had busted inside me. I turned off the light and sat down in the chair by the window. My legs were shaking and I was so tired I could have bawled. The room was cold and dark. I sat there for a long time and smoked a squashed cigarette I had saved. Outside the yard was black and quiet. After a while I heard Sucker lie down.

I wasn't mad anymore, only tired. It seemed awful to me that I had talked like that to a kid only twelve. I couldn't take it all in. I told myself I would go over to him and try to make it up. But I just sat there in the cold until a long time had passed. I planned how I could straighten it out in the morning. Then, trying not to squeak the springs, I got back in bed.

Sucker was gone when I woke up the next day. And later when I wanted to apologize as I had planned he looked at me in this new hard way so that I couldn't say a word.

All of that was two or three months ago. Since then Sucker has grown faster than any boy I ever saw. He's almost as tall as I am and his bones have gotten heavier and bigger. He won't wear any of my old clothes any more and has bought his first pair of long pants—with some leather suspenders to hold them up. Those are just the changes that are easy to see and put into words.

Our room isn't mine at all any more. He's gotten up this gang of kids and they have a club. When they aren't digging trenches in some vacant lot and fighting they are always in my room. On the door there is some foolishness written in Mercurochrome saying "Woe to the Outsider who Enters" and signed with crossed bones and their secret initials. They have rigged up a radio and every afternoon it blares out music. Once as I was coming in I heard a boy telling something in a low voice about what he saw in the back of his big brother's automobile. I could guess what I didn't hear. *That's what her and my brother do. It's the truth—parked in the car.* For a minute Sucker looked surprised and his face was almost like it used to be. Then he got hard and tough again. "Sure, dumbbell. We know all that." They didn't notice me. Sucker began telling them how in two years he was planning to be a trapper in Alaska.

But most of the time Sucker stays by himself. It is worse when we are alone together in the room. He sprawls across the bed in those long corduroy pants with the suspenders and just stares at me with that hard, half sneering look. I fiddle around my desk and can't get settled because of those eyes of his. And the thing is I just have to study because I've gotten three bad cards this term already. If I flunk English I can't graduate next year. I don't want to be a bum and I just have to get my mind on it. I don't care a flip for Maybelle or any particular girl any more and it's only this thing between Sucker and me that is the trouble now. We never speak except when we have to before the family. I don't even want to call him Sucker any more and unless I forget I call him by his real name, Richard. At night I can't study with him in the room and I have to hang around the drug store, smoking and doing nothing, with the fellows who loaf there.

More than anything I want to be easy in my mind again. And I miss the way Sucker and I were for a while in a funny, sad way that before this I never would have believed. But everything is so different that there seems to be nothing I can do to get it right. I've sometimes thought if we could have it

out in a big fight that would help. But I can't fight him because he's four years younger. And another thing—sometimes
this look in his eyes makes me almost believe that if Sucker
could he would kill me.

Understanding
the Story

1. What is the origin of the name "Sucker"?
   Where is it explained in the story?
2. Why is Maybelle brought into the story?
   What role does she play in the relationship
   of Pete and Sucker?
3. Explain the following remarks by Pete:
   a. "If the person admires you a lot you despise
      him and don't care—and it is the person
      who doesn't notice you that you are apt to
      admire."
   b. "Anyway I guess you understand people
      better when you are happy than when
      something is worrying you."
   c. "If I'd talked loud or hit him it wouldn't
      have been so bad. But my voice was slow
      and like I was very calm."
4. Why doesn't Pete apologize after the outburst
   that ends with the words . . . "a dumb Sucker"?
5. Who is really the "sucker" in the story? Defend your answer.

Appreciating
the Story

1. Why is Pete telling the story? Why doesn't the
   author use an objective narrator?
2. How are we made to see the character of
   Sucker, in spite of Pete's judgments?
3. How does the author keep the reader interested in the outcome of the story, in spite of
   the fact that there is not too much real action?

4. Contrast the conversations between the two boys at the start and at the end of the story. How does the tone of each reflect the change in the relationship between them?
5. What evidence is given in the story of the author's insight into the hearts and minds of adolescents?
6. How does the author illustrate the "funny, sad way" Sucker and Pete "were for a while"?
7. Would the ending have been more satisfying if the cousins had made up? Defend your answer with examples from the story.

A
Start
in
Life

RUTH SUCKOW

*Approaching
the Story ...*

GOOD looks, money, education, good health, a
cheerful disposition, good parents—all these can
give a person a good start in life. But poor Daisy
Switzer has none of these. What will her start
be like?

Ruth Suckow, the author of this story, wrote
mainly of simple, poor people. She captures the
rhythms and idiom of their speech. The details
she includes show her knowledge of the locale
and the ways of the people in the Midwest, in
the earlier part of the twentieth century. Although she wrote about the people and the land
she knew best, Ruth Suckow succeeded in making Daisy's start in life moving to anyone who
reads the story.

*... And Keep
in Mind*

THIS is the story of the changing role in life of
a poor, homely girl and her slow realization of
what the change means. Try to put yourself in

Daisy's place as this understanding slowly comes
to her. At the day's beginning, "she was important in her small world." By late afternoon, "she
was an outsider." Try to understand what each
carefully planned section of the story contributes
to making you identify with Daisy—the picture
of poverty in the Switzer household, the trip to
her employer's home, her first hours on her new
job. You will realize how successfully the author
gets us to feel with Daisy and to share her "start
in life."

THE SWITZERS
were scurrying around to get Daisy ready by the time that
Elmer Kruse should get through in town. They had known all
week that Elmer might be in for her any day. But they hadn't
done a thing until he appeared. "Oh, it was so rainy today,
the roads were so muddy, they hadn't thought he'd get in
until maybe next week." It would have been the same any
other day.

Mrs. Switzer was trying now at the last moment to get all
of Daisy's things into the battered telescope [1] that lay on the
bed. The bed had not "gotten made"; and just as soon as
Daisy was gone, Mrs. Switzer would have to hurry off to the
Woodworths, where she was to wash today. Daisy's things
were scattered over the dark brown quilt and the rumpled
sheet that were dingy and clammy in this damp weather. So
was the whole bedroom with its sloping ceiling, and old-fashioned square-paned windows, the commode that they used

[1] *Telescope:* an adjustable traveling bag consisting of two cases, the
larger slipping over the smaller.

for a dresser littered with pin trays, curlers, broken combs, ribbons, smoky lamp, all mixed up together; the door of the closet open, showing the confusion of clothes and shabby shoes. . . . They all slept in this room—Mrs. Switzer and Dwight in the bed, the two girls in the cot against the wall.

"Mama, I can't find the belt to that plaid dress."

"Oh, ain't it somewheres around? Well, I guess you'll have to let it go. If I come across it I can send it out to you. Someone'll be going past there."

She had meant to get Daisy all mended and "fixed up" before she went out to the country. But somehow . . . oh, there was always so much to see to when she came home. Gone all day, washing and cleaning for other people; it didn't leave her much time for her own home.

She was late now. The Woodworths liked to have her get the washing out early so that she could do some cleaning too before she left. But she couldn't help it. She would have to get Daisy off first. She had already had on her wraps ready to go, when Elmer came—her cleaning cap, of a blue faded almost gray, and the ancient black coat with gathered sleeves that she wore over her work dress when she went out to wash.

"What's become of all your underclothes? They ain't all dirty, are they?"

"They are, too. You didn't wash for us last week, mama."

"Well, you'll have to take along what you've got. Maybe there'll be some way of getting the rest to you."

"Elmers come in every week, don't they?" Daisy demanded.

"Yes, but maybe they won't always be bringing you in."

She jammed what she could into the telescope, thinking with her helpless, anxious fatalism that it would have to do somehow.

"Daisy, you get yourself ready now."

"I am ready, mama, I want to put on my other ribbon."

"Oh, that's 'way down in the telescope somewhere. You

needn't be so anxious to fix yourself up. This ain't like going visiting."

Daisy stood at the little mirror preening herself—such a homely child, "all Switzer," skinny, with pale sharp eyes set close together and thin, stringy, reddish hair. But she had never really learned yet how homely she was. She was the oldest, and she got the pick of what clothes were given to the Switzers. Goldie and Dwight envied her. She was important in her small world. She was proud of her blue coat that had belonged to Alice Brooker, the town lawyer's daughter. It hung unevenly above her bony little knees, and the buttons came down too far. Her mother had tried to make it over for her.

Mrs. Switzer looked at her, troubled, but not knowing how she could tell her all the things she ought to be told. Daisy had never been away before except to go to her Uncle Fred's at Lehigh. She seemed to think that this would be the same. She had so many things to learn. Well, she would find them out soon enough—only too soon. Working for other people— she would learn what that meant. Elmer and Edna Kruse were nice young people. They would mean well enough by Daisy. It was a good chance for her to start in. But it wasn't the same.

Daisy was so proud. She thought it was quite a thing to be "starting in to earn." She thought she could buy herself so much with her dollar and a half a week.[2] The other children stood back watching her, round-eyed and impressed. They wished that they were going away, like Daisy.

They heard a car come splashing through the mud on low. "There he is back! Have you got your things on? Goldie—go out and tell him she's coming."

[2] *Dollar and a half a week:* in the 1920's, when the events of this story take place, this amount could buy more than the same amount today, but it was still a low wage.

"No, me tell him, me!" Dwight shouted jealously.

"Well—both of you tell him. Land! . . ."

She tried hastily to put on the cover of the bulging tele-scope and to fasten the straps. One of them broke.

"Well, you'll have to take it the way it is."

It was an old thing, hadn't been used since her husband, Mert, had "left off canvassing" [3] before he died. And he had worn it all to pieces.

"Well, I guess you'll have to go now. He won't want to wait. I'll try and send you out what you ain't got with you." She turned to Daisy. Her face was working. There was noth-ing else to do, as everyone said. Daisy would have to help, and she might as well learn it now. Only, she hated to see Daisy go off, to have her starting in. She knew what it meant. "Well—you try and work good this summer, so they'll want you to stay. I hope they'll bring you in sometimes."

Daisy's homely little face grew pale with awe, suddenly, at the sight of her mother crying, at something that she dimly sensed in the pressure of her mother's thin strong arms. Her vanity in her new importance was somehow shamed and dampened.

Elmer's big new Buick, mud-splashed but imposing, stood tilted on the uneven road. Mud was thick on the wheels. It was a bad day for driving, with the roads a yellow mass, water lying in all the wheel ruts. The little road that led past these few houses on the outskirts of town, and up over the hill, had a cold, rainy loneliness. Elmer sat in the front seat of the Buick, and in the back was a big box of groceries.

"Got any room to sit in there?" he asked genially. "I didn't get out, it's so muddy here."

"No, don't get out," Mrs. Switzer said hastily. "She can put this right on the floor there in the back." She added, with

---

[3] *Canvassing:* working as a traveling salesman.

a timid attempt at courtesy, "Ain't the roads pretty bad out that way?"

"Yes, but farmers get so they don't think so much about the roads."

"I s'pose that's so."

He saw the signs of tears on Mrs. Switzer's face, and they made him anxious to get away. She embraced Daisy hastily again. Daisy climbed over the grocery box and scrunched herself into the seat.

"I guess you'll bring her in with you some time when you're coming," Mrs. Switzer hinted.

"Sure. We'll bring her."

He started the engine. It roared, half died down as the wheels of the car spun in the thick wet mud.

In that moment, Daisy had a startled view of home—the small house standing on a rough rise of land, weathered to a dim color that showed dark streaks from the rain; the narrow sloping front porch whose edge had a soaked, gnawed look; the chickens, grayish-black, pecking at the wet ground; their playthings, stones, a wagon, some old pail covers littered about; a soaked, discolored piece of underwear hanging on the line in the back yard. The yard was tussocky and overhung the road with shaggy long grass where the yellow bank was caved in under it. Goldie and Dwight were gazing at her solemnly. She saw her mother's face—a thin, weak, loving face, drawn with neglected weeping, with its reddened eyes and poor teeth . . . in the old coat and heavy shoes and cleaning cap, her work-worn hand with its big knuckles clutching at her coat. She saw the playthings they had used yesterday, and the old swing that hung from one of the trees, the ropes sodden, the seat in crooked. . . .

The car went off, slipping on the wet clay. She waved frantically, suddenly understanding that she was leaving them. They waved at her.

Mrs. Switzer stood there a little while. Then came the harsh rasp of the old black iron pump that stood out under the box elder tree. She was pumping water to leave for the children before she went off to work.

Daisy held on as the car skidded going down the short clay hill. Elmer didn't bother with chains. He was too used to the roads. But her eyes brightened with scared excitement. When they were down, and Elmer slowed up going along the tracks in the deep wet grass that led to the main road, she looked back, holding on her hat with her small scrawny hand.

Just down this little hill—and home was gone. The big car, the feel of her telescope on the floor under her feet, the fact that she was going out to the country, changed the looks of everything. She saw it all now.

Dunkels' house stood on one side of the road. A closed-up white house. The windows stared blank and cold between the old shutters. There was a chair with a broken straw seat under the fruit trees. The Dunkels were old Catholic people who seldom went anywhere. In the front yard was a clump of tall pines, the rough brown trunks wet, the green branches, dark and shining, heavy with rain, the ground underneath mournfully sodden and black.

The pasture on the other side. The green grass, lush, wet and cold, and the outcroppings of limestone that held little pools of rain water in all the tiny holes. Beyond, the low hills gloomy with timber against the lowering sky.

They slid out onto the main road. They bumped over the small wooden bridge above the swollen creek that came from the pasture. Daisy looked down. She saw the little swirls of foam, the long grass that swished with the water, the old rusted tin cans lodged between the rocks.

She sat up straight and important, her thin, homely little face strained with excitement, her sharp eyes taking in everything. The watery mud holes in the road, the little thickets of plum trees, low and wet, in dark interlacings. She held on fiercely, but made no sound when the car skidded.

She felt the grandeur of having a ride. One wet Sunday, Mr. Brooker had driven them all home from church, she and Goldie and Dwight packed tightly into the back seat of the car, shut in by the side curtains, against which the rain lashed, catching the muddy scent of the roads. Sometimes they could plan to go to town just when Mr. Pattey was going to work in his Ford. Then they would run out and shout eagerly, "Mr. Pattey! Are you going through town?" Sometimes he said, with curt good nature, "Well, pile in"; and they all hopped into the truck back. "He says we can go along with him."

She looked at the black wet fields through which little leaves of bright green corn grew in rows, at showery bushes of sumac along the roadside. A gasoline engine pumping water made a loud desolate sound. There were somber-looking cattle in the wet grass, and lonely, thick-foliaged trees growing here and there in the pastures. She felt her telescope on the floor of the car, the box of groceries beside her. She eyed these with a sharp curiosity. There was a fresh pineapple —something the Switzers didn't often get at home. She wondered if Edna would have it for dinner. Maybe she could hint a little to Edna.

She was out in the country. She could no longer see her house even if she wanted to—standing dingy, streaked with rain, in its rough grass on the little hill. A lump came into her throat. She had looked forward to playing with Edna's children. But Goldie and Dwight would play all morning without her. She was still proud of being the oldest, of going out with Elmer and Edna; but now there was a forlornness in the pride.

She wished she were in the front seat with Elmer. She

didn't see why he hadn't put her there. She would have liked to know who all the people were who lived on these farms; how old Elmer's babies were; and if he and Edna always went to the movies when they went into town on Saturday nights. Elmer must have lots of money to buy a car like this. He had a new house on his farm, too, and Mrs. Metzinger had said that it had plumbing. Maybe they would take her to the movies, too. She might hint about that.

When she had to visit Uncle Fred, she had had to go on the train. She liked this better. She hoped they had a long way to go. She called out to Elmer:

"Say, how much farther is your place?"

"What's that?" He turned around. "Oh, just down the road a ways. Scared to drive in the mud?"

"No, I ain't scared. I like to drive most any way."

She looked at Elmer's back, the old felt hat crammed down carelessly on his head, the back of his neck with the golden hair on the sunburned skin above the blue of his shirt collar. Strong and easy and slouched a little over the steering wheel that he handled so masterly. Elmer and Edna were just young folks; but Mrs. Metzinger said that they had more to start with than most young farmers did, and that they were hustlers. Daisy felt that the pride of this belonged to her too, now.

"Here we are!"

"Oh, is this where you folks live?" Daisy cried eagerly.

The house stood back from the road, beyond a space of bare yard with a little scattering of grass just starting—small, modern, painted a bright new white and yellow. The barn was new, too, a big splendid barn of frescoed brick, with a silo of the same. There were no trees. A raw, desolate wind blew across the back yard as they drove up beside the back door.

Edna had come out on the step. Elmer grinned at her as

he took out the box of groceries, and she slightly raised her eyebrows. She said kindly enough:

"Well, you brought Daisy. Hello, Daisy, are you going to stay with us this summer?"

"I guess so," Daisy said importantly. But she suddenly felt a little shy and forlorn as she got out of the car and stood on the bare ground in the chilly wind.

"Yes, I brought her along," Elmer said.

"Are the roads very bad?"

"Kind of bad. Why?"

"Well, I'd like to get over to mama's some time today."

"Oh, I guess they aren't too bad for that."

Daisy pricked up her sharp little ears. Another ride. That cheered her.

"Look in the door," Edna said in a low fond voice, motioning with her head.

Two little round, blond heads were pressed tightly against the screen door. There was a clamor of "Daddy, daddy!" Elmer grinned with a bashful pride as he stood with the box of groceries, raising his eyebrows with mock surprise and demanding, "Who's this? What you shoutin' 'daddy' for? You don't think daddy's got anything for you, do you?" He and Edna were going into the kitchen together, until Edna remembered and called back hastily:

"Oh, come in, Daisy!"

Daisy stood, a little left out and solitary, there in the kitchen, as Billy, the older of the babies, climbed frantically over Elmer, demanding candy, and the little one toddled smilingly about. Her eyes took in all of it. She was impressed by the shining blue-and-white linoleum, the range with its nickel and enamel, the bright new woodwork. Edna was laughing and scolding at Elmer and the baby. Billy had made his father produce the candy. Daisy's sharp little eyes looked hungrily at the lemon drops and Edna remembered her.

"Give Daisy a piece of your candy," she said.

He would not go up to Daisy. She had to come forward and take one of the lemon drops herself. She saw where Edna put the sack, in a dish high in the cupboard. She hoped they would get some more before long.

"My telescope's out there in the car," she reminded them.

"Oh, Elmer, you go and get it and take it up for her," Edna said.

"What?"

"Her valise—or whatever it is—out in the car."

"Oh, sure," Elmer said with a cheerful grin.

"It's kind of an old telescope," Daisy said conversationally. "I guess it's been used a lot. My papa used to have it. The strap broke when mama was fastening it this morning. We ain't got any suitcase. I had to take this because it was all there was in the house, and mama didn't want to get me a new one."

Edna raised her eyebrows politely. She leaned over and pretended to spat the baby as he came toddling up to her, then rubbed her cheek against his round head with its funny fuzz of hair.

Daisy watched solemnly. "I didn't know both of your children was boys. I thought one of 'em was a girl. That's what there is at home now—one boy and one girl."

"Um-hm," Edna replied absently. "You can go up with Elmer and take off your things, Daisy," she said. "You can stop and unpack your valise now, I guess, if you'd like to. Then you can come down and help me in the kitchen. You know we got you to help me," she reminded.

Daisy, subdued, followed Elmer up the bright new stairs. In the upper hall, two strips of very clean rag rug were laid over the shining yellow of the floor. Elmer had put her telescope in one of the bedrooms.

"There you are!"

She heard him go clattering down the stairs, and then a kind of murmuring and laughing in the kitchen. The back door slammed. She hurried to the window in time to see Elmer go striding off toward the barn.

She looked about her room with intense curiosity. It, too, had a bright varnished floor. She had a bed all her own—a small, old-fashioned bed, left from some old furnishings, that had been put in this room that had the pipes and the hot water tank. She had to see everything, but she had a stealthy look as she tiptoed about, started to open the drawers of the dresser, looked out of her window. She put her coat and hat on the bed. She would rather be down in the kitchen with Edna than unpack her telescope now.

She guessed she would go down where the rest of them were.

Elmer came into the house for dinner. He brought in a cold, muddy, outdoor breath with him. The range was going, but the bright little kitchen seemed chilly, with the white oil-cloth on the table, the baby's varnished high chair and his little fat mottled hands.

Edna made a significant little face at Elmer. Daisy did not see. She was standing back from the stove, where Edna was at work, looking at the baby.

"He can talk pretty good, can't he? Dwight couldn't say anything but 'mama' when he was that little."

Edna's back was turned. She said meaningly:

"Now, Elmer's come in for dinner, Daisy, we'll have to hurry. You must help me get on the dinner. You can cut bread and get things on the table. You must help, you know. That's what you are supposed to do."

Daisy looked startled, a little scared and resentful. "Well, I don't know where you keep your bread."

"Don't you remember where I told you to put it this morning? Right over in the cabinet, in that big box. You must watch, Daisy, and learn where things are."

Elmer, a little embarrassed at the look that Edna gave him, whistled as he began to wash his hands at the sink.

"How's daddy's old boy?" he said loudly, giving a poke at the baby's chin.

As Edna passed him, she shook her head and her lips just formed, "Been like that all morning!"

He grinned comprehendingly. Then both their faces became expressionless.

Daisy had not exactly heard, but she looked from one to the other, silent and dimly wondering. The queer ache that had kept starting all through the morning, under her interest in Edna's things and doings, came over her again. She sensed something different in the atmosphere than she had ever known before—some queer difference between the position of herself and of the two babies, a faint notion of what mama had meant when she had said that this would not be visiting.

"I guess I'm going to have the toothache again," she said faintly.

No one seemed to hear her.

Edna whisked off the potatoes, drained the water. . . . "You might bring me a dish, Daisy." Daisy searched a long time while Edna turned impatiently and pointed. Edna put the rest of the things on the table herself. Her young, fresh, capable mouth was tightly closed, and she was making certain resolutions.

Daisy stood hesitating in the middle of the room, a scrawny, unappealing little figure. Billy—fat, blond, in funny, dark blue union-alls [4]—was trotting busily about the kitchen. Daisy swooped down upon him and tried to bring him to the table. He set up a howl. Edna turned, looked astonished, severe.

[4] *Union-alls:* one piece underwear.

"I was trying to make him come to the table," Daisy explained weakly.

"You scared him. He isn't used to you. He doesn't like it. Don't cry, Billy. The girl didn't mean anything."

"Here, daddy'll put him in his place," Elmer said hastily.

Billy looked over his father's shoulder at Daisy with suffused, resentful blue eyes. She did not understand it, and felt strangely at a loss. She had been left with Goldie and Dwight so often. She had always made Dwight go to the table. She had been the boss.

Edna said in a cool, held-in voice, "Put these things on the table, Daisy."

They sat down. Daisy and the other children had always felt it a great treat to eat away from home instead of at their own scanty, hastily set table. They had hung around Mrs. Metzinger's house at noon, hoping to be asked to stay, not offended when told that "it was time for them to run off now." Her pinched little face had a hungry look as she stared at the potatoes and fried ham and pie. But they did not watch and urge her to have more, as Mrs. Metzinger did, and Mrs. Brooker when she took pity on the Switzers and had them there. Daisy wanted more pie. But none of them seemed to be taking more, and so she said nothing. She remembered what her mother had said, with now a faint comprehension. "You must remember you're out working for other folks, and it won't be like it is at home."

After dinner Edna said, "Now you can wash the dishes, Daisy."

She went into the next room with the children. Daisy, as she went hesitatingly about the kitchen alone, could hear Edna's low contented humming as she sat in there rocking the baby in her lap. The bright kitchen was empty and lonely now. Through the window, Daisy could see the great barn looming up against the rainy sky. She hoped that they would drive to Edna's mother's soon.

She finished as soon as she could and went into the dining room where Edna was sewing on the baby's rompers. Edna went on sewing. Daisy sat down disconsolately. That queer low ache went all through her. She said in a small dismal voice:

"I guess I got the toothache again."

Edna bit off a thread.

"I had it awful hard awhile ago. Mama come pretty near taking me to the dentist."

"That's too bad," Edna murmured politely. But she offered no other condolence. She gave a little secret smile at the baby asleep on a blanket and a pillow in one corner of the shiny leather davenport.

"Is Elmer going to drive into town tomorrow?"

"Tomorrow? I don't suppose so."

"Mama couldn't find the belt of my plaid dress and I thought if he was, maybe I could go along and get it. I'd like to have it."

Daisy's homely mouth drooped at the corners. Her toothache did not seem to matter to anyone. Edna did not seem to want to see that anything was wrong with her. She had expected Edna to be concerned, to mention remedies. But it wasn't toothache, that strange lonesome ache all over her. Maybe she was going to be terribly sick. Mama wouldn't come home for supper to be told about it.

She saw mama's face as in that last glimpse of it—drawn with crying, and yet trying to smile, under the old cleaning cap, her hand holding her coat together. . . .

Edna glanced quickly at her. The child was so mortally un-attractive, unappealing even in her forlornness. Edna frowned a little, but said kindly:

"Now you might take Billy into the kitchen out of my way, Daisy, and amuse him."

"Well, he cries when I pick him up," Daisy said faintly.

"He won't cry this time. Take him out and help him play with his blocks. You must help me with the children, you know."

"Well, if he'll go with me."

"He'll go with you, won't he, Billy boy? Won't you go with Daisy, sweetheart?"

Billy stared and then nodded. Daisy felt a thrill of comfort as Billy put his little fat hand in hers and trotted into the kitchen beside her. He had the fattest hands, she thought. Edna brought the blocks and put the box down on the floor beside Daisy.

"Now, see if you can amuse him so that I can get my sewing done."

"Shall you and me play blocks, Billy?" Daisy murmured.

He nodded. Then he got hold of the box with one hand, tipped out all the blocks on the floor with a bang and a rattle, and looked at her with a pleased proud smile.

"Oh no, Billy. You mustn't spill out the blocks. Look, you're too little to play with them. No, now—now wait! Let Daisy show you. Daisy'll build you something real nice—shall she?"

He gave a solemn nod of consent.

Daisy set out the blocks on the bright linoleum. She had never had such blocks as these to handle before. Dwight's were only a few old, unmatched, broken ones. Her spirit of leadership came back, and she firmly put away that fat hand of Billy's whenever he meddled with her building. She could make something really wonderful with these blocks.

"No, Billy, you mustn't. See, when Daisy's got it all done, then you can see what the lovely building is."

She put the blocks together with great interest. She knew what she was going to make—it was going to be a new house;

no, a new church. Just as she got the walls up, in came that
little hand again, and then with a delighted grunt Billy swept
the blocks pellmell about the floor. At the clatter, he sat back,
pursing his mouth to give an ecstatic "Ooh!"

"Oh, Billy—you mustn't, the building wasn't done! Look,
you've spoiled it. Now, you've got to sit 'way off here while I
try to build it over again."

Billy's look of triumph turned to surprise and then to vocif-
erous protest as Daisy picked him up and firmly transplanted
him to another corner of the room. He set up a tremendous
howl. He had never been set aside like that before. Edna came
hurrying out. Daisy looked at Edna for justification, but
instinctively on the defensive.

"Billy knocked over the blocks. He spoiled the building."

"Wah! Wah!" Billy gave loud heartbroken sobs. The tears
ran down his fat cheeks and he held out his arms piteously
toward his mother.

"I didn't hurt him," Daisy said, scared.

"Never mind, lover," Edna was crooning. "Of course he
can play with his blocks. They're Billy's blocks, Daisy," she
said. "He doesn't like to sit and see you put up buildings. He
wants to play, too. See, you've made him cry now."

"Do' wanna stay here," Billy wailed.

"Well, come in with mother then." She picked him up,
wiping his tears.

"I didn't hurt him," Daisy protested.

"Well, never mind now. You can pick up the blocks and
then sweep up the floor, Daisy. You didn't do that when you
finished the dishes. Never mind," she was saying to Billy.
"Pretty soon daddy'll come in and we'll have a nice ride."

Daisy soberly picked up the blocks and got the broom.
What had she done to Billy? He had tried to spoil her building. She had always made Dwight keep back until she had
finished. Of course it was Daisy, the oldest, who should lead

and manage. There had been no one to hear her side. Everything was different. She winked back tears as she swept, poorly and carelessly.

Then she brightened up as Elmer came tramping up on the back porch and then through the kitchen.

"Edna!"

"She's in there," Daisy offered.

"Want to go now? What? Is the baby asleep?" he said blankly.

Edna gave him a warning look and the door was closed.

Daisy listened hard. She swept very softly. She could catch only a little of what they said—"Kind of hate to go off . . . I know, but if we once start . . . not a thing all day . . . what we got her for. . . ." She had no real comprehension of it. She hurried and put away the broom. She wanted to be sure and be ready to go.

Elmer tramped out, straight past her. She saw from the window that he was backing the car out from the shed. She could hear Edna and Billy upstairs, could hear the baby cry a little as he was wakened. Maybe she ought to go out and get her wraps, too.

Elmer honked the horn. A moment later Edna came hurrying downstairs, in her hat and coat, and Billy in a knitted cap and a red sweater crammed over his union-alls, so that he looked like a little brownie. The baby had on his little coat, too.

Edna called out, "Come in and get this boy, daddy." She did not look at Daisy, but said hurriedly, "We're going for a little ride, Daisy. Have you finished the sweeping? Well, then, you can pick up those pieces in the dining room. We won't be gone so very long. When it's a quarter past five, you start the fire, like I showed you this noon, and slice the potatoes that were left, and the meat. And set the table."

The horn was honked again.

"Yes! Well, we'll be back, Daisy. Come, lover, daddy's in a hurry."

Daisy stood looking after them. Billy clamored to sit beside his daddy. Edna took the baby from Elmer and put him beside her on the back seat. There was room—half of the big back seat. There wasn't anything, really, to be done at home. That was the worst of it. They just didn't want to take her. They all belonged together. They didn't want to take anyone else along. She was an outsider. They all—even the baby—had a freshened look of expectancy.

The engine roared—they had started; slipping on the mud of the drive, then forging straight ahead, around the turn, out of sight.

She went forlornly into the dining room. The light from the windows was dim now in the rainy, late afternoon. The pink pieces from the baby's rompers were scattered over the gay rug. She got down on her hands and knees, slowly picking them up, sniffing a little. She heard the Big Ben clock in the kitchen ticking loudly.

That dreadful ache submerged her. No one would ask about it, no one would try to comfort her. Before, there had always been mama coming home, anxious, scolding sometimes, but worried over them if they didn't feel right, caring about them. Mama and Goldie and Dwight cared about her—but she was away out in the country, and they were at home. She didn't want to stay here, where she didn't belong. But mama had told her that she must begin helping this summer.

Her ugly little mouth contorted into a grimace of weeping. But silent weeping, without any tears; because she already had the cold knowledge that no one would notice or comfort it.

1. The title has at least two possible meanings. What are they?
2. "Mrs. Switzer looked at her, troubled, but not knowing how she could tell her all the things she ought to be told." If you could speak to Daisy, what would you have told her before she left home to go to work?
3. Describe Daisy's relationship with her younger sister and brother. Compare Daisy's place in the Kruse household with that of the Kruse children. What differences do you find?
4. Why does Daisy keep complaining of a toothache?
5. What does the incident of the blocks contribute to the story?
6. Explain the meaning of the final paragraph.

1. There are several dramatic moments in Daisy's day. Which affects you most deeply? Why?
2. There are three acts in the drama of Daisy's start in life: the parting with her family; her ride to her new home for the summer; her first hours on her new job. What does each tell us of Daisy's growing awareness of her changing circumstances?
3. A number of people are mentioned incidentally: the Brookers; Mr. Pattey; Mrs. Metzinger. What do they add to our understanding of the Switzer family's place in the community?
4. The author has a fine sense of detail. Show how this is evident in the story in
   a. the poverty of the Switzers,

    b. the final view Daisy has of her home,

    c. the description of the countryside.

5. The author uses the "omniscient" point of view; that is, she speaks through the thoughts of a number of characters in the story, moving from one to the other as she feels necessary. She might have attempted to present the story through Daisy alone, in the first person. Which method do you think makes a more effective story? Why?

One Friday Morning

LANGSTON HUGHES

Approaching the Story ...

"ONE FRIDAY MORNING" is a story of prejudice against a talented high school student because she is Negro. It will recall to each of us the first time we realized that we were not being judged for what we were as individuals. We were being *pre*-judged because of some accident of birth. The unreasoned failure to accept people as they really are is not inborn. It is learned. It is learned by imitation of others who are prejudiced, or it is taught by them. Only if we understand the devastating effects of prejudice, only if we fully realize how un-American prejudice is can we fully devote ourselves to fighting it. This story by Langston Hughes, an outstanding black poet and essayist, effectively provides us with this understanding of the nature of prejudice.

... And Keep in Mind

As you read the story, note how the author builds up the dreams and expectations of Nancy and her parents. Notice how he stresses the positive qualities in her life—her pride in her country, her

pride in her race, her sensitivity to beauty. Notice
the roles played by her understanding art teacher
and the vice-principal of the school. Ask yourself
why the author chose to make these the principal
characters in his drama of prejudice. And keep
in mind Miss O'Shay's reactions to Nancy's keen
disappointment and Nancy's own feelings toward
the courageous vice-principal. In the capable
hands of Langston Hughes what might be a de-
pressing story of man-made injustice becomes a
call for us to work to achieve "liberty and justice
for all."

THE NEWS DID NOT COME
directly to Nancy Lee, but it came in little indirections that
finally added themselves up to one tremendous fact: she had
won the prize! But being a calm and quiet young lady, she
did not say anything although the whole high school buzzed
with rumors, guesses, reportedly authentic announcements
on the part of the students who had no right to be making
announcements at all—since no student really knew yet who
had won this year's art scholarship.

But Nancy Lee's drawing was so good, her lines so sure,
her colors so bright and harmonious that certainly no other
student in the senior art class at George Washington High
was thought to have very much of a chance. Yet you never
could tell. Last year nobody had expected Joe Williams to win
the Artist Club scholarship with that funny modernistic water
color he had done of the high-level bridge. In fact, it was
hard to make out there was a bridge until you had looked at
the picture a long time. Still, Joe Williams got the prize, was

feted by the community's leading painters, club women, and society folks at a big banquet at the Park-Rose Hotel, and was now an award student at the Art School—the city's only art school.

Nancy Lee Johnson was a colored girl, a few years out of the South. But seldom did her high-school classmates think of her as colored. She was smart, pretty and brown, and fitted in well with the life of the school. She stood high in scholarship, played a swell game of basketball, had taken part in the senior musical in a soft velvety voice, and had never seemed to intrude or stand out except in pleasant ways, so it was seldom even mentioned—her color.

Nancy Lee sometimes forgot she was colored herself. She liked her classmates and her school. Particularly she liked her art teacher, Miss Dietrich, the tall red-haired woman who taught her to keep her brush strokes firm and her colors clean, who taught her law and order in doing things; and the beauty of working step by step until a job is done; a picture finished; a design created; or a block print carved out of nothing but an idea and a smooth square of linoleum, inked, proofs made, and finally put down on paper—clean, sharp, beautiful, individual, unlike any other in the world, thus making the paper have a meaning nobody else could give it except Nancy Lee. That was the wonderful thing about true creation. You made something nobody else on earth could make—but you.

Miss Dietrich was the kind of teacher who brought out the best in her students—but their own best, not anybody else's copied best. For anybody else's best, great though it might be, even Michelangelo's, wasn't enough to please Miss Dietrich dealing with the creative impulses of young men and women living in an American city in the Middle West, and being American.

Nancy Lee was proud of being American, a Negro American with blood out of Africa a long time ago, too many gener-

ations back to count. But her parents had taught her the
beauties of Africa, its strength, its song, its mighty rivers, its
early smelting of iron, its building of the pyramids, and its
ancient and important civilizations. And Miss Dietrich had
discovered for her the sharp and humorous lines of African
sculpture, Benin, Congo, Makonde.[1] Nancy Lee's father was
a mail carrier, her mother a social worker in a city settlement
house. Both parents had been to Negro colleges in the South.
And her mother had gotten a further degree in social work
from a Northern university. Her parents were, like most
Americans, simple ordinary people who had worked hard
and steadily for their education. Now they were trying to
make it easier for Nancy Lee to achieve learning than it had
been for them. They would be very happy when they learned
of the award to their daughter—yet Nancy did not tell them.
To surprise them would be better. Besides, there had been a
promise.

Casually, one day, Miss Dietrich asked Nancy Lee what
color frame she thought would be best on her picture. That
had been the first inkling.

"Blue," Nancy Lee said. Although the picture had been
entered in the Artist Club contest a month ago, Nancy Lee
did not hestitate in her choice of a color for the possible frame
since she could still see her picture clearly in her mind's eye—
for that picture waiting for the blue frame had come out of
her soul, her own life, and had bloomed into miraculous being
with Miss Dietrich's help. It was, she knew, the best water
color she had painted in her four years as a high-school art
student, and she was glad she had made something Miss
Dietrich liked well enough to permit her to enter in the contest before she graduated.

It was not a modernistic picture in the sense that you had to
look at it a long time to understand what it meant. It was just

[1] *Benin, Congo, Makonde:* centers in Africa of outstanding art.

a simple scene in the city park on a spring day with the trees still leaflessly lacy against the sky, the new grass fresh and green, a flag on a tall pole in the center, children playing, and an old Negro woman sitting on a bench with her head turned. A lot for one picture, to be sure, but it was not there in heavy and final detail like a calendar. Its charm was that everything was light and airy, happy like the spring, with a lot of blue sky, paper-white clouds, and air showing through. You could tell that the old Negro woman was looking at the flag; and that the flag was proud in the spring breeze; and that the breeze helped to make the children's dresses billow as they played.

Miss Dietrich had taught Nancy Lee how to paint spring, people and breeze on what was only a plain white piece of paper from the supply closet. But Miss Dietrich had not said make it like any other spring-people-breeze ever seen before. She let it remain Nancy Lee's own. That is how the old Negro woman happened to be there looking at the flag—for in her mind the flag, the spring and the woman formed a kind of triangle holding a dream Nancy Lee wanted to express. White stars on a blue field, spring, children, ever-growing life, and an old woman. Would the judges at the Artist Club like it?

One wet rainy April afternoon Miss O'Shay, the girl's vice-principal, sent for Nancy Lee to stop by her office as school closed. Pupils without umbrellas or raincoats were clustered in doorways hoping to make it home between showers. Outside the skies were gray. Nancy Lee's thoughts were suddenly gray, too.

She did not think she had done anything wrong, yet that tight little knot came in her throat just the same as she approached Miss O'Shay's door. Perhaps she had banged her locker too often and too hard. Perhaps the note in French she had written to Sallie halfway across the study hall just for fun had never gotten to Sallie but into Miss O'Shay's hands instead. Or maybe she was failing in some subject and wouldn't be allowed to graduate. Chemistry! A pang went through the pit of her stomach.

She knocked on Miss O'Shay's door. That familiarly solid and competent voice said, "Come in."

Miss O'Shay had a way of making you feel welcome even if you came to be expelled.

"Sit down, Nancy Lee Johnson," said Miss O'Shay. "I have something to tell you." Nancy Lee sat down. "But I must ask you to promise not to tell anyone yet."

"I won't Miss O'Shay," Nancy Lee said, wondering what on earth the principal had to say to her.

"You are about to graduate," Miss O'Shay said. "And we shall miss you. You have been an excellent student, Nancy, and you will not be without honors on the senior list, as I am sure you know."

At that point there was a light knock on the door. Miss O'Shay called out, "Come in," and Miss Dietrich entered. "May I be a part of this, too?" she asked, tall and smiling.

"Of course," Miss O'Shay said. "I was just telling Nancy Lee what we thought of her. But I hadn't gotten around to giving her the news. Perhaps, Miss Dietrich, you'd like to tell her yourself."

Miss Dietrich was always direct. "Nancy Lee," she said, "your picture has won the Artist Club Scholarship."

The slender brown girl's eyes widened, her heart jumped, then her throat tightened again. She tried to smile, but instead tears came in her eyes.

"Dear Nancy Lee," Miss O'Shay said, "we are so happy for you." The elderly white woman took her hand and shook it warmly while Miss Dietrich beamed with pride.

Nancy Lee must have danced all the way home. She never remembered quite how she got there through the rain. She hoped she had been dignified. But certainly she hadn't stopped to tell anybody her secret on the way. Raindrops, smiles, and tears mingled on her brown cheeks. She hoped her mother hadn't yet gotten home and that the house was empty. She wanted to have time to calm down and look natural before she had to see anyone. She didn't want to be bursting with excitement—having a secret to contain.

Miss O'Shay's calling her to the office had been in the nature of a preparation and a warning. The kind, elderly vice-principal said she did not believe in catching young ladies unawares, even with honors, so she wished her to know about the coming award. In making acceptance speeches she wanted her to be calm, prepared, not nervous, overcome, and frightened, so Nancy Lee was asked to think what she would say when the scholarship award was conferred upon her a few days hence, both at the Friday morning high-school assembly hour when the announcement would be made, and at the evening banquet of the Artist Club. Nancy Lee promised the vice-principal to think calmly about what she would say.

Miss Dietrich had then asked for some facts about her parents,.her background and her life, since it would probably all be desired for the papers. Nancy Lee had told her how, six years before, they had come up from Deep South, her father having been successful in achieving a transfer from one post office to another, a thing he had long sought in order to give Nancy Lee a chance to go to school in the North. Now, they lived in a modest Negro neighborhood, went to see the best plays when they came to town, and had been saving to send Nancy Lee to art school, in case she were permitted to enter. But the scholarship would help a great deal, for they were not rich people.

"Now Mother can have a new coat next winter," Nancy Lee thought, "because my tuition will all be covered for the first year. And once in art school, there are other scholarships I can win."

Dreams began to dance through her head, plans and ambitions, beauties she would create for herself, her parents and the Negro people—for Nancy Lee possessed a deep and reverent race pride. She could see the old woman in her picture (really her grandmother in the South) lifting her head to the bright stars on the flag in the distance. A Negro in America! Often hurt, discriminated against, sometimes lynched—but always there were the stars—the blue body of the flag. Was there any other flag in the world that had so many stars? Nancy Lee thought deeply but she could remember none in all the encyclopedias or geographies she had ever looked into.

"Hitch your wagon to a star," [2] Nancy Lee thought, dancing home in the rain. "Who were our flag makers?"

Friday morning came, the morning when the world would know—her high-school world, the newspaper world, her mother and dad. Dad could not be there at the assembly to hear the announcement, nor see her prize picture displayed on the stage, nor listen to Nancy Lee's little speech of acceptance, but Mother would be able to come, although Mother was much puzzled as to why Nancy Lee was so insistent she be at school on that particular Friday morning.

When something is happening, something new and fine, something that will change your very life, it is hard to go to sleep at night for thinking about it, and hard to keep your heart from pounding, or a strange little knot of joy from gathering in your throat. Nancy Lee had taken her bath, brushed her hair until it glowed, and had gone to bed thinking about the next day, the big day when, before three thousand students, she would be the one student honored, her painting the one painting to be acclaimed as the best of the year from all the art classes of the city. Her short speech of gratitude was ready. She went over it in her mind, not word for word (be-

[2] "*Hitch your wagon to a star*": phrase of Ralph Waldo Emerson advising high goals and lofty ideals.

cause she didn't want it to sound as if she had learned it by heart) but she let the thoughts flow simply and sincerely through her consciousness many times.

When the president of the Artist Club presented her with the medal and scroll of the scholarship award, she would say:

"Judges, and members of the Artist Club. I want to thank you for this award that means so much to me personally and through me to my people, the colored people of this city who, sometimes, are discouraged and bewildered, thinking that color and poverty are against them. I accept this award with gratitude and pride, not for myself alone but for my race that believes in American opportunity and American fairness—and the bright stars in our flag. I thank Miss Dietrich and the teachers of this school who made it possible for me to have the knowledge and training that lie behind this honor you have conferred upon my painting. When I came here from the South a few years ago, I was not sure how you would receive me. You received me well. You have given me a chance, and helped me along the road I wanted to follow. I suppose the judges know that every week here at assembly the students of this school pledge allegiance to the flag. I shall try to be worthy of that pledge, and of the help and friendship and understanding of my fellow citizens of whatever race or creed, and of our American dream of 'Liberty and justice for all!' "

That would be her response before the students in the morning. How proud and happy the Negro pupils would be, perhaps as proud as they were of the one colored star on the football team. Her mother would probably cry with happiness. Thus Nancy Lee went to sleep dreaming of a wonderful tomorrow.

The bright sunlight of an April morning woke her. There was breakfast with her parents—their half-amused and puzzled faces across the table, wondering what could be this secret that made her eyes so bright. The swift walk to school;

the clock in the tower almost nine; hundreds of pupils streaming into the long rambling old building that was the city's
largest high school; the sudden quiet of the home room after
the bell rang; then the teacher opening her record book to
call the roll. But just before she began, she looked across the
room until her eyes located Nancy Lee.

"Nancy," she said, "Miss O'Shay would like to see you in
her office, please."

Nancy Lee rose and went out while the names were being
called and the word "present" added its period to each name.
Perhaps, Nancy Lee thought, the reporters from the papers
had already come. Maybe they wanted to take her picture
before assembly, which wasn't until ten o'clock. (Last year
they had had the photograph of the winner of the award in
the morning papers as soon as the announcement had been
made.)

Nancy Lee knocked at Miss O'Shay's door.

"Come in."

The vice-principal stood at her desk. There was no one else
in the room. It was very quiet.

"Sit down, Nancy Lee," she said. Miss O'Shay did not smile.
There was a long pause. The seconds went by slowly. "I do
not know how to tell you what I have to say," the elderly
woman began, her eyes on the papers on her desk. "I am in-
dignant and ashamed for myself and for this city." Then she
lifted her eyes and looked at Nancy Lee in the neat blue dress
sitting there before her. "You are not to receive the scholarship this morning."

Outside in the hall the electric bells announcing the first
period rang, loud and interminably long. Miss O'Shay remained silent. To the brown girl there in the chair, the room
grew suddenly smaller, smaller, smaller, and there was no air.
She could not speak.

Miss O'Shay said, "When the committee learned that you were colored they changed their plans."

Still Nancy Lee said nothing, for there was no air to give breath to her lungs.

"Here is the letter from the committee, Nancy Lee." Miss O'Shay picked it up and read the final paragraph to her.

"It seems to us wiser to arbitrarily rotate the award among the various high schools of the city from now on. And especially in this case since the student chosen happens to be colored, a circumstance which unfortunately, had we known, might have prevented this embarrassment. But there have never been any Negro students in the local art school and the presence of one there might create difficulties for all concerned. We have high regard for the quality of Nancy Lee Johnson's talent, but we do not feel it would be fair to honor it with the Art Club award." Miss O'Shay paused. She put the letter down.

"Nancy Lee, I am very sorry to have to give you this message."

"But my speech," Nancy Lee said, "was about..." The words stuck in her throat. "...about America...."

Miss O'Shay had risen, she turned her back and stood looking out the window at the spring tulips in the school yard.

"I thought, since the award would be made at assembly right after our oath of allegiance," the words tumbled almost hysterically from Nancy Lee's throat now, "I would put part of the flag salute in my speech. You know, Miss O'Shay, that part about 'liberty and justice for all.' "

"I know," said Miss O'Shay slowly facing the room again. "But America is only what we who believe in it, make it. I am Irish. You may not know, Nancy Lee, but years ago, we were called the dirty Irish, and mobs rioted against us in the big cities, and we were invited to go back where we came from. But we didn't go. And we didn't give up, because we believed in the American dream, and in our power to make that dream come true. Difficulties, yes. Mountains to climb, yes. Discouragements to face, yes. Democracy to make, yes. That is it, Nancy Lee! We still have in this world of ours, democracy *to make*. You and I, Nancy Lee. But the premise and the base is here, the lines of the Declaration of Independence and the words of Lincoln are here, and the stars in our flag. Those who deny you the scholarship do not know the meaning of those stars, but it's up to us to make them know. As a teacher in the public schools of this city, I myself will go before the school board and ask them to remove from our system the offer of any prizes or awards denied to any student because of race or color." Suddenly Miss O'Shay stopped speaking. Her clear, clear blue eyes looked into those of the girl before her. The woman's eyes were full of strength and courage. "Lift up your head, Nancy Lee, and smile at me."

Miss O'Shay stood against the open window with the green lawn and the tulips beyond, the sunlight tangled in her gray hair, her voice an electric flow of strength to the hurt spirit of Nancy Lee. The Abolitionists who believed in freedom when there was slavery must have been like that. The first white teachers who went into the Deep South to teach the freed slaves must have been like that. All those who stand against ignorance, narrowness, hate, and mud on stars must be like that.

Nancy Lee lifted her head and smiled. The tears were only drops of April rain.

The bell for assembly rang. Nancy Lee went through the long hall filled with students toward the auditorium.

"There will be other awards," Nancy Lee thought. "There're schools in other cities. This won't keep me down. But when I'm a woman, I'll fight to see that these things don't happen to other girls as this has happened to me. And men and women like Miss O'Shay will help me."

She took her seat among the seniors. The doors of the auditorium closed. As the principal came onto the platform the students rose and turned their eyes to the flag on the stage with its red and white stripes and the stars on its field of blue.

One hand went to the heart, the other outstretched toward the flag. Three thousand voices spoke. Among them was the voice of a dark girl whose cheeks were suddenly wet with tears.

"I pledge allegiance to the flag of the United States of America and to the Republic for which it stands." The words grew stronger, the dark girl's voice stronger, too. "One nation indivisible,[3] with liberty and justice for all."

"That is the land we must make," she thought.

Understanding the Story

1. Describe the character of Nancy Lee. Give evidence from the story that indicates the kind of person she is.
2. Why is Nancy proud to be an American? Why is she proud to be a Negro?
3. What does the scholarship mean to Nancy financially? What does it mean to her emotionally?
4. What is Nancy's immediate reaction to being denied the scholarship? What is her later reaction? Are these reactions true to life? Explain your answer.
5. Comment on Miss O'Shay's promise: "I myself will go before the school board and ask them to remove from our .system the offer of any prizes or awards denied to any student be-

[3] "One nation indivisible . . .": in 1954, after this story was written, an act of Congress added the words "under God" immediately after "one nation."

cause of race or color." Are any students still
denied prizes and awards for this reason?

*Appreciating
the Story*

1. What is the author's purpose in the story?
   How well does he succeed? Give evidence to
   justify your evaluation.
2. What positive elements balance the description of the ugly effects of prejudice? What do
   they add to the story?
3. Why does the author include Nancy's pro-
   posed speech and her thoughts on her second
   visit to Miss O'Shay's office?
4. What are the effects of prejudice in the story
   on Nancy? Miss O'Shay? George Washington
   High School?
5. What does Nancy Lee mean when she thinks,
   "That is the land we must make"? What contrast is the author pointing out?
6. When do you think this story was written?
   Have conditions changed since then? What
   would Nancy do now?

Reviewing the Unit

For Comparative Study

1. In each of these stories, the leading character changes (or grows) as a result of the action. Give examples of such development from the stories you have read.
2. In some stories, what is important is suggested rather than stated outright. Show this with reference to the stories in the unit.
3. Why do none of these stories have "happy endings"? Does this make them less enjoyable to read?
4. Each leading character in these stories faces a problem. Define each problem in a general way. Which problems do you find in your own life? Which do you find are presented in the most moving way? Did you, as the reader, identify with the character and become involved in the problems?
5. Are the girls or the boys more favorably depicted in these stories? Why do you think so?
6. Each story is based on a single incident—a quarrel, leaving home for work, being denied a scholarship. How is each of these incidents developed into a significant story? What suspense element is present in each?
7. What do you think becomes of the leading characters in each of the stories after the ending of the story as written? Justify your answer with evidence from the stories.

The following descriptive words are to be found
in the stories of this unit. Copy the sentences in
your notebook, filling in the appropriate words.

arbitrary	interminable
authentic	modernistic
casual	sarcastic
dignified	solemn
indignant	timid

1. When someone pushed in front of her on the
   line, the ____ shopper complained to the
   manager of the store.
2. The expert confirmed the fact that the autograph of Babe Ruth was ____.
3. The visitor to the museum could make no
   sense of the ____ painting.
4. The ____ child was afraid to ask his father
   for an increase in his allowance.
5. The husband had to wait for an ____ time to
   hear news of his wife's health from the doctor.
6. The class felt that the decision to cancel the
   field day was ____ and unjust.
7. When he went to the principal's office, the
   student tried to appear ____ but he was, in
   fact, very nervous.
8. The priest was ordained during a ____ ceremony.
9. When the girl refused to dance with him, the
   boy made a ____ remark.
10. The hostess asked her guests to dress in a
    ____ way for the barbecue.

For Creative Writing

Use one of the following sentences as the opening for a short story.

1. The moment of decision had come.
2. Why did it have to happen to me?
3. I dreaded having to tell my parents.
4. The first dollar I earned was the (hardest, easiest).
5. Life began for me when . . .
6. I wish I hadn't said it, but I did.
7. "What should I do?" I asked my father, (mother, parents).
8. At last, I was on my own.
9. It was a secret between me and my father (mother, brother, sister).
10. Kid brothers (sisters) are (great, pests).
11. I never really knew my (brother, sister).

MEETING
OUR
FATE

As we go through life, we are faced with decisions. We feel we can make the right or the wrong choice. Or has the choice been made for us by fate, by chance, by destiny, by a power beyond us?

The stories in this unit deal with the events that either shape or allow one to shape his destiny. The events may not seem very important at the time they occur, but they turn out to be decisive—for better or for worse. A nurse's aide meets a patient who changes her entire future; a boy on a bike runs into and kills a chicken; a boy decides to drop out of school. In all the stories, something else might have happened—but it didn't. Why didn't it? Decide whether you believe, as some do, that you can control your own life, or, as others do, that you are fated to live as you do.

The locale of the stories is varied: one takes place in Ireland; one is set in an American hospital; one takes place in a New York apartment. The characters include a nurse's aide of 24, a professor, a widow with a fourteen-year-old son, and a college student.

In a sense, you, the reader, are living out the story of your own life, and each day may be the

day that decides the turn your life will take. Will
you persist in the right decision as Sirene does,
or will you yield to impulse, as Donald finds himself doing? It's up to you. Or is it?

A
Firm
Word
or
Two

NATHANIEL BENCHLEY

Approaching the Story . . .

ONE of the problems in the United States today is the high school dropout. Year after year, thousands of American teen-agers leave school and lose the opportunities that education brings. They are then inadequately prepared for work. Why does it happen? This story offers an important reason. You will meet Donald, an eighteen-year-old college freshman, who comes to his parents with a proposal. It's a thought that has occurred to many students in high school and college. As he puts it, "It's just that I thought I might take a year off."

Nathaniel Benchley's sensitive handling of Donald and his parents will impress you with its honesty. You'll find yourself taking sides and wondering "What if I were in Donald's position?"

*... And Keep
in Mind*

THE problem Donald brings to his parents is the
crisis in the story. Study the motives of all three
characters as they explore Donald's idea. They
all mean well; they all want to do the right thing.
Yet they all see the problem differently. As you
read, try to see the situation as Donald does;
then as Donald's father does; and finally as Donald's mother does. What reasons are offered for
and against Donald's proposition? Think through
the problem and ask yourself: "If I were Donald,
what would I do? If I were one of Donald's parents, how would I handle this?"

Try to decide which of the three has the best
solution for the circumstances. Is it too late for
Donald and his parents to change?

STEWART FLEMING
put on his topcoat, tossed his hat onto the hall table, and
looked at his watch. "Ten minutes to eight!" he called.

"I'll be right there," his wife, Dorothy, answered, from the
back of the apartment. "I'm just finishing my face."

Fleming went into the living room and dropped into a
chair. He knew it should take no more than half an hour to
get to the theatre, and the curtain was at eight-thirty, so
there still was plenty of time. Nevertheless, he hated being
late and he hated to rush, and for that reason, when he and
Dorothy went to the theatre, they always had their dinner
afterward.

There was a thud, followed by a scraping noise, outside
the front door, and then the door opened and Donald, the

Flemings' eighteen-year-old son, came in, dragging a monstrous suitcase behind him. He was tall and muscular, and his shirt collar was open and his necktie pulled down. His coat flapped loosely about him. In spite of his general state of disarray, he looked clean and powerful, like an athlete muffled in towels and blankets.

"Well, *hello!*" Fleming exclaimed, with pleasure. "We didn't expect you until tomorrow!"

They shook hands, and Donald smiled and said, "They changed the exam schedule. My last one was this morning, instead of this afternoon."

"How were they?"

"Not too tough."

Fleming smiled reminiscently. "I can still remember *my* freshman mid-years. I was scared senseless."

"These weren't too bad." Donald casually shook a cigarette out of a pack, offered it to his father, and, when Fleming refused, put it in his own mouth.

"How are things?" Fleming asked. "Everything all right?"

"Yes, I guess so." Donald glanced around the room. "Where's Mother?"

"She's dressing. She'll be right out."

"I gather you two are going out for a do, or something."

"We're going to the theatre. As I said, we didn't expect you back until tomorrow. By the way, if you'd like to take my ticket, I'll be glad to—"

"Oh, no. Don't be silly." Donald walked around the room, looking at the bookshelves as though he had never seen them before. "Are you going out afterward?" he asked.

"Just to have some dinner. Why?"

"Nothing. I'd like to talk to you some time, but it can wait."

"What about? What's on your mind?"

"Nothing special," Donald said. "There isn't time for it now."

"What's the matter? Are you in any trouble?"

"No, of course not. It's not any trouble."

"Well, you might as well tell me now as later. What is it?"

"Let's let it pass, shall we? I'm sorry I brought it up."

Dorothy's footsteps sounded down the hall, and she came into the room and gave a shriek, and ran to Donald and kissed him. "Look at *you!*" she said. "Where did *you* come from?"

"Down the road a piece," Donald replied, laughing. "People with two heads were allowed to cut all their exams."

"I think this is perfectly *marvellous!* Do you want to come along, and see if we can get an extra seat for you?"

"No, thanks. I think I'll stay here and throw together some chow. I'll see you when you come back."

"He has something he wants to tell us," Fleming said. "But he doesn't think we ought to hear about it until later."

"What is it?" Dorothy asked, suddenly serious. "Are you all right?"

"Sure I'm all right. I'm fine. This is just an idea I had, that's all."

"Well, if it's just an idea, it certainly can't hurt us to know about it now," said Fleming. "Maybe we'll need some time to think about it."

"Yes, please tell us," said Dorothy. "Then we have to go or we'll be late." She held her coat out to Fleming and he helped her into it.

"Maybe you're right, at that," said Donald. "Well . . ." He hesitated, and then, in as offhand a manner as he could, he said, "It's just that I thought I might take a year off."

Fleming stared at him. "What do you mean?" he said.

"Just that. Not go back next semester."

"Have you been thrown out?"

"No, no." Donald smiled, and started to push them toward the door. "It's just that I thought I might do better to take the money you'd spend on college and go around the world for a year, or something. We can talk about it later."

"What in the world gives you the idea that—" Fleming began, but Dorothy took his arm and pulled him to the door.

"Come on, dear," she said. "We'll be late. We can talk about this later."

"That's right, Mother," said Donald, laughing. "You simmer him down, and I'll wait for you here."

"Simmer *who* down?" said Fleming, holding back.

"Stewart!" said Dorothy. "Come on!"

Fleming reached for his hat, and slammed it on his head. He and Dorothy went out, and Donald said, "Have a good time," and closed the door behind them. Through the door they heard him whistling as he went to the kitchen to make his supper.

"It's the darndest thing I ever heard!" Fleming said after he had given the cab driver the address of the theatre. "What possibly makes him think he can take a year off?"

"I don't know," Dorothy replied. "We'll find out when we talk to him later."

"Well, I'm not going to let him do it," Fleming said. "He's out of his mind."

"I wouldn't just forbid him to do it. I think it would be better if you tried to reason with him."

"Of course I'll try to reason with him. But if reason fails, then I'm dammed well going to forbid him."

She was quiet for a moment. "I'm not sure that would be a good idea," she said, at last.

"Why not? Have you a better idea?"

"No, but we haven't very many noes left, as far as he's concerned."

"What do you mean?"

"Just that. He's at the age when we can't say 'no' much more, and I don't think it would be good for our last 'no' to be based on money. I mean, we can stop him just by not giving him the money to do it, and I don't think our last 'no' should be on that basis."

"All right—what do you suggest, then?"

"I don't know. But don't forbid him. Let him see for himself that it's not a good idea."

Fleming fidgeted and fumed throughout the play, and although the rest of the audience seemed to enjoy it, he could find nothing amusing or interesting in it. During the second-act intermission, he and Dorothy went out to the lobby and he said, "How about it? Do you want to go back for the last act?"

"Why, of course!" she said. "I'm having a wonderful time —aren't you?"

"I just don't get it, that's all. I cannot understand it."

"There's nothing hard to understand about it. It's more or less straight from the novel, and this is—"

"I'm not talking about the play," Fleming cut in impatiently. "I'm talking about Donald. I cannot understand what would make him want to do a thing like that."

"Oh," she said. "Well, there's nothing we can do until we hear his side of it."

"There is no 'his side of it,'" Fleming said. "It's sheer lunacy, that's all."

"Listen to me," Dorothy said. "It may be lunacy, but you've got to hear him out. You've got to listen to him, or he'll never again respect a thing you say. You cannot forbid him to do things, as if he were still a child."

"He never *has* been forbidden to do things, as I remember it. You've always said we had to reason with him, no matter what it was."

"Stewart, I'm not going to argue with you any more!" she said sharply. "You're going to be reasonable about this. I'm going to take *his* side and tell him to go ahead."

Fleming started for the door. "That's great," he said. "That's just fine. Here you spend eighteen years saying we've got to stick together on these things—saying we can never have any divided authority—and now, when something important comes up, you offer to go over to his side."

"Just keep on talking," she said as she followed him out. "Keep on talking to me, and maybe you'll get it out of your system enough so that you can be civil to your son when we get home."

Neither Fleming nor Dorothy even considered going to a restaurant when the play was over. They got into a cab, and Fleming gave the driver their home address, dug his hands into his pockets, and settled back in the seat. There was a long silence, and then Dorothy said, "Are you going to listen to his side of it?"

"Yes, I'll listen," Fleming replied.

"If you'll treat him as though he were a full, grown-up adult, then that's all I ask."

When they got home, Donald was sitting in the living room, listening to the phonograph. The volume was turned up high, and the room quivered with the beat of the music Donald smiled and stood up as they came in. "Hi," he said. "How was it?"

Fleming said nothing, and Dorothy said, "I just loved it. I thought it was wonderful."

"Aren't you home a little early?" Donald asked. "I thought you were going on for dinner afterward."

Dorothy hesitated. "We thought we'd rather eat at home," she said. "What with its being your first night back, and everything."

"I didn't mean to louse up your evening," said Donald. "You didn't have to worry about me."

"You didn't louse up a thing," Dorothy replied gaily. "Come on—let's all go in the kitchen while I cook something." She turned to Fleming, who was mixing himself a drink at the bar. "Would you make one for me, too?" she asked. "A long one, if you please." Fleming nodded, and Dorothy went into the kitchen, followed slowly by Donald.

When Fleming joined them, and he and Donald were seated at the kitchen table, Dorothy, who was melting butter in a pan, said, "Well, now—let's hear some more about this idea of yours."

"Well, I'll tell you," Donald said slowly. "It just seemed to me that I wasn't getting any place in college, and—"

"You haven't had a chance," Fleming cut in. "It's only been four—"

"Stewart!" said Dorothy. "Let him finish."

"I don't know," Donald went on. "It just seemed that maybe if I got around a little, and saw some other things, it might give me some sort of direction—I don't know—a goal, or a point, or something. I just don't feel there's any point in what I'm doing."

"May I ask a question?" Fleming said, gently, to Dorothy. She nodded, and he turned to Donald and asked, "Did you intend to go back to college after this—this year of looking around, or did you intend to keep on until you found something?"

"Oh, sure, I think I'd go back," Donald replied. "At least I think now that I would. I guess it would all depend."

"And how did you intend to get back?" Fleming asked. "Just tell the college that you were ready to come in again?"

"Well, sure," Donald said. "Guy I heard of got thrown out last year, and they told him he could come back provided he got a job for a year. I figure it would amount to the same thing."

"I see. And do you know how many people failed to get

into college last fall? Do you know how lucky you are to be there at all?"

"Stewart, that's not the point," said Dorothy. "The point is what he wants to accomplish if he takes a year off."

"I figure if they've let you in once, they'll let you in again," Donald said. "Provided you tell them what you're planning to do, and all. Anyway, I've completed one semester, so I'd have those credits behind me, and—"

"Provided you've passed your exams, you'll have those credits behind you," Fleming interrupted.

"I got through, all right," Donald said. "Anyway, what I want to accomplish is just what I said—I want to get a point of view, or a philosophy, or something, that'll give me a reason for being there. I don't want to go to college just to say that I've been to college. I want to go to college to get something out of it—something good, and solid."

"And you don't feel you're getting that now?"

"No, sir. I don't."

"Do you mind telling us why? Do you have any specific reasons you can give us?"

Donald shrugged, and spread his hands. "It's just what I feel," he said. "I can't explain it more than that."

Fleming looked at Dorothy. "Have you any suggestions?" he asked.

She looked blank, and Donald said, "Maybe this will explain it. The guys who come from California, they have a Californian point of view. The guys from the Middle West, a Midwestern point of view. I don't feel that I've got *any* point of view. If I could get *out* a little, and look around, I think I'd probably get the maturity I need to appreciate what's going on around me. Does that make sense?"

Fleming said to Dorothy, "Your witness."

"Yes, of course it makes sense," she said. "In a way, that is.

But just how did you figure you'd go about taking this year off? What is it that you intend to do?"

"I don't know," Donald said. "Get a job, or something. Maybe be a cruise director, or even just a sailor. Go around the world. I can get work wherever I go."

"Enough work to support yourself?" Fleming asked. "I hate to point this out, but jobs aren't as easy to get as they once were."

"Well, that brings up the next point," Donald said. "I've been thinking about this for some time now, and it occurred to me—as I said—that if you give me what you'd spend for the year at college, then that would be enough to get started on, and I could make my own way from there. But just to be on the safe side, I wrote to Mr. Blackwood and asked him if there was a job I could get with his line."

"You wrote to *Howard Blackwood?*" Fleming said, shocked. "Did you tell him who you were?"

"Well, sure. I mean—what with the name, and all, I figured he was bound to guess. There's no reason for it to be a secret, is there?"

"Did he answer you? What did he say?"

"He said they had all the cruise directors they needed but that I could come and talk to him after exams, and he'd see what else he could find for me. I mean, if I can get on a ship that's going some place in the Orient, or to the Mediterranean, then I can leave it wherever I want and pick up another job."

"There's a little matter of working papers, passports, and permits," said Fleming tartly. "And there are countries that wouldn't give you the time of day, much less a job."

"A guy from college got a job with one of the oil companies," Donald replied, as though that disposed of the whole problem. "They sent him all over the Middle East."

"Then maybe you'd better look for work in an oil company," said Fleming. "I don't think your steamship approach is going to get you anywhere."

"Maybe not," Donald said. "Do you know anybody in an oil company that I might write to?"

"No, I don't!" Fleming said. "And I think that if you're going to do this, it would be better you did it on your own, without using my name."

"I didn't mean to use your *name*," said Donald, with a trace of anger. "I just wanted to know whom to write to."

"Write to the Director of Personnel," said Fleming. "That's where you'll end up anyway, no matter whom you write to."

"Are you sure you've thought this all through?" Dorothy asked Donald. "Do you realize how hard it may be, and how badly you may disappointed?"

"I don't care how hard it may be," said Donald. "That part of it doesn't worry me at all. I just want to get around."

"Even at the expense of a college education?" Fleming asked, forcing himself to sound mild.

"It won't *be* at the expense of a college education!" Donald said heatedly. "But even suppose I *get* a job with an oil company—suppose I decide to stay with it the rest of my life—what's the difference? A guy I heard of got thrown out sophomore year, and six months later he was making two hundred dollars a week."

"It seems to me you know a remarkably fortunate group of young men," said Fleming.

Dorothy ladled scrambled eggs onto two plates, gave one to Fleming, and took the other herself. "Well, this is nothing we have to decide right here and now," she said. "I think the thing to do is for Donald to see what he can find, and then we'll know better what the prospects are. Don't you agree?" She looked at Fleming, and smiled.

"Yes," said Donald to his father. "It's all right with you if

I *talk* to Mr. Blackwood, isn't it? I mean, you don't *mind* if I
go and see him?"

Fleming shrugged. "You can do whatever you like," he said.
"Whatever you think is best."

The next day from his office, Fleming called Blackwood.
When Blackwood answered the phone, Fleming still hadn't
decided just what he was going to say. They exchanged
greetings, and then Fleming said, "Howard, I gather that my
son and heir has been in touch with you about a possible job,
or something."

"Yes," said Blackwood. "What's all this about, anyway? Is
he in trouble in college?"

"Not that I can gather—no. Its just that he wants to—"
Fleming paused, wondering how to phrase it without sound-
ing ridiculous. "It appears that what he wants is to see a little
bit of the world before going on with his studies. It sounds
crazy to me, but that's the way I understand it."

"And you don't want him to do it—is that it?"

"Hell, Howard, I think it's an insane idea. But Dorothy is
all against our forbidding him to do anything. She wants him
to find out for himself how stupid it is. I don't know what's
got into him—all this business about getting a point of view,
and a goal, and everything. Hell, *we* weren't worried about
that kind of stuff when *we* were freshmen."

"No, but this group is different," Blackwood said. "I've
seen a good many of them, and they've got a lot more on
their minds than we had at the same age."

"Well, what do *you* think? Does it sound like a good idea?"

"Stu, I'm not going to run your son's life for him. If you
think he ought to find out the hard way, I'll see what I can do
for him. If you want me to turn him down, I can do that just
as easily."

"That puts it right back in my lap, then"

"That's where you want it to be, isn't it?"

Fleming hesitated, and took a deep breath. "All right," he said. "Turn him down. But don't tell him that I told you to. Or that I even talked to you."

"Obviously not."

"O.K., then, Howard," Fleming said. "Thanks—and I'm sorry to have put you to all this trouble."

Fleming hung up, feeling a mixture of relief and guilt. I hope that will take care of it, he thought. I hope that when this doesn't work out, he'll give up and go back to college.

That night, when Fleming got home from work, he found Donald in his old room, going through his desk and looking at old letters and papers, and whistling a brisk tune. He glanced up as Fleming came in. "Hi, Sport," he said.

"Hi," said Fleming amiably. "How goes it?"

"Great. Keeneroo."

"Did you see Mr. Blackwood?"

"Uh-huh." Donald skimmed one page of a letter, tore it up, and dropped it in the wastebasket.

"What did he say?"

"He said there wasn't anything." Donald picked up another letter, opened it, and chuckled.

There was a pause, and then Fleming said, "You seem to be kind of happy about it. Was it a relief to get it over with?"

Donald looked at him. "What do you mean?" he asked.

"I mean—well, I just mean it doesn't look as though you were too depressed about it, that's all."

"Oh, that." Donald tossed the letter onto the desk and picked up another. "No—that didn't make any difference one way or the other. I got a lead onto something really hot."

"Oh? What kind of thing?"

"Well, it's not definite yet," Donald said, "so I'd rather not talk about it."

"I see." Fleming cleared his throat. "But it's the same general idea, I gather?"

Donald nodded, still reading. "More or less, yes," he said.
There was a silence. "Well," Fleming said, and hesitated.
"We're always interested in—I mean, any time you feel like
telling us . . ." He let the sentence trail off.

Donald laughed. "Don't worry. You'll be first to hear."

"Good," said Fleming, and he cleared his throat again.
Good. That's nice to know." He tried to think of something
else to say, but couldn't. Standing mute in the middle of the
room, he suddenly felt ill at ease and slightly lost. "Well—"
he said, and then turned and left, trying to look as though he
had just remembered something he had to do.

The subject of Donald's plans was not mentioned during
the next several days. Donald was busy with his friends—so
busy, in fact, that it looked as if he had forgotten his scheme.
Fleming knew he had not forgotten, but he thought that perhaps it had fallen through, and that Donald was simply ig-
noring the whole thing to cover his disappointment. Let's
hope that's what it is, anyway, Fleming thought. About all
that anyone can do at this point is hope.

Then, late one afternoon, Donald came home beaming and
rubbing his hands. "Well, it's all set," he announced as he
strode into the living room, where Fleming and Dorothy were
sitting. "I take off a week from tomorrow."

"Take off?" Fleming said, looking up from his paper. "Is
this an airplane trip?"

"Just a figure of speech. No—here's the deal. I've signed
on a freighter that's going through the Canal [1] and around to
the West Coast."

In the ringing silence that followed, Donald looked first at
his mother and then at Fleming. He smiled, and said, "You
were right about that working-in-Europe deal. It's no good.
So what I did was get in touch with a guy I know, who lined
me up with a job in a logging camp in Oregon. The ship goes

[1] *Canal:* the Panama Canal.

as far as San Pedro,[2] and I get off there and work my way up the coast." He grinned.

"What kind of logging camp works in the winter?" Fleming asked quietly.

"Oh, the logging job doesn't start right away," Donald replied. "I'll have a couple of months to look around. I thought I might go to Hollywood and see if there's any action there, and then—who knows? But at that point I'll have enough money so I won't have to worry."

"Oh?" said Fleming. "Where from?"

"Well, I'll have whatever I make on the ship, and then I figure that what's left over from college will come to about fifteen hundred bucks—so that, and whatever else I make, will be more than enough. For one thing, you can make twenty bucks a day as an extra in the movies."

"To narrow this down to just one point," Fleming said, "you will not have any fifteen hundred bucks left over from college. It probably hasn't occurred to you, but I am committed to paying a number of your college bills for the full year, whether you are there or not. The sum you call 'what's left over from college' will most likely be four or five hundred dollars. If you're lucky."

"Oh," said Donald. He thought for a moment. "Well—that's O.K.," he said. "That won't make much difference. I can get along on five hundred, if I make enough on the side."

"As for your remark about extras in the movies," Fleming went on, "that's so idiotic I won't even bother to comment on it."

Donald laughed. "No," he said. "I didn't really mean working as an extra. I wouldn't do anything in the movies unless it was a regular part. Something with lines."

"Good God Almighty," Fleming said, and closed his eyes.

[2] *San Pedro:* former city in California, now the port section of Los Angeles.

"Donald, darling, are you sure you've thought about this?" Dorothy asked, leaning forward. "Are you *sure* it's what you want to do?"

"Yes, Mother. I am—I have—it is." Donald smiled, and she sat back slowly.

"May I say I think you're crazy?" Fleming said.

"I don't. I think this is going to be the best thing I've ever done," said Donald.

Fleming took a deep breath. "All right, then," he said. "That would seem to settle it. I can't give you all the money right now, but I'll give you what I can, and send the rest later. I just hope you know what you're doing."

Donald laughed. "Don't worry about that," he said. "I do."

It was cold the day the ship sailed, and a light rain was falling. Dorothy said goodbye to Donald in the living room, and then ran into the back of the apartment while Donald and Fleming went out and waited for the elevator. Donald was quiet, and Fleming could see that he was nervous, and even downcast, but that seemed natural in the circumstances, and Fleming didn't think much about it. He offered to help with the suitcase, but Donald wouldn't let him, so he just stood there and pretended not to be aware that anything was amiss.

Donald's depression became more and more evident on the taxi ride to Brooklyn, where his ship was docked. Finally, as the cab threaded its way along the wet cluttered waterfront, he spoke. Without looking at Fleming, he said, "That logging job fell through."

"Oh?" said Fleming. "When did you find this out?"

"I got a letter yesterday. They seem to be cutting down, or something. Anyway, they said they had all the men they could use."

"What are you going to do?"

Donald shrugged. "This guy I know said there was a chance of something else."

"But there's nothing definite?"

Donald shook his head.

"Well," said Fleming, "if you need anything—" he stopped, and thought for a few minutes, and then, trying to sound as casual as he could, he said, "You really don't have to go through with this, you know."

Donald said nothing, and the rest of the trip went by in silence.

The pier was cold and dark, and as they walked to the end where the freighter was berthed their footsteps had a hollow ring. The decks of the ship glistened with rain and oil, and there were long, tapering smears of rust beneath each porthole. The air was filled with clanking, grinding noises, punctuated by shouts and whistles and crashes, as the cargo was loaded. Donald stopped when they came to the narrow gangplank, and put his suitcase down. He and Fleming stared at the ship for a minute or two, and then Donald took out a cigarette and lighted it. He inhaled, and let the smoke come out slowly. "You really didn't want me to do this, did you?" he said.

Fleming looked at him in surprise. "Hell, no," he said. "Of course we didn't."

"Why didn't you say so?"

"Why didn't I *say* so? I thought it was obvious!"

There was a pause, and then Donald said, "Sometimes it's hard to tell, with all the talk that goes on."

"We were just trying to get you to make up your mind."

"Well, a firm word or two might have helped. Something definite, one way or the other."

"I'm sorry."

"That's all right."

"I suppose it's too late now?" Fleming said.

"It would look that way."

"Whatever you say. It's your decision."

"As usual," said Donald.

"What do you want me to do? Do you want me to forbid you to go? Right here and now, do you want me to take you by the arm and lead you back home?"

There was a long silence, and then Donald said, "I guess that would look kind of silly, wouldn't it?"

"If you want me to, I'll do it."

Donald flipped his cigarette into the water, held out his hand, and smiled. "Thanks, anyway," he said. "If I change my mind, I'll let you know."

They shook hands, and then Donald picked up his suitcase and went down the wet, glistening gangplank and onto the ship. He didn't look back, and Fleming turned and walked, with his hands in his pockets, into the cold darkness of the pier.

Understanding the Story

1. Explain the meaning of the following observations from the story:
   a. Mrs. Fleming: "If you'll treat him as though he were a full, grown-up adult, then that's all I ask."
   b. Mrs. Fleming: "... we haven't very many noes left, as far as he's concerned."
   c. Donald: "Well, a firm word or two might have helped."
   d. Mr. Fleming: "Whatever you say. It's your decision." Donald: "As usual."
2. Describe the relationship between Donald and his parents. Cite passages from the story to support your views.
3. What purpose does the visit of the parents to

the theatre serve in the development of the story?

4. List the arguments for and against Donald's leaving school. Which are more impressive to you? Why?

5. What does Mr. Fleming mean when he uses the words "divided authority?"

6. Find evidence that Donald's firmness in his decision wavers as he approaches the moment of leaving.

7. What is the meaning of the title?

8. What kind of person is Donald? Cite passages from the story to support your view.

Appreciating the Story

1. What evidence in the story indicates that the author has a point of view he is trying to get across to the reader?

2. How true-to-life is the ending? Give reasons for your opinion.

3. With whose point of view do you agree most fully—Donald's, Mr. Fleming's, Mrs. Fleming's? Give reasons for your answer.

4. One problem currently under much discussion is "the generation gap." What indication of this can be found in the story? What do you think is the cause of this "gap"?

5. What values guide each of the characters in this story? How do they, in a sense, make the outcome of the story unavoidable?

6. Write another possible ending to the story.

7. Add a paragraph to the story describing the thoughts of Donald as he watches his father leave, or of the father as he walks away from his son.

The Chance
of a
Lifetime

MONTY CULVER

*Approaching
the Story . . .*

To many Americans, the goal of equality of opportunity is as distant as ever. They may lack the
education to compete for good jobs or the money
to get that education. Yet, even with skills and
knowledge, many fail to take advantage of the
opportunities that present themselves. They do
not have the determination to overcome obstacles
or confidence in their own ability. The main character in the story you are about to read is a young
black woman serving as a nurse's aide in a hospital. Sirene's education had ended with high
school, despite the fact that she was a good student. In a sense, she represents all those who can
achieve a great deal, but for one reason or another, find themselves trapped by circumstances.
How can they be ready for opportunity's knock?

*. . . And Keep
in Mind*

THE meeting with a patient turns out to be the
chance for which Sirene has been hoping. But
will Sirene be able to take advantage of "the

chance of a lifetime"? As you read, try to put yourself in Sirene's place. What qualities of character give promise of success? Which stand in her way? There is a tug of war within Sirene. Will her determination and keen intelligence win out over her sensitivity and her feelings of inferiority? Or, to put it another way, will she do what is necessary to shape her own destiny, or will she resign herself to her fate?

THE MAN WHO CHANGED Sirene's life came into it through the front door of the hospital in which she worked, late one afternoon in January. At that time, Sirene—a tall, trim Negro girl with large, downcast eyes—was twenty-four and in need of a change. She occasionally imagined, without much enthusiasm, that a man might someday come into her life and rescue her from the nurse's-aide routine, but she never imagined—although her imagination was active—that the man would be who he was, or that the change would be what it was.

A few seconds before she first saw him, Sirene hurried out of the hospital's main kitchen and crossed into the first-floor lobby. She was hearing the kitchen supervisor's falsely cheery "Bye, Miss Scott" echoing in her head. She disliked being called "Miss Scott" almost as much as she disliked being called "Sirene." Her first name had been something to be borne ever since her earliest childhood; and, in later years, she had come to associate the "Miss Scott" with the starched-white nurses and supervisors who smiled stiffly at a point somewhere over her shoulder and were always asking her for, handing to her or putting her name down on mimeo-graphed charts.

She wrinkled her nose now at the meal-cart charts—a sheet for each cart, with spaces to check off "Knives," "Forks," "Spoons." Even if you assumed you were dealing with mor-ons, mightn't "Silverware" be enough?

Crossing the lobby, she saw Miss Ingram's finger crooked at her. Miss Ingram, a coldly beautiful, light-colored girl, could be counted on not to remember anyone's name, first or last. She called to Sirene, "Miss—ah, please take this gentle-man up to room 612."

Sirene dropped her eyes and shuffled toward the desk with a pang of shame for her own sulkiness. She sneaked a glance at the gentleman—a tall white man in a gray overcoat. When he smiled tentatively at her, she dropped her gaze again. Without saying anything, she took his admission form off Miss Ingram's counter and read the name on the top line—A. E. Brant. (Another of the mimeographed instructions stated that aides, when possible, should call the patient by name.) Then she reached down for his overnight case ("Always carry the patient's luggage") and, at the handlegrip, she touched his warm hand.

She jerked her hand back. Then, feeling her dark face burning, she mumbled, "I'm sorry," and turned toward the elevator, catching, as she turned, a flashed impression of Miss Ingram's lovely faint-tan face, the small, Caucasian [1] features fixed in the expression of a sniff.

At the elevator door, she jabbed the button and stood look-ing nervously at the nurses who passed and then at Mr. Brant's case; she wished he would set it down. Thinking of her recoil from his hand, she blushed again.

"Oh! I'm sorry, miss," he said suddenly. "I didn't think. Is there some rule about my carrying my suitcase?"

[1] *Caucasian:* of the white race.

Surprised, she risked a glance at him; he looked concerned. She said, "Well, yes, sir"—she had to look at the form again—"Mr. Brant."

He set the case down, saying, "Far be it from me."

They got on the elevator, the only riders. With the suitcase in her own hand, she felt more comfortable, and grateful to him. Then, however, he let her down. "Don't you think it's nice of them," he said casually, "to put a colored girl right out there at the desk?"

Her eyes fixed on the control panel, she felt a rush of embarrassment and of disappointment in him, and was surprised at the strength of her feelings. "Yes, sir," she mumbled.

"Makes you feel proud" he said, and his tone made her look at him sharply. He was watching the elevator door, his eyebrows up a little. "It's just a shame they couldn't get Lena Horne [2] for the job."

He looked at her then, and his mouth curved a little. After a moment, he said, "It's the same way where I work. Everybody gets together and decides to go all out for equality of opportunity. Then the personnel man goes out and looks for somebody who looks sort of white."

She smiled toward the floor. Then she suddenly realized that he was talking a little nervously because she had not answered; it seldom occurred to her that anyone was waiting for *her* to say something. She muttered, "No sense being *too* equal." But he seemed to have heard her.

"Um-hum." He nodded. "You have to approach these things with a certain moderation."

The elevator had taken them up six floors; Sirene felt as though they had traveled a great distance farther together.

Miss Bowles, one of the floor nurses, was waiting in the hall, a busty blonde in white, holding her clipboard jutting out

[2] *Lena Horne:* popular singer, noted for her beauty.

from her waist as though she stood behind a Dutch door [3] with a counter at the middle. She smiled broadly and briefly without opening her lips, then said, "Mr. Brant? Yes indeedy, we're all ready for you." She checked off his name on the entering list and scribbled it into a blank space on her floor diagram.

She led them into 612, a semiprivate room with both beds empty. "See, you even get your choice," she chirped. "The one by the window?" She darted to the bed nearer the window and printed his name on the chart at the foot.

Mr. Brant was frowning around the room.

"The view here is lovely," Miss Bowles went on, "and we'll try to make you comfortable."

"Well, yes, but excuse me," Mr. Brant said, "but aren't there any telephones in the rooms?"

Miss Bowles's brow wrinkled briefly at this reminder that her floor of the old building was not yet as thoroughly modernized as some of the others. "I'm sorry to say that only the rooms on the other side of the hall have their own telephones. But you'll be very comfortable."

He hesitated. "Well—is there an empty room across the hall? My children are too small to visit me, but they get a kick out of calling me up during the day."

"I'm sorry, Mr. Brant," Miss Bowles said with a smile, "but we've registered you." She turned away to the window, opening the curtains wider. "The sun rooms at the end of each hall have telephones for—"

Mr. Brant wet his lips, looked around and strode into the hall.

Sirene was left standing just inside the door, still holding the overnight case and looking at Miss Bowles's broad back. Choked by a sudden nervous hilarity, she wondered what she

[3] *Dutch door:* a door divided horizontally so that the lower part can be shut while the upper remains open.

ought to say: "He's gone, Miss Bowles"? "After him, Miss Bowles"? Fortunately, just at the moment beyond which Sirene would have *had* to say something, Miss Bowles turned in midspeech, stopped talking, and stared at the door "Mr. Brant," she said, in a tiny voice, and hurried, behind her clipboard, out into the hall. Sirene went after her in time to see Mr. Brant, removing his overcoat, swerve into 605 in a swirl of gray. She was reminded of a time in her childhood when a bird had got down the chimney, and the family, in single file, and ranked according to age and speed, had chased it from room to room.

When she followed Miss Bowles into 605, she saw Mr. Brant's overcoat across a chair; he was peeling off his suit jacket, and smiling at the telephone on the stand between the two empty beds. "This will be fine," he said cheerfully to Miss Bowles. "The kids are used to calling me up once a day down at school."

"Mr. Brant, if you had specified a telephone—"

"Oh, it never occurred to me there wouldn't be a telephone," he said, smiling and lowering his eyes, as if to say, Don't be embarrassed; I know it's not your fault.

He gripped the straight top fold of the hospital-made bed, yanked both the top sheet and the blanket firmly down, and sat down on the bed; Sirene, who had moved in far enough to watch them both, choked again at the dumbfounded expression on Miss Bowles's face.

"Mr. Brant," Miss Bowles said, "you are *registered* for 612 on the *charts.*"

He loosened his necktie and opened his collar. "Well, of course, those charts are in your control, nurse," he said. "I mean, I wouldn't ask a favor if you didn't have the authority."

Miss Bowles said, "But it's all entered down*stairs!*"

"Well, you could call them downstairs. This room's obviously empty." He bent to untie his shoes and smiled up into

her face. "Go ahead," he said quietly. "All it needs is a couple
of scratchings out. Please."

When he had held her gaze this way for a few seconds, he
stood up and walked around the bed to the bathroom door.
"Excuse me," he said, and went in and closed the door.

Miss Bowles shook herself and said, "Well, Miss Scott. . . ."
with a jumpy laugh, trying for a note of we-know-how-
patients-are. She wrote Mr. Brant's name on the chart at the
foot of the bed and went out. Sirene looked at the overnight
case in her hand and swung it up onto the visitor's chair. She
smiled.

After a few moments, Mr. Brant came out of the bathroom.
"You know, I hate doing things like that," he said seriously,
taking his tie the rest of the way off. "I used to be the type
who wouldn't even have tried it. But the kids *do* like to call
up."

Sirene thought: I'm still the type who wouldn't even try it.
"I'm sure they do," she said.

"I thought the bed was a nice touch," he said judiciously.
"Course, I could have taken my shoes off and put my feet up
on it."

She wanted to say: Well, you have to approach these
things with a certain moderation; but she only smiled.

After a second, he grinned. "Well, we've had a long day,
Miss—ah," he said, opening his case and taking out a pair of
pajamas. "What *is* your name, for when I see you again?"

She considered "Miss Scott," but it was inappropriate to
the way she felt. "Sirene," she said, a little extra loudly and
clearly.

"Really?" He glanced up from his cuff links. "I know how
that is. I'm Aloysius."

It was time for Sirene to think of lining up the meal carts
and getting out the linens, but she stood a moment trying to
think of something else to say. In his overnight case she saw

two sacks of folded single sheets of white paper, each en-
dorsed and dated on the outside—apparently student themes
or quizzes. "Do you teach school?"

"I teach out at City."

She thought for a few seconds about people she knew who
had gone to the City University—chattering girls and one
hulking tackle from her high-school class and a few little
gum-chewers who worked part-time as nurses' aides to help
pay their tuition. She wanted to ask him if they didn't drive
him crazy—she knew he wouldn't think the question too personal—but she didn't speak. After a second, she faltered,
"Well. . . ." and started out. He waved to her and winked;
and she went up the hall and down the right-angled passage
to the sixth-floor kitchen.

So this was the kind of person who taught in college.

She went at her pre-dinner arranging and checklisting with
an air of bemusement which changed, just as the trays were
coming up on the dumbwaiter, to a sudden fretfulness when
she realized that she didn't know why Mr. Brant was hospital-
ized. She fussed and snapped at the other aides until all the
carts were trundled away, and she had time to go out to the
desk.

Mr. Brant's doctor, she learned, planned to remove a cyst.
Minor surgery, no serious illness. Sirene, while relieved, realized she was disappointed to know that he would be there
only a day or two. Suddenly she laughed at herself (although
to anyone who might have glanced at her there at the desk,
she would have presented the same downcast, faintly sullen
expression); she could always, she thought, plant his footstool
in the doorway of his bathroom and hope he'd trip over it and
break his leg.

She remained bemused throughout the evening's chart-
initialing. She left when her shift ended at midnight, drove
her old car home over the icy streets to a darkened house (her

mother was in bed, her father gone to work at twelve, her sister still out) and, still thoughtful, prepared for bed.

Her feelings surprised her. She knew that, like a character in a Thurber [4] story she'd enjoyed, she never liked anyone she hadn't met before—that is, until Mr. Brant. Somehow, the few minutes of talking with him and seeing him in action had affected her life. The shadow of loneliness and the everpresent prison of the organizers and chart-mimeographers seemed a little withdrawn and shrunken. Because of a man who taught in a college.

Though her grades had been consistently excellent through high school, Sirene had not thought of going on to college. The high school's "guidance counselor" had opened their only conversation by saying, "I don't suppose you'll be able to go to college," and her parents had spoken only of how much easier things would be when Sirene was bringing in a little money. The few classmates of hers who crossed the river to City were considered by the neighborhood to be either grinds or flibbertigibbets, and, from what she knew of them, Sirene concurred.

Yet, when she woke up the morning after meeting Mr. Brant, Sirene found herself thinking about college. It was crazy even to consider it, but she couldn't shut off the questions. True, there was more money now, with her job and her savings, but was it enough? How much did college cost? And would she be able to keep her job? Her four-to-twelve schedule was in her favor, but could you work full-time when you were going to school? How could you have time to go to classes and get your studying done? (You could, she reflected wryly, draw up a chart of your week's time, with a little box for each hour.)

She would be even lonelier and more thoroughly organized

[4] *Thurber:* American humorist, author of "The Secret Life of Walter Mitty."

than before, conspicuous for her advanced age. Was it worth it for the privilege of filling out forms, attending to mimeographed assignment sheets and reading lists, sitting in large classes where the teachers knew the students only by number? She would be as she had been in high school, too timid to ask questions in the classes or to speak to other students in the halls.

No. You were better off to stick to what you were doing: you might not like it, but you knew what to expect from it.

The next day, she spent the early afternoon in the library, rereading Hemingway's *The Sun Also Rises*,[5] and went to work at four with the feeling that all business was well off her mind. Still, she was disappointed to find, upon arriving, that Mr. Brant had just been brought upstairs from his examination, and was sleeping. At eight, with most of the day's checklists disposed of, she drifted to the end of the hall again, encouraged by the full light she saw shining from the doorway. She looked in and saw him awake and reading, and saw also—a possibility that had never occured to her, although it was an obvious one—that the other bed in the semiprivate room was occupied. A middle-aged man lay there, his hands behind his head, looking gloomily up at the ceiling.

So of course it was impossible to talk to Mr. Brant in any privacy; and he would go home the next morning. As she went on with her evening's job, she became more and more discouraged, and decided it was no use approaching him. She couldn't have, even if she had wanted to.

At ten, most of the aides, who worked six-hour shifts, had left, and the two who remained slipped off, as soon as possible, to sneak a cigarette on the back stairway. Sirene, fiddling about in the sixth-floor kitchen, heard a repeated buzz from the nurses' board out at the desk; she went out, saw no nurses in sight, and went herself down to 657 to deliver a pitcher of

[5] Hemingway's *The Sun Also Rises:* novel by Ernest Hemingway.

water. Then she went back past the desk into the angled corridor which led to the kitchen, actually a food-receiving
room—a large space containing a sink, a four-burner hot plate
where the nurses' coffeepot sat and broad wall tables adja-
cent to the dumbwaiter which brought the food up from the
main kitchen on the first floor. Sirene, turning the last corner,
was startled to find the room not empty as she had left it:
leaning against the edge of the sink, reading, with a steaming
coffee cup beside him, was Mr. Brant.

He looked up at her and said, "OK, I'll go quietly," and she
felt an ugly thrill of certainty that he did not remember her
at all. But, as she moved into the stronger light, he smiled
and said, "Oh, hello, Sirene."

She smiled faintly, realizing that she had been called
nothing but Miss Scott since she had left home that morning,
and remembering her old distaste for her first name. She knew
that she should say, "Hello, Aloysius," or at least say *something*, but she didn't.

"I figured maybe I could scrounge a little coffee out here,"
he said after a moment. "Whyn't you have some?" He waved
at the hot plate, and she, feeling ridiculously like a guest, relit
the fire under the pot and took a cup from the cupboard.

After a second of the old struggle to force her mind and
voice to produce something worth listening to, she said miser-
ably, "How do you feel?"

He laughed. "I feel fine now, thank you. They're throwing
me out tomorrow."

The subject seemed closed. After pouring herself a cup of
coffee, she noticed his book on the table where he had placed
it—the new nine-hundred-page novel by a well-known "serious" author. "I didn't care for that," she said, touching it.
"He doesn't know what he's up to, so he just bunches it all
up and chucks it at you."

He looked at it and back at her. "Oh—you think so?"

He was doubtless wondering who she thought *she* was. "Well, we hadn't ought to talk about it before you finish it," she said desperately. She fumbled again in her mind and produced—still a platitude, but one at least closer to what she wanted to talk about—"Do you like teaching?"

"Yes."

She hesitated. "From what you hear. . . ." He looked up at her over his cup, and she faltered. "I mean, I know some people who go out there and I always thought—" She plunged on into it. "If they're all like that, I mean the ones I know, I'd think they'd drive you crazy."

He thrust one hand high into the air and said, "Better to light one little candle. . . ." He lowered the hand and grinned sheepishly. "No," he said. "I really like it very much."

They both looked up as official-sounding heel-clicks came down the main hall, grew louder at the mouth of the kitchen corridor, and then faded. They both breathed deeply, and Sirene said reluctantly, "You better get on back. They'll bawl you out."

"Um-hum. Rules and regulations."

And Sirene realized hazily that the subject was irretrievably changed, that she would not get to the words that would return them to it. He would go tomorrow, before she even got to work. He was not, of course, going around the world, but she would never call him at the university, never go out to visit his office. She would stay where she was, knowing what to expect.

There in the kitchen—in the silence, emphatic and eerie, after the passing of the heel-clicking, he said, "Why'd you ask, Sirene? Were you thinking of going to school out there? You ought to try it sometime."

At last, she began pouring out her questions, and he answered them patiently and easily. The costs were such-and-such, and by keeping her job she could afford them. Yes, lots of people worked and went to school; she probably shouldn't start out with a full schedule, but she could take at least three courses; some people even managed with full schedules. True, most of the students were younger than she, but at a school like City she would find plenty of people her age and even older.

Would she have to wait until next fall to start? No; the winter term was just about to begin. Regular freshman-class admissions were closed, but she could enter as a non-degree student, part-time, right up through the week before classes started, and transfer to degree status later.

They might ask for records from her high school; she could get her principal to fill out a form for her—or did she still have her diploma and report cards stuck around somewhere? Yes, well, just bundle them up and take them in with her. She could go in tomorrow, for that matter; the offices were open till noon on Saturdays.

"The Administration Building," he said. "You can't miss it; it's stuck right there in the center of the square with everything else around it."

She asked, much more easily now, "And you really think I ought to do it? You know how you get to thinking that going to school isn't much use. I mean"—she waved around her at the hospital—"if college turned out to be just like every place else—well, I might as well have my time in the library."

"I think you ought to try it," he said. "And don't be too disappointed if it's not *too* different; there's a lot of red tape around. Wherever there are large numbers of people, there's red tape."

He drank from his third cup of coffee. "But the thing to remember is, you will learn things you never heard about; you will read things you've never read. I know you like to read what you damn please, but the truth is you miss things you ought to read. And you'll meet a dozen people you'd never meet anywhere else, and you'll be able to talk to them all the rest of your life. You know what that is?" He saw her face. "Or maybe you don't, but I know what it is. I never used to talk to anybody, either. I still can't, to some people. But, all in all, I probably talk too damn much now. Go on, get on out there."

Then the heels began to click again, and this time did turn into the kitchen corridor. Sirene stiffened against the edge of the table, but Mr. Brant quickly refilled his cup, winked at her and hurried around the corner toward the footsteps.

Sirene heard the head nurse's heavy voice: "Against the rules for patients to be back here, Mr. Brant."

"Yes, ma'am," he said cheerfully. "That's what the lady was just telling me."

As the padding of his slippers faded, the nurse pivoted through the doorway. She bustled over to the hot plate and turned up the fire. "Let's be sure to keep the patients where they belong, Miss Scott."

"Yes'm," Sirene said happily. "That's what I told him."

But she did not go out to City the next morning. She woke up in the middle of the night and, feeling her way toward the bathroom, was wretchedly sick.

In the morning, the doctor was reassuring, if not particularly helpful, and the week she spent with the virus, or whatever it was, turned out to be, weakness and discomfort aside, a lazily pleasant one. Her mother agreeably walked to the library with a list, made up almost entirely of books Sirene had read before. When Sirene opened *Pride and Prejudice*,[6] the remote world of the story somehow became interchangeable with the world of the university; she wondered drowsily if she would find anything there to surprise her as much as Mr. Darcy had surprised Elizabeth.[7]

[6] *Pride and Prejudice*: novel by Jane Austen.
[7] *Mr. Darcy, Elizabeth*: leading characters in *Pride and Prejudice*.

She went back to work on Sunday. About ten-thirty on Monday morning, with her high-school diploma and report cards in a neat bundle, she left home in her old, secondhand car to drive across town to where the university buildings clustered in and around a city-block quadrangle.

Parking turned out to be a problem; ice and plowed snow lined the curbs, and all the spaces that looked empty had sports cars in them. She drove around and around. Finally, after waiting for some time behind a parked car before realizing that the boy inside was reading a book, she successfully followed another student to his car and pulled into the space he left. She shut off the motor and sighed so deeply that she laughed at herself. Her mood of increasing tenseness swung back to its earlier lightness.

The students she passed on the university walks looked animated and cheerful, and no one stared at her. She felt that she *ought* to be worried. What would be her first words to the man who would take her application? What would be her first words to Mr. Brant if she should see him?—and, picking at the very back of her mind, the timid person's deepest fear: Does he really remember me? Does anyone remember me when I'm not right there?

Remembering what Mr. Brant had said, she headed for the building in the center. She had been afraid that there would be more than one building in the center, or something. But there it was, by itself, and as she neared its entrance, she could read the carving in the stones above its doors—"Administration Building."

It did not occur to her to wonder why, if the winter term had not yet started, so many students crowded the walks.

Hanging from the ceiling just inside the Administration Building were signs with arrows on them, one reading "Admissions." She walked in the direction of the arrow, through a pair of swinging glass doors and up to a counter, behind which people were working at desks. To the smiling young man who rose and came toward her, she said, "I'd like to make out an application, please."

He was a tall, stooped young man with glasses. He said, "An application for the summer session, miss?"

What did that mean? "Well, I'm not—I'd like to start to school in this new term."

"I'm afraid applications for this winter are closed," he said.

She was ready for that one. "Yes, but I wanted to apply as a non-degree student. Part time."

"Well, yes. We were taking non-degree students right up till Thursday, when registration closed. But now the term's started, you see. Classes started today."

The typewriters clattered and the ventilators hummed loudly; Sirene felt herself holding her smile in place. After a deep breath, she said, "Thank you very much."

"I'm sorry," he said. "Can I give you an application form for summer?"

"I'll have to make plans. Thank you." She turned away, thinking savagely, I always *thank* people. She knew that in the four months between now and the summer session her impulse to act would disappear; she felt it ebbing now.

With an angry wrench, she turned back to the counter. She caught the young man as he began to lower himself into his swivel chair; he looked at her, eyebrows up, and came back toward her. She thought, He's not the only one surprised.

"Excuse me," she said, trying to keep her voice cheerful, "but if classes just started—if I could get fixed up today, I'd only have to miss a day or two. Is there no chance at all?"

"I'm terribly sorry."

"You said you were taking people up through Thursday; is there really that much difference?"

He smiled tightly. "Our closing date was Thursday. We have to stick to our rules."

She remembered Mr. Brant and the hospital room without a telephone. "Please," she said. "You could do it all today. I have my high-school diploma and my report cards right here. Please."

His eyes were now flittering from spot to spot on the counter, his brow deeply wrinkled. Sirene realized that he would rather help her than not. For the first time since her return to the counter, she felt a spark of real hope. "Mr. Brant was specially hoping I would come," she said, not even feeling ashamed. "Mr. Brant of your staff said I could use his name."

His gaze jerked up to her. "Do you know Al Brant?"

"Yes, I know Mr. Brant."

"So do I, as it happens." He really smiled now. He pulled a telephone toward him, flipped the pages of a small, paperbound directory and concentrated upon the dialing with the intense self-satisfaction of someone who has been handed a way out. "Maybe . . . we . . . can . . . just . . . settle this . . . right . . . now."

He waited. For that instant, Sirene felt as she remembered feeling one night in her early teens when, urged by her sisters, she had given a birthday party, and no one had arrived until a few minutes past the hour. She had been convinced that the carefully written invitations, the remarks exchanged with classmates about the coming occasion, had been cheerfully and casually forgotten by all but herself. Does anyone really remember me?

"Oh, what is your name?" the young man whispered.

"Scott. Miss Sirene Scott."

The telephone squawked. "Hello, Al?" he said, "This is Tony Mewhirter. Fine, thanks. Say, what can you tell me about a girl named Scott?"

A silence, then a squawk.

"Well, there's a young lady here named Scott who wants to enter late, says she has your recommendation."

A squawk, a silence, a series of grating syllables.

The young man frowned importantly. "OK, Al, thank you. Sorry to bother."

He hung up the phone. Sirene, watching him numbly, was still able to notice that he was just as happy as he had been before; his job was to settle things, and this thing was settled.

"I'm sorry, Miss Scott," he said. "I thought with a faculty member's recommendation we just might have made an exception. But Mr. Brant says your name is not familiar."

He watched her, his head bowed a little, looking up through the glasses. Sirene, as if standing outside her own swirl of emotion, saw his lively interest in what she would do. She said, "Thank you for the trouble."

We're all so polite, she thought as she pushed through the doors and took slow, careful steps down the paneled hall.

Then, for a moment, she excused Mr. Brant for forgetting. After all, he talked every day with people who were in college or wanted to go to college; he had no reason to be impressed by her.

But why should he forget? *She* had remembered; and that seemed suddenly to be a profound reason why he should have, too. When, in her slow walk, she reached the outside doors where the hall crossed another, she thought, the hell with being polite.

She took two steps up the intersecting hall to what looked like a cashier's window and said to the woman behind the marble counter, "Can you tell me where Mr. Brant's office is?"

"Who?" The woman picked up one of the paper-bound directories. "What department is he in, hon?"

"He teaches here."

"I know, but what department?" At Sirene's blank stare, the woman said, "What subject does he teach?"

"I don't know." The fact surprised her; she had thought of him as a wonderful teacher without knowing what he taught.

The woman flipped the pages and tossed the book away. "Sorry, hon, can't even look it up. They haven't even got the damn directory in alphabetical order. It's all arranged according to departments."

"Thank you," Sirene said. She could go back and inquire of the young man in the admissions office, but she'd told him that she *knew* Mr. Brant. She went out down the crosswalk.

As she passed a young couple swinging their clasped hands, she swerved toward them and said, "Could you tell me—" but her voice creaked in her throat, and they were already past her. Sirene was directly in front of an advancing pair of young men, and she said more successfully, "Can you tell me where Mr. Brant's office is?"

The taller one asked, "What department?" The shorter one said, "I'm sorry, I don't know the name." And after halting in their stride, they went on past, the taller one looking back.

Sirene hurried on into the building that rose before her, and found herself in a cafeteria line that crept between steel rails toward a clanging cash register. She dodged outside the rails and into the area of booths and tables. There she stopped in front of a noisy, semicircular booth. The faces began to turn, one by one, toward her, and then the whole booth seemed to swing toward her like a scythe. She said, in a voice only slightly raised, although she thought she was shouting, "Excuse me, but can any of you tell me where Mr. Brant's office is?"

The noise faded, and a girl giggled sharply; but a pale-faced girl at one end of the semicircle glared at the giggler and shouted to the booth, "Mr. Brant! Does anyone know?"

Sirene looked around the curve of faces that seemed to advance and recede. A boy in the middle said, "I'm sorry, miss. Ask around; someone'll know."

She took a step toward the next booth and stopped, seeing everyone there already looking at her. She turned again, not thinking but just turning, as though in a maze. She bumped into a boy rising from the small table behind her, a massive six-foot-five boy with the face of a peaceful child. She did not realize that his huge hand on her elbow was anything more than polite until he pointed her toward the door and said, "Look, miss, through that door over there. See that diagonal walk and the building it leads to? You can't miss it, a ten-story building, taller than any of the others. You walk over there and find 617; that's Mr. Brant."

The crosswalk was a blur of faces that looked at her; the elevator very nearly made her sick, and she leaned against its wall, feeling herself drain away toward her toes. After getting off, she turned right toward 650 and walked to 622 before she realized that she was seeing only even numbers. She stopped, turned back, and walked on without knowing whether she was doubling back or not. After a while she saw 601 and went on to 613, 615, 617.

Beyond the open door, slouched in a swivel chair, listening with a smile to a student who sat leaning across the corner of the desk toward him, sat Mr. Brant.

Without thinking even to knock, Sirene strode across the threshold, a set smile on her face. She heard herself say bitterly, "Please don't get up."

He looked, then scrambled up out of the chair. He smiled happily at her and said, "Why, hi, Sirene!"

She suddenly understood everything that had happened. She remembered the exact words of the young man's telephone call, and she saw with relief, and even amusement, the collapse of Mr. Brant's face. Sirene loved the quickness with which he understood, too. He said, "Oh, no, Sirene, are you Miss Scott?"

And she was giggling helplessly and sitting in the chair vacated by the student, a big-nosed boy who smiled at her hesitantly. Mr. Brant was reaching for the phone and saying, "Oh, Lord. Sirene, this is Irving. Irv, this is Miss Scott, Sirene Scott. Don't ever call her anything but Sirene."

Giddily, she thrust out her hand to the boy. He grinned, took her hand, waved, and left. Beside her, Mr. Brant had hung up and was saying, "Come on, let's go over. They're supposed to close from twelve to one, but I told Mewhirter the system wouldn't collapse if he stayed open till we got there."

Sirene, standing, suddenly felt timid again, but she said firmly, "I'm so glad to have influential friends."

Understanding the Story

1. To a reader, what is the effect of the first paragraph?
2. List the duties of a nurse's aide, as they are indicated or suggested in the story. What are Sirene's reactions as she performs them?
3. Find evidence of Sirene's sensitivity to the people with whom she comes into contact.
4. What is the importance in the story of Mr. Brant's determination to have a telephone in his room?
5. How is Sirene's attitude toward college determined? How does Mr. Brant's view affect her attitude?
6. What obstacles are in Sirene's way when she gets to City? How does she overcome them? Explain the misunderstanding about her name.

*Appreciating
the Story*

1. How does the author change the tone of the story to reveal the thoughts of Sirene, the hospital personnel, and Mr. Brant?
2. Sirene's character is built for the reader through carefully selected details. Select the details you think are particularly effective in revealing character and indicate what they add to your undestanding of Sirene.
3. The relationship between Sirene and Mr. Brant seems quite natural to the reader. How does the author make this relationship real? What interaction between the two does he describe?
4. Through Sirene's eyes, we get a number of criticisms of her world. What criticisms are suggested of high school guidance? Of hospital routine? Of college students? To what extent are these true or just a reflection of Sirene's own attitude toward herself?
5. Locate evidences of humor in the story. What do they add or detract?
6. Notice where the author chooses to end the story. Would you have ended it sooner? Later? Justify your answer.

The Story
of the
Widow's
Son

MARY LAVIN

*Approaching
the Story . . .*

MANY of us often wish that we had a second
chance to do either the right thing, after we realize we have acted wrongly, or the better thing,
after we have behaved not so well. But what
would happen if that second chance came?
Would we be prepared for it? Are we certain
that we would indeed do the right thing, the
better thing? Or are we fated to repeat the errors
we have already made in a different form?

"The Story of the Widow's Son" is really two
stories, because Mary Lavin has given her characters a second chance to do it over differently.
The second ending will surprise you and leave
you thinking about whether yourself or fate is
your worst enemy.

The story is set in Ireland; the characters are
an Irish widow, her fourteen-year-old son, and
her neighbors. The conversation is typical of
rural Ireland. Yet the story has appeal for all
those of us who have wished we might be able

to improve on the past. And who among us has not had that secret wish?

... And Keep
in Mind

THE key to the story is the character of the widow. There is a double relationship between the widow and her son, Packy, a public relationship—the one shown to the neighbors—and a very private relationship. The widow has trouble making her feelings clear to her son in their private relationship. As you read, find the most important ingredients of her personality and see how they affect her actions to her son. Note, too, the question that unifies the two different endings: "Why did he put the price of one old hen above the price of his own life?"

You should find this story moving. After you have finished reading it, ask yourself how the author has been able to make it so.

T HIS IS THE STORY of a widow's son, but it is a story that has two endings.

There was once a widow, living in a small neglected village at the foot of a steep hill. She had only one son, but he was the meaning of her life. She wore herself out working for him. She made a hundred sacrifices in order to keep him at a good school in the town, four miles away, because there was a better teacher there than the village dullard that had taught herself.

She made great plans for Packy, but she did not tell him

about her plans. Instead she threatened him, day and night, that if he didn't turn out well, she would put him to work on the roads, or in the quarry under the hill.

But as the years went by, everyone in the village, and even Packy himself, could tell by the way she watched him out of sight in the morning, and watched to see him come into sight in the evening, that he was the beat of her heart, and that her gruff words were only a cover for her pride and her joy in him.

It was for Packy's sake that she walked for hours along the road, letting her cow graze the long acre of the wayside grass, in order to spare the few poor blades that pushed up through the stones in her own field. It was for his sake she walked back and forth to the town to sell a few cabbages as soon as ever they were fit. It was for his sake that she got up in the cold dawning hours to gather mushrooms to take the place of foods that had to be bought.

She bent her back daily to make every penny she could, and as often happens, she made more by industry, out of her few bald acres, than many of the farmers around her made out of their great bearded meadows. Out of the money she made by selling eggs alone, she paid for Packy's clothes and for the greater number of his books.

When Packy was fourteen, he was in the last class in the school, and the master had great hopes of his winning a scholarship to a big college in the city. He was getting to be a tall lad, and his features were beginning to take a strong cast. His character was strengthening too, under his mother's sharp tongue. The people of the village were beginning to give him the same respect they gave to the sons of the farmers who came from their fine colleges in the summer, with blue suits and bright ties. And whenever they spoke to the widow, they praised him to the skies.

One day in June, when the air was so heavy the scent that rose up from the grass was imprisoned under the low clouds

and hung in the air, the widow was waiting at the gate for
Packy. There had been no rain for some days and the hens
and chickens were pecking irritably at the dry ground and
wandering up and down the road in bewilderment. A neighbor passed.

"Waiting for Packy?" said the neighbor, pleasantly, and
he stood for a minute to take off his hat and wipe the sweat
of the day from his face. He was an old man.

"It's a hot day!" he said. "It will be a hard push for Packy
on that battered old bike of his. I wouldn't like to have to
face into four miles on a day like this!"

"Packy would travel three times that distance if there was
a book at the other end!" said the widow, with the pride of
those who cannot read more than a line or two.

The minutes went by slowly. The widow kept looking up at
the sun. "I suppose the heat is better than the rain!"

"The heat can do a lot of harm, too, though," said the
neighbor, absent-mindedly, as he pulled a long blade of grass
from between the stones of the wall and began to chew the
end of it. "You could get sunstroke on a day like this!"

The widow strained out further over the gate. She looked
up the hill in the direction of the town.

"He will have a good cool breeze on his face coming down
the hill, at any rate," she said.

The man looked up the hill. "That's true. On the hottest
day of the year you would get a cool breeze coming down
that hill on a bicycle. You would feel the air streaming past
your cheeks like silk. And in the winter it's like two knives
flashing to either side of you, and peeling off your skin like
you'd peel the bark off a sally-rod.[1] " He chewed the grass
meditatively. "That must be one of the steepest hills in Ireland," he said. "That hill is a hill worthy of the name of a

---

[1] *Sally-rod:* branch of a willow tree that grows in Ireland.

hill. It's my belief that that hill is to be found marked with a name in the Ordinance Survey map!"[2]

"If that's the case," said the widow, "Packy will be able to tell you all about it. When it isn't a book he has in his hand, it's a map."

"Is that so?" said the man. "A map is a great thing. It isn't everyone can make out a map."

"I think I see Packy!" the widow said.

At the top of the hill there was a glitter of spokes as a bicycle came into sight. Then there was a flash of blue jersey as Packy came flying downward, gripping the handlebars of the bike, with his bright hair blown back from his forehead. The hill was so steep, and he came down so fast, that it seemed to the man and woman at the bottom of the hill that he was not moving at all, but that it was the bright trees and bushes, the bright ditches and wayside grasses that were streaming away to either side of him.

The hens and chickens clucked and squawked and ran along the road looking for a safe place in the ditches. Packy waved to his mother. He came nearer and nearer. They could see the freckles on his face.

"Shoo!" cried Packy, at the squawking hens. They ran with their long necks straining forward.

"Shoo!" said Packy's mother, lifting her apron and flapping it in the air to frighten them out of his way.

It was only afterwards, when the harm was done, that the widow began to think that it might, perhaps, have been the flapping of her own apron that frightened the old clucking hen, and sent her flying out into the middle of the road.

Packy jammed on the brakes. The widow screamed. There was a flurry of white feathers and a spurt of blood. The bicycle swerved and fell. Packy was thrown over the handlebars.

[2] *Ordinance Survey map:* map based on an official government survey of the United Kingdom.

It was such a simple accident that, although the widow screamed, and although the old man looked around to see if there was help near, neither of them thought that Packy was very badly hurt, but when they ran over and lifted his head, and saw that he could not speak, they wiped the blood from his face and looked around, desperately, to measure the distance they would have to carry him. It was only a few yards to the door of the cottage, but Packy was dead before they got him across the threshold.

"He's only in a weakness!" screamed the widow, and she urged the crowd that had gathered outside the door to do something for him. "Get a doctor!" she cried. "Hurry! Hurry! The doctor will bring him around."

But the neighbors that kept coming in the door, quickly, from all sides, were crossing themselves, one after another, and falling on their knees, as soon as they laid eyes on the boy stretched out flat on the bed, with the dust and dirt and the sweat marks of life on his dead face.

When at last the widow was convinced that her son was dead, the other women had to hold her down. She waved her arms and cried out aloud, and wrestled to get free. She wanted to wring the neck of every hen in the yard.

"I'll kill every one of them. What good are they to me, now? That old clucking hen wasn't worth more than six shillings, at the very most. What is six shillings? Is it worth poor Packy's life?"

But after a time she stopped raving, and looked from one face to another. "Why didn't he ride over the old hen?" she asked. "Why did he try to save an old hen that wasn't worth more than six shillings? Didn't he know he was worth more to his mother than an old hen? Why did he do it? Why did he put on the brakes going down one of the worst hills in the country? Why? Why?"

The neighbors patted her arm. "There now!" they said.

"There now!" and that was all they could think of saying.

And years afterwards, whenever the widow spoke of Packy to the neighbors who dropped in to keep her company for an hour or two, she always had the same question to ask.

"Why did he put the price of an old clucking hen above the price of his own life?"

And the people always gave the same answer.

"There now!" they said. "There now!" And they sat as silently as the widow herself, looking into the fire.

But surely some of those neighbors must have been stirred to wonder what would have happened had Packy not yielded to his impulse of fear, and had, instead, ridden boldly over the old clucking hen. And surely some of them must have stared into the flames and pictured the scene of the accident again, altering a detail here and there as they did so, and giving the story a different end.

For these people knew the widow, and they knew Packy, and when you know people well it is as easy to guess what they would say and do in certain circumstances as it is to remember what they actually did say and do in other circumstances. In fact, it is sometimes easier to invent than to remember accurately, and were this not so two great branches of creative art would wither in an hour: the art of the storyteller and the art of the gossip.

So, perhaps, if I try to tell you what I myself think might have happened had Packy killed that cackling old hen, you will not accuse me of abusing my privileges as a writer. After all, what I am about to tell you is no more of a fiction than what I have already told, and I lean no heavier now upon your credulity than, with your full consent, I did in the first instance.

Moreover, in many respects the new story is the same as the old. It begins in the same way.

There is the widow, grazing her cow by the wayside, and

walking the long roads to the town, weighted down with
sacks of cabbages that will pay for Packy's schooling. There
she is fussing over Packy in the mornings in case he would be
late for school. There she is in the evening watching the battered clock on the dresser for the hour when he will return.
And there too, on a hot day in June, is the old laboring man
coming up the road, and pausing to talk to her. There he is
dragging a blade of glass from between the stones of the wall,
and putting it between his teeth to chew, before he opens his
mouth. And when he opens his mouth at last, it is to utter the
same remark.

"Waiting for Packy?" said the old man, and then he took
off his hat and wiped the sweat from his forehead. "It's a hot
day," he said.

"It's very hot," said the widow, looking anxiously up the
hill. "It's a hot day to push a bicycle four miles along a bad
road with the dust rising to choke you, and sun striking spikes
off the handlebars!"

"The heat is better than the rain, all the same," said the
old man.

"I suppose it is," said the widow. "All the same, there were
days when Packy came home with the rain dried into his
clothes so bad they stood up stiff like boards against the wall,
for all the world as if he was still standing in them!"

"Is that so?" said the old man. "You may be sure he got a
good petting on those days. There is no son like a widow's
son. A ewe lamb!"

"Is it Packy?" said the widow, in disgust. "Packy never got
a day's petting since the day he was born. I made up my mind
from the first that I'd never make a soft one out of him."

The widow looked up the hill again, and set herself to
raking the gravel outside the gate as if she were in the road
for no other purpose. Then she gave another look up the hill.

"Here he is now!" she said, and she raised such a cloud of

dust with the rake that they could hardly see the glitter of
the bicycle spokes, and the flash of blue as Packy came down
the hill at a breakneck speed. Nearer and nearer he came,
faster and faster, waving his hand to the widow, shouting at
the hens to leave the way!

The hens ran for the ditches, stretching their necks in
gawky terror. And then, as the last hen squawked into the
ditch, the way was clear for a moment before the whirling
silver spokes. Then, unexpectedly, up from nowhere it
seemed, came an old clucking hen and, clucking despairingly,
it stood for a moment on the top of the wall and then rose into
the air with the clumsy flight of a ground fowl.

Packy stopped whistling. The widow screamed. Packy
yelled and the widow flapped her apron. Then Packy swerved
the bicycle, and a cloud rose from the braked wheel.

For a minute it could not be seen what exactly had happened, but Packy put his foot down and dragged it along the
ground in the dust till he brought the bicycle to a sharp stop.
He threw the bicycle down with a clatter on the hard road
and ran back. The widow could not bear to look. She threw
her apron over her head.

"He's killed the clucking hen!" she said. "He's killed her!
He's killed her!" and then she began to run up the hill.

"Did you kill it?" screamed the widow, and as she got near
enough to see the blood and feathers she raised her arm over
her head, and her fist was clenched till the knuckles shone
white. Packy cowered over the carcass of the fowl and
hunched up his shoulders as if to shield himself from a blow.
His legs were spattered with blood, and the brown and white
feathers of the dead hen were stuck to his hands, and stuck
to his clothes, and they were strewn all over the road. Some of
the short white inner feathers were still swirling with the dust
in the air.

"I couldn't help it Mother. I couldn't help it. I didn't see her till it was too late!"

The widow caught up the hen and examined it all over, holding it by the bone of the breast, and letting the long neck dangle. Then, catching it by the leg, she raised it suddenly above her head, and brought down the bleeding body on the boy's back, in blow after blow, spattering the blood all over his face and his hands and over his clothes.

"How dare you lie to me!" she screamed, gaspingly, between the blows. "You saw the hen. I know you saw it. You stopped whistling! You called out! We were watching you. We saw." She turned upon the old man. "Isn't that right?" she demanded. "He saw the hen, didn't he?"

"It looked that way," said the old man, uncertainly.

"There you are!" said the widow. She threw the hen down on the road. "You saw the hen in front of you on the road, as plain as you see it now," she accused, "but you wouldn't stop to save it because you were in too big a hurry home to fill your belly! Isn't that so?"

"No, mother. No! I saw her all right but it was too late to do anything."

"He admits now that he saw it," said the widow, turning and nodding triumphantly at the onlookers who had gathered at the sound of the shouting.

"I never denied seeing it!" said the boy, appealing to the onlookers as to his judges.

"He doesn't deny it!" screamed the widow. "He stands there as brazen as you like, and admits for all the world to hear that he saw the hen as plain as the nose on his face, and he rode over it without a thought!"

"But what else could I do?" said the boy, throwing out his hand; appealing to the crowd now, and now appealing to the widow. "If I'd put on the brakes going at such a speed I would have been put over the handlebars!"

"And what harm would that have done you?" screamed the widow. "I often saw you taking a toss when you were wrestling with Jimmy Mack and I heard no complaints afterwards, although your elbows and knees would be running blood, and your face scraped like a gridiron!"

She turned to the crowd. "That's as true as God. I often saw him come in with his nose spouting blood like a pump, and one eye closed as tight as the eye of a corpse. My hand was often stiff for a week from sopping out wet cloths to put poultices on him and try to bring his face back to rights again."

She swung back to Packy again. "You're not afraid of a fall when you go climbing trees, are you? You're not afraid to go up on the roof after a cat, are you? You killed that hen on purpose—that's what I believe! You're tired of going to school. You want to get out of going away to college. That's it! You think if you kill the few poor hens we have there will be no money when the time comes to pay for books and classes. That's it!" Packy began to redden.

"It's late in the day for me to be thinking of things like that," he said. "It's long ago I should have started those tricks if that was the way I felt. But it's not true, I want to go to college. The reason I was coming down the hill so fast was to tell you that I got the scholarship. The teacher told me as I was leaving the schoolhouse. That's why I was waving my hand. Didn't you see me waving my hand from the top of the hill?"

The widow's hands fell to her sides. The wind of words died down within her and left her flat and limp. She didn't know what to say. She could feel the neighbors staring at her. She wanted to throw out her arms to the boy, to drag him against her heart and hug him like a small child. But she thought of how the crowd would look at each other and nod and snigger. A ewe lamb! If she gave in to her feelings now they would know how much she had been counting on his getting the scholarship.

She looked at Packy, and when she saw him standing before her, spattered with the furious feathers and crude blood of the dead hen, she felt a fierce disappointment for the boy's own disappointment, and a fierce resentment against him for killing the hen on this day of all days, and spoiling the great news of his success.

Her mind was in confusion. She stared at the blood on his face, and all at once it seemed as if the blood was a bad omen of the future that was for him. Disappointment,. fear, resentment, and above all defiance, raised themselves within her. She looked from Packy to the onlookers.

"Scholarship! Scholarship!" she sneered, putting as much derision as she could into her voice and expression.

"I suppose you think you are a great fellow now? I suppose you think you are independent now? I suppose you think you can go off with yourself now, and look down on your poor slave of a mother who scraped and sweated for you with her cabbages and her hens? Is that the way? Well, let me tell you this! You're not as independent as you think. The scholarship may pay for your books and your teacher's fees but who will pay for your clothes? Ah-ha, you forgot that, didn't you?"

She put her hands on her hips. Packy hung his head. He no longer appealed to the gawking neighbors. They might have been able to save him from blows but he knew that no one could save him from shame.

The widow's heart burned at sight of his shamed face, as her heart burned, with grief, but her temper, too, burned fiercer, and she came to a point at which nothing could quell the blaze till it had burned itself out.

"Who'll buy your suits?" she yelled. "Who'll buy your boots?" She paused to think of more humiliating accusations. "Who'll buy your breeches?" What would wound deepest?

What shame could she drag upon him? "Who'll buy your nightshirts or will you sleep in your skin?"

The neighbors laughed at that, and the tension was broken. The widow herself laughed. She held her sides and laughed, and as she laughed everything seemed to take on a newer and simpler significance. Things were not as bad as they seemed a moment before. She wanted Packy to laugh too. She looked at him. But as she looked at Packy, her heart turned cold with a strange new fear.

"Get into the house!" she said, giving him a push. She wanted him safe under her own roof. She wanted to get him away from the gaping neighbors. She hated them, man, woman and child. She felt that if they had not been there things would have been different. And she wanted to get away from the sight of the blood on the road. She wanted to mash a few potatoes and make a bit of potato cake for Packy. That would comfort him. He loved that.

Packy hardly touched the food. And even after he had washed and scrubbed himself there were stains of blood turning up in the most unexpected places: behind his ears, under his fingernails, inside the cuff of his sleeve.

"Put on your good clothes," said the widow, making a great effort to be gentle, but her manners had become as twisted and as hard as the branches of the trees across the road. Even the kindly offers she made sounded harsh.

The boy sat on the chair in a slumped position that kept her nerves on edge and set up a further conflict of irritation and love in her heart. She hated to see him slumping there in the chair, not asking to go outside the door, but still she was uneasy whenever he as much as looked in the direction of the door. She felt safe while he was under the roof, inside the lintel, under her eyes.

Next day she went in to wake him for school, but his room was empty; his bed had not been slept in, and when she ran out into the yard and called him there was no answer. She ran up and down. She called at the houses of the neighbors, but he was not in any house.

She thought she could hear sniggering behind her in each house that she left, as she ran to another one. He wasn't in the village. He wasn't in the town. The master of the school said that she should let the police have a description of him. He said he never met a boy as sensitive as Packy. A boy like that took strange notions into his head.

The police did their best but there was no news of Packy that night. A few days later there was a letter saying that he was well. He asked his mother to notify the master that he would not be coming back, so that some other boy could claim the scholarship. He said that he would send the price of the hen as soon as he made some money.

Another letter in a few weeks said that he had got a job on a trawler, and that he would not be able to write very often but that he would put aside some of his pay every week and send it to his mother whenever he got into port. He said that he wanted to pay her back for all she had done for him. He gave no address. He kept his promise about the money, but he never gave any address when he wrote.

... And so the people may have let their thoughts run on, as they sat by the fire with the widow, many a night, listening to her complaining voice saying the same thing over and over. "Why did he put the price of one old hen above the price of his own life?"

And it is possible that their version of the story has a certain element of truth about it, too. Perhaps all our actions have this double quality about them, this possibility of alternative, and that it is only by careful watching and absolute sincerity, that we follow the path that is destined for us, and, no matter how tragic that may be, it is better than the tragedy we bring upon ourselves.

1. Cite several examples of the widow's devotion to her son.
2. What qualities of the widow's character are shown in her conversation with her neighbor? Which qualities emerge from the tragic incident itself?
3. Show how the qualities you have identified determine the outcome in the second telling of the story.
4. Explain the following:
   a. "She had only one son, but he was the meaning of her life."
   b. "The boy sat on the chair in a slumped position that kept her nerves on edge and set up a further conflict of irritation and love in her heart."
   c. "In fact, it is sometimes easier to invent than to remember accurately, and were this not so two great branches of creative art would wither in an hour: the art of the storyteller and the art of the gossip."
5. Show the difference between the widow's outward and inward reactions to the news of Packy's scholarship. Why are they different?
6. Explain the final sentence of the story. What is the author saying about the nature of destiny?

1. There is a poetic quality about the writing of this story. Give examples of poetic expression from the story.
2. Study the structure of this sentence. "It's long ago I should have started those tricks if that's

the way I felt." How does the statement capture the quality of rural Irish speech?

3. How does the author move from the first ending of the story to the second? What makes this transition effective?

4. What role do the neighbors play in the story? Would the story have been less effective without them? Why or why not?

5. Think through the entire story after reading it. Then rewrite it from Packy's point of view, keeping the double-ending technique.

6. What is the effect of the question, "Why did he put the price of one old hen above the price of his own life?" after the first ending? The second?

Reviewing
the
Unit

For Comparative Study

1. Contrast Donald and Sirene with respect to:
   a. their outlook on life.
   b. their attitude toward themselves.
   c. their attitude toward education.
2. Compare the attitude of the Flemings toward Donald with the Widow's toward Packy.
3. Each of the stories has a character who acts under pressure. What does each crisis reveal about Mrs. Fleming? Mr. Fleming? Sirene? The Widow?
4. In a sense, Mr. Brant is an instrument of fate for Sirene. For the Widow, the hen serves the same purpose. Explain.
5. To what extent do the characters determine the outcome of the stories? What part does fate play? Explain your answers.
6. Some of the characters have difficulty communicating their thoughts—Donald to his parents, the Widow to Packy. Why is this so? How can this difficulty be overcome?
7. What do you think becomes of Donald? Packy? Sirene? Explain your answers.

Building Your Vocabulary

The following descriptive words are found in the stories of this unit. Copy the sentences in your notebook, filling in the appropriate adjective.

animated   irretrievable
brazen   judicious
derisive   sullen
downcast   tentative
fretful   wry

1. The _____ boys crashed the party and refused to leave.
2. The wise man made a _____ decision.
3. The disappointed bride had a _____ expression.
4. She put a _____ toe into the icy water.
5. When the guest on the television talk show entered, the discussion grew _____.
6. Babies with colic are usually _____.
7. When insulted, children will become _____.
8. After tasting the new bride's cooking, her husband made a _____ face.
9. The ring that fell down the drain is _____.
10. _____ laughter greeted his stupid suggestion.

For Creative
Writing
of Original
Short Stories

Use one of the following as the title for an original short story.

1. A Stranger Knocks
2. My Biggest Mistake
3. A Gamble Pays Off
4. Born Under a Lucky Star
5. Master of My Fate
6. How _____ Beat His (Her) Handicap
7. Opportunity Only Knocks Once
8. Fortune or Failure?
9. The Big Chance
10. A Second Chance

UNDERSTANDING
OURSELVES

"MAN doth not live by bread only," says the Bible. In addition to the physical needs for food and shelter, we have emotional needs that have to be satisfied. The "poor little rich boy" is an example of the person who has wealth and is still unhappy because he may be without friends, unloved, or not recognized as an individual. In other words, although his physical needs are satisfied, his emotional needs are not.

What are our emotional needs? Some are the need to have a feeling of belonging—to a family group, to a club, to a community; the need to be loved—by parents, by brothers and sisters, by a member of the opposite sex; the need to achieve, to accomplish something of worth. Everyone needs to be accepted for himself,, as a unique individual. The need exists, too, to find release from the pressures of daily living by escape to the world of the imagination.

The stories in this unit deal with people who seek, consciously or unconsciously, to satisfy their emotional needs. Jeanie, who lives in a world of asphalt ugliness, wants to see the sky. Tommie and Margie yearn for teachers who are people. The search for emotional satisfaction will become part of you, as you find yourself identifying with the characters in these stories. You should begin to recognize your own feelings and their importance in your life. As a result you will understand yourself better and be on the way to fulfilling the age-old advice, "Know thyself."

The Fun
They Had

ISAAC ASIMOV

*Approaching
the Story . . .*

Isaac Asimov is one of the foremost American
writers of science fiction. In many instances, however, his tales of the future have a good deal to
say about the present. In this story, you are asked
to project yourself nearly two hundred years into
the future. You will see words you won't find in
any dictionary—words like telebook, but you
won't have any difficulty in figuring out what
they mean. Young Margie and Tommy are talking about the schools of today—hundreds of years
in the past to them. It will be a strange sensation
to read about your kind of schools discussed by
children who can't imagine what they are like.

This is a short short story. A short short story
comes to the point with as few words as possible.
It usually places the emphasis on the story, rather
than on character or setting and often ends with
an unexpected surprise twist.

*. . . And Keep
in Mind*

As you read, you will recognize certain familiar
things; others will seem strange in the school
setting. The author intends you to compare your
school of today with the school that Tommy and
Margie attend. Note how they are alike and differ-

ent and ask yourself why the author has stressed the differences. Remember, too, that with the fewest words possible, the author is building up to a conclusion that will surprise and amuse you. It will also leave you thinking about your relationship with your teacher in the world of today.

$\mathbf{M}$ARGIE EVEN WROTE IT that night in her diary. On the page headed May 17, 2155, she wrote, "Today Tommy found a real book!"

It was a very old book. Margie's grandfather once said that when he was a little boy *his* grandfather told him there was a time all stories were printed on paper.

They turned the pages, which were yellow and crinkly, and it was awfully funny to read words that stood still instead of moving the way they were supposed to—on a screen, you know. And then, when they turned back to the page before, it had the same words on it that it had had when they read it the first time.

"Gee," said Tommy, "what a waste. When you're through with the book, you just throw it away, I guess. Our television screen must have had a million books on it and it's good for plenty more. I wouldn't throw it away.

"Same with mine," said Margie. She was eleven and hadn't seen as many telebooks [1] as Tommy had. He was thirteen.

She said, "Where did you find it?"

"In my house." He pointed without looking, because he was busy reading. "In the attic."

---

[1] *Telebooks:* word made up to indicate books shown on a television screen rather than printed and bound.

"What's it about?"

"School."

Margie was scornful. "School? What's there to write about school? I hate school." Margie always hated school, but now she hated it more than ever. The mechanical teacher had been giving her test after test in geography and she had been doing worse and worse until her mother had shaken her head sorrowfully and sent for the County Inspector.

He was a round little man with a red face and a whole box of tools with dials and wires. He smiled at her and gave her an apple, then took the teacher apart. Margie had hoped he wouldn't know how to put it together again, but he knew how all right and after an hour or so, there it was again, large and black and ugly with a big screen on which all the lessons were shown and the questions were asked. That wasn't so bad. The part she hated most was the slot where she had to put homework and test papers. She always had to write them out in a punch code they made her learn when she was six years old, and the mechanical teacher calculated the mark in no time.

The Inspector had smiled after he was finished and patted her head. He said to her mother, "It's not the little girl's fault, Mrs. Jones. I think the geography sector was geared a little too quick. Those things happen sometimes. I've slowed it up to an average ten-year level. Actually, the over-all pattern of her progress is quite satisfactory." And he patted Margie's head again.

Margie was disappointed. She had been hoping they would take the teacher away altogether. They had once taken Tommy's teacher away for nearly a month because the history sector had blanked out completely.

So she said to Tommy, "Why would anyone write about school?"

Tommy looked at her with very superior eyes. "Because

it's not our kind of school, stupid. This is the old kind of school that they had hundreds and hundreds of years ago." He added loftily, pronouncing the word carefully, "*Centuries* ago."

Margie was hurt. "Well, I don't know what kind of school they had all that time ago." She read the book over his shoulder for a while, then said, "Anyway, they had a teacher."

"Sure they had a teacher, but it wasn't a *regular* teacher. It was a man."

"A man? How could a man be a teacher?"

"Well, he just told the boys and girls things and gave them homework and asked them questions."

"A man isn't smart enough."

"Sure he is. My father knows as much as my teacher."

"He can't. A man can't know as much as a teacher."

"He knows almost as much, I betcha."

Margie wasn't prepared to dispute that. She said, "I wouldn't want a strange man in my house to teach me."

Tommy screamed with laughter. "You don't know much, Margie. The teachers didn't live in the house. They had a special building and all the kids went there."

"And all the kids learned the same thing?"

"Sure, if they were the same age."

"But my mother says a teacher has to be adjusted to fit the mind of each boy and girl it teaches and that each kid has to be taught differently."

"Just the same they didn't do it that way then. If you don't like it, you don't have to read the book."

"I didn't say I didn't like it," Margie said quickly. She wanted to read about those funny schools.

They weren't even half finished when Margie's mother called, "Margie! School!"

Margie looked up. "Not yet, Mamma."

"Now," said Mrs. Jones. "And it's probably time for Tommy, too."

Margie said to Tommy, "Can I read the book some more with you after school?"

"Maybe," he said nonchalantly. He walked away whistling, the dusty old book tucked beneath his arm.

Margie went into the schoolroom. It was right next to her bedroom, and the mechanical teacher was on and waiting for her. It was always on at the same time every day except Saturday and Sunday, because her mother said little girls learned better if they learned at regular hours.

The screen was lit up, and it said: "Today's arithmetic lesson is on the addition of proper fractions. Please insert yesterday's homework in the proper slot."

Margie did so with a sigh. She was thinking about the old schools they had when her grandfather's grandfather was a little boy. All the kids from the whole neighborhood came, laughing and shouting in the schoolyard, sitting together in the schoolroom, going home together at the end of the day. They learned the same things so they could help one another on the homework and talk about it.

And the teachers were people. . . .

The mechanical teacher was flashing on the screen: "When we add the fractions ½ and ¼—"

Margie was thinking about how the kids must have loved it in the old days. She was thinking about the fun they had.

Understanding the Story

1. What is school like in the year 2155? How is it different from school today?
2. What is Margie's attitude towards school? To what extent is it justified?
3. Comment on each of the following:
   a. ". . . my mother says a teacher has to be

adjusted to fit the mind of each boy and
girl it teaches and that each kid has to be
taught differently."

b. "... her mother said little girls learned better if they learned at regular hours."

c. "They learned the same things so they could
help one another on the homework and talk
about it."

4. Explain the meaning of the final paragraph.

5. What are the arguments for and against auto-
mated teaching?

*Appreciating
the Story*

1. What is the purpose of the story? Why is the
method the author has used to achieve it effective?

2. Identify the elements of good science fiction.
How do they figure in this story?

3. Find evidence of humor. How does it add to
the effectiveness of the story?

4. How well does the author succeed in condens-
ing his story into a "short short"? What single
incident sets the whole story into motion?

5. In the final paragraph the author suggests
more than he states. How does this contribute
to the surprise ending?

Beauty
Is Truth

ANNA GUEST

*Approaching
the Story . . .*

MOST of us go through the day totally unaware
of the beauty that is around us—a bird's call, a
falling leaf, a perfectly shaped skyscraper, a plane
in flight, a flaming sunset. At times we consciously seek out the beautiful, by a visit to a
museum, for example. The author of "Beauty is
Truth" is very much concerned with awareness
of everyday life and the beauty in it. Before you
read this story, look around you. Pick out something you feel is beautiful. It may be the tree
outside your window or the smile on your
mother's face. Perhaps you have difficulty finding
anything you consider beautiful. All of us, however, have a particular thing we turn to when
we need something pleasing to the eye or to the
ear.

*. . . And Keep
in Mind*

JEANIE is a student in an urban high school. She
travels "downtown" to school by train and re-
turns by train when her classes are over. Like
many high school girls, she has duties at home.
But what does a sensitive girl do when she lives
in a poverty-stricken neighborhood and realizes
that everything around her is ugly and hateful?

As you read, try to join Jeanie in her search for
beauty in her life. Early in the story you will find
that the odds are against her. You will admire her
strength and her honesty in facing and trying to
overcome the terrible reality that could easily
crush anyone without Jeanie's character. This is
a story that, like the composition Jeanie writes as
her homework assignment, is "pain and truth and
beauty."

Aт 125тн street,[1]
they all got off—Jeanie and her friend, Barbara, and a crowd
of other girls and boys coming home from the same downtown
high school. Through the train window, Jeanie thought she
saw the remaining passengers look at them with relief and
disdain. Around her, the boys and girls pressed forward with
noisy gaiety. They were all friends now. They were home
again. A tall boy detached himself from a group, bowed low
and swept his cap before him in a courtly salute.

"Greetings, Lady Jeanie. Greetings, Barbara."

Jeanie bit her lip. Frowning, she pulled her coat closer and
shrugged. Barbara smiled and dimpled, pleased for her friend.

"I told you he likes you," she whispered. "Look, he's waiting. Want me to go on ahead?"

Jeanie really was wasting an opportunity, Barbara thought.
Norman was keen. She saw Jeanie's head, slightly bowed and
thrust forward. It was no use. She was an odd girl, but Barbara
liked her anyway. The boy swung gracefully back to his
group.

"Coming to the show tonight?" Barbara asked.

[1] 125th Street: subway station located in Harlem in New York City.

Jeanie still frowned.

"No, I can't," she said. "I'm so far behind in my homework, I'd better try to do some before they decide to throw me out."

"Want a Coke or something?" asked Barbara as they passed the big ice cream parlor window, cluttered with candy boxes and ornate with curly lettering. They could see the jukebox near the door and some boys and girls sitting down at a table. It looked warm and friendly.

Jeanie shook her head, one brief shake. "I think I'll stop in. I'm thirsty," said Barbara.

Jeanie shrugged.

"So long, then."

"So long."

Jeanie walked along the busy street, aimlessly looking in the store windows. She turned the corner and walked the few blocks to her house. Though it was chilly, each brownstone or gray stoop had its cluster of people clinging to the iron railings. Some children on skates played a desperate game of hockey with sticks that were not hockey sticks. When a car approached, they did not interrupt their game until it was almost too late. Amid shouts from the driver and wild jeers from the children, the car passed, and the game was resumed in all its concentrated intensity.

Her little brother Billy was playing in front of the stoop with three or four other children. They were bending over something on the sidewalk, in a closed circle. Pitching pennies again, she thought with repugnance! She was going to pass them, and started up the three stone steps to the doorway. A window on the ground floor opened, and Fat Mary leaned out, dressed only in a slip and a worn, brown sweater.

"Now you're going to catch it, Billy Boy. Your sister's going to tell your mama you've been pitching pennies again."

Jeanie did not pause.

Billy sprang up. "Hi, Jeanie, gimme a nickel. I need a nickel. A nickel, a nickel, I gotta have a nickel."

The other little boys took up the chant. "A nickel, a nickel, Billy needs a nickel."

She threw them a furious glance and went in. Two little girls sat on the second landing, playing house. They had a set of toy dishes spread out on the top stair and each held a doll in her lap. Jeanie stepped over them, careful not to disturb their arrangements.

The kitchen smelled dank and unused, and the opening of the door dislodged a flake of green-painted plaster. It fell into the sink with a dry powdering. A black dress someone had given her mother lay over the chair before the sewing machine. It reminded her that her own dress sleeve had torn half out, dressing after health ed. She really should sew it, but the sight of the black dress waiting to be made over made her dislike the thought of sewing. She would just have to wear her coat in school tomorrow. Lots of other girls had to do that, too.

She hung her coat on a hook in the room she shared with her mother and stood irresolute. Her mother would be coming in soon and would expect to find the potatoes peeled and the table laid. She caught sight of a comic book and, unwillingly attracted by the garish colors, read one side. "Ah!" she thought in disgust. "Billy!" She thought of her homework. She was so far behind in social studies, she could probably never make it up. It was hardly worth trying. Mercantilism.[2] The rise of the merchant class. She would probably fail. And health education, all those cuts in health ed. Miss Fisher, her course counselor, had called her down yesterday and warned her. "Ah" she said again. Miss Fisher was all right. She had

[2] *Mercantilism:* economic policy of building a nation's wealth by having more exports than imports.

even been encouraging. "I know you can do it," Miss Fisher had said.

She sat down on the bed and opened her looseleaf notebook at random. A page fell out. She was about to jam it back in, when the freshly inked writing caught her eye. Today's English. Some poem about a vase and youths and maidens. Miss Lowy had brought in some pictures of vases with people on them, dressed in togas or whatever they were, spinning and reading from scrolls. Why did everybody get so excited about the Greeks? It was so long ago. "Wonderful!" Miss Lowy had exclaimed. How could anybody get so stirred up about a poem? She meant it, too. You could tell from her expression. "Listen, boys and girls. Listen." A lifted arm enjoined them.

"Beauty is truth, truth beauty,—that is all
Ye know on earth, and all ye need to know." [3]

There it was, copied into her notebook. Caught by something in the lines, she tried to find the poem in her tattered anthology, not bothering about the index, but turning the pages to and fro. John Keats, at last.

"Write about beauty and truth. About life," Miss Lowy had said.

Jeanie tore a page out of her notebook and opened her pen. Pulling over a chair, she rested her book on the sooty window sill. She stared out at the dusk falling sadly, sadly, thickening into darkness over the coalyards.

A crash of the kitchen door caused a reverberation in the window sill. The notebook slipped out of her hands.

"Where'd you get that bottle of pop?" she heard her mother's voice.

A high-pitched, wordless sniveling came in reply.

[3] *"Beauty is truth . . .":* lines from "Ode on a Grecian Urn" by John Keats (1795–1821), British poet.

"I asked you where'd you get that pop? You better tell me."

"A lady gave me a nickel. A lady came down the street and asked me. . . ."

"You're lying. I know where you got that money. Gambling, that's what you were doing."

"I was only pitching pennies, Ma. It's only a game, Ma."

"Gambling and stealing and associating with bad friends! I told you to stay away from them boys. Didn't I? Didn't I?" Her mother's voice rose. "I'm going to give you a beating you aren't going to forget."

Billy wailed on a long descending note.

Jeanie could hear the impact of the strap and her mother's heavy breathing.

"I want you to grow up good, not lying and gambling and stealing," her mother gasped, "and I'm going to make you good. You aren't ever going to forget this. And you aren't going to get any supper either. You can go now. You can go to bed and reflect on what I told you."

He stumbled past her, whimpering, fists grinding into eyes, and into the dark little alcove which was his room. Jeanie heard the groan of the bed as he threw himself on it. She felt the pain in her fingers and saw them still pressed tightly around the pen.

Her mother appeared in the doorway. She wore her hat and coat.

"Come and help me get supper, Jeanie. You should have got things started." Her voice was tired and tremulous and held no reproach.

"I don't want any supper, Ma."

Her mother came in and sat down heavily on the bed, taking off her hat and letting her coat fall open.

"I had a hard day. I worked hard every minute," she said. "I brought you something extra nice for dessert. I stood on line to get some of these tarts from Sutter's."

Jeanie rose and silently put her mother's hat on the shelf.
She held out her hand for her mother's coat and hung it up.
Together they opened the paper bags on the kitchen table.
She set the water to boil.

As they ate in silence, the three tarts shone like subtle
jewels on a plate, at one end of the chipped porcelain table.
Her mother looked tired.

"You better fix your brother up a plate," her mother said.
"Put it on a tray. Here, take this." And she put on the tray
the most luscious, the most perfect of the tarts. "Wait." She
went heavily over to her swollen black handbag, took out a
small clasp purse, opened it, and carefully, seriously, deliberately, picked out a coin, rejected it, and took out another.
"Give him this." It was a quarter.

After the dishes were washed, Jeanie brought her books
into the kitchen and spread them out under the glaring overhead light. Billy had been asleep, huddled in his clothes.
Tears had left dusty streaks on his face.

Her mother sat in the armchair, ripping out the sides of the
black dress. Her spectacles made her look strange. *Beauty is
truth*, Jeanie read in her notebook. Hastily, carelessly,
defiantly disregarding margins and doubtful spellings, letting
her pen dig into the paper, she began to write: *Last night my
brother got a terrible beating. . . .*

Scramble to borrow the social studies homework from a
girl in her home room, say hello to Barbara, dress for health
ed, dress again, the torn sleeve, bookkeeping—a blot, get
another piece of ledger paper. "This is the third I've given
you. You might say thank you." Get to English early. Slip her
composition in under the others, sit in the last seat. Don't
bother me. I am in a bad mood. Rows and rows of seats! Rows
and rows of windows opposite! She could even read the
writing on some of the blackboards, but who cared? A boy
leaned far out of the window before closing it. Other heads

were turning. Would he fall? No, he was safe. Heads turned back. A poem about a skylark! [4] From where she sat, she could see about a square foot of sky, drained of all color by the looming school walls.

Miss Lowy read clearly, standing all alone at the front of the room in her clean white blouse, her blonde hair smoothed down.

Miss Lowy, maybe you see skylarks. Me, I'd like to see some sky, Jeanie thought and nearly uttered it. Around her, students were writing in their notebooks. Miss Lowy was about to speak to her. Better start writing something. Sullen, Mr. MacIver had called her last week. She felt about for her notebook and pen. It had been a mistake to write as she had done about her brother's beating. They would laugh if they knew, Shirley, who was class secretary, and Saul, with the prominent forehead. No, he would not laugh. He was always writing about spaceships and the end of the world. No danger, though, that her story would be read. Only the best manuscripts were read. She remembered keenly the blotched appearance of the paper, the lines crossed out and the words whose spelling she could never be sure of. Oh, well, she didn't care. Only one more period and then the week end. "Lady Jeanie's too proud to come to our party. Jeanie, what are you waiting for? Jeanie's waiting for a Prince Charming to come and take her away." If Barbara asked her again, she would go with her, maybe. There was going to be a party at Norma's Saturday night, with Cokes and sandwiches and records and dancing, everybody chipping in. Jeanie, I need a nickel. Mama, I need a dollar. I need, I need.

The bell rang and the pens dropped and the books were closed with a clatter. She slipped out ahead of the pushing, jostling boys and girls.

---

[4] *Poem about a skylark:* both William Wordsworth (1770–1850) and Percy Bysshe Shelley (1792–1822) wrote poems "To a Skylark."

Monday, Miss Lowy had on still another perfect white blouse. She stood facing the class, holding a sheaf of papers in her hand. Most of the students looked at her expectantly. Marian, who nearly always got 90, whispered to her neighbor. Michael, who had but recently come from Greece—ah, but that was a different Greece—grumbled and shifted in his seat. He would have to do his composition over. He always did.

"I spent a very enjoyable time this week end, reading your work," said Miss Lowy, waiting for the class to smile.

"Seriously, though, many of your pieces were most interesting, even though they were a trifle unconventional about spelling and punctuation." A smile was obviously indicated here too, and the class obeyed. She paused. "Sometimes, however, a piece of writing is so honest and human, that you have to forgive the technical weaknesses. Not that they aren't important," she said hastily, "but what the writer has to say is more significant."

The three best students in the class looked confused. It was their pride not to have technical errors.

"When you hear this," Miss Lowy continued, "I think you'll agree with me. I know it brought tears to my eyes."

The class looked incredulous.

"It's called 'Evening Comes to 128th Street.'"

Jeanie's heart beat painfully. She picked up a pencil, but dropped it, so unsteady were her fingers. Even the back of Shirley's head was listening. Even the classes in the other wing of the building, across the courtyard, seemed fixed, row on row, in an attitude of listening. Miss Lowy read on. It was all there, the coalyards and Fat Mary, the stoop and the tarts from Sutter's, Billy asleep with the tears dried on his face, the shabby purse and the quarter.

"The funny part of it was, when I woke him, Billy wasn't angry. He was glad about the quarter and ate his supper, dessert and all, but mama never did eat her tart, so I put it away." Miss Lowy stopped reading.

A poignancy of remembrance swept over Jeanie, the shame and regret. It was no business of theirs, these strange people.

No one spoke. The silence was unbearable. Finally, Marian, the incomparable Marian, raised her hand.

"It was so real," she said, "you felt you were right in that kitchen."

"You didn't know whom to feel sorry for," said another student. "You wanted to cry with the mother and you wanted to cry with Billy."

"With the girl, too," said another.

Several heads nodded.

"You see," said Miss Lowy. "It's literature. It's life. It's pain and truth and beauty."

Jeanie's heart beat so, it made a mist come before her eyes. Through the blur she heard Miss Lowy say it was good enough to be sent in to Scholastic.[5] It showed talent, it showed promise. She heard her name called and shrank from the eyes turned upon her.

After school, she hurried out and caught the first train, the one you could catch only if you left immediately and did not stroll or stop the least little bit to talk to someone. She did not want to meet anyone, not even Barbara.

Was that Billy among the children on the stoop?

"Billy," she called. "Billy."

What would she say to him? *Beauty is truth, truth beauty?*

"Billy," she called again urgently.

Billy lifted his head and, seeing who it was, tore himself reluctantly away from his friends and took a step toward her.

---

[5] *Scholastic:* magazine that offers awards to encourage promising young high school writers.

1. At the opening of the story, what do Jeanie's refusals to join her schoolmates show about her character? Describe her relationship with the other students.
2. Find evidence of Jeanie's poverty in the story. What kind of neighborhood does she live in? How do you know?
3. Explain Jeanie's thought: "Miss Lowy, maybe you see skylarks. Me, I'd like to see some sky." What emotional need is Jeanie expressing?
4. Explain the title as it applies to the story. In what way does Jeanie's accurate description of the ugliness of life around her become a thing of beauty?
5. To what extent do you agree or disagree with the comments made by her classmates about Jeanie's composition?
6. Contrast what Jeanie studies and her school environment with her environment at home.
7. Explain Jeanie's first reaction when her paper is read: "It was no business of theirs, these strange people."
8. Find evidence of Jeanie's family's spirit and unity despite poverty.

1. What are the advantages in the author's having us see things through Jeanie's eyes?
2. How is Jeanie's awareness of her environment shown? Why is this awareness important?
3. What are the standards by which Miss Lowy judges the writing of the students in the class? Why do you agree or disagree with them?

4. What purpose is there in Jeanie's setting down
   in writing the events that started with Billy's
   beating? Justify your answer.
5. Do you think that the truth about anything is
   beautiful, even if the thing itself is ugly?
   Defend your answer.

Reviewing the Unit

For Comparative Study

1. The characters in both stories have longings. They yearn for things they do not have. What are these things? What do they have in common?
2. Both stories are critical of the society they describe. What criticisms are made in each story?
3. Compare the robot's teaching with the teaching of Miss Lowy. What are the advantages of each? What are the disadvantages of each?
4. Compare the attitudes towards school of Margie and Jeanie. How are they similar? How are they different?
5. If Margie and Tommie found themselves in a class like Jeanie's, what would their reactions be? Justify your answer.
6. How do you think Jeanie would feel in a situation like Tommie's and Margie's? Explain.
7. Which story is more effective in making its point—"The Fun They Had" or "Beauty Is Truth"? Why?

Building Your Vocabulary

In your notebook, match the adjectives from the stories with the nouns they describe.

Column A	Column B
1. courtly	a. windowsill
2. dank	b. paper
3. garish	c. class
4. crinkly	d. colors
5. luscious	e. forehead
6. ornate	f. smell
7. prominent	g. tart
8. tattered	h. voice
9. tremulous	i. salute
10. sooty	j. lettering
	k. anthology

For Creative Writing

Use one of the following as the ending for an original short story.
1. I really felt pride, after that, in being _____.
2. I had gotten what I wanted, at last.
3. That's how I achieved love (acceptance).
4. That's what happens when you let your imagination run loose.
5. I finally found out what made our family tick.
6. I was no longer ashamed.
7. Now, I knew why _____.
8. I knew I would never fulfill my dream, but I was satisfied that I had tried.
9. I was happy I had been able to help.
10. I had seen the light.

SHAPING
IDEALS

IN the Bible, the prophet, Micah, says: "It hath been told thee, O man, what is good . . . Only to do justly, and to love mercy, and to walk humbly with thy God."

Man must make ideals such as these part of his code of behavior if he is to survive and achieve peace of mind and peace of soul. Micah stresses justice, mercy, and humility. The stories in this unit include and go beyond the ideals of the prophet. One holds forth the ideal of peace and a better world for all, an ideal we have yet to reach. The other shows us that respect for the dignity of the individual is necessary if man is to live with his fellow man.

If these ideals seem to be vague and removed from our everyday affairs, the stories in this unit breathe life into them in terms of people. The narrator in "The Taste of Melon," and Papa in "Papa and the Bomb" have one thing in common— each has an ideal that is part of him, an ideal to which he wishes to remain true.

While both of these stories have a moral and point the way to moral behavior, each holds our interest because of the story-telling skill of the writer. It may seem strange that such widely different objects as a watermelon and a used coffee can can move us to live a good life, but that is exactly what the stories in which they appear try to do. The attentive and sensitive reader will come away a better person for having read them.

The Taste of Melon

BORDEN DEAL

*Appreciating
the Story*

WE are all familiar with the forbidden fruit of the Garden of Eden. This story deals with a modern-day forbidden fruit, "the greatest watermelon ever seen" by a typical sixteen-year-old. Why, even his own father had said, "No melon tastes as sweet as a stolen one." Yet this watermelon leads to an experience that this teen-ager will never forget.

The watermelon is a vine. One seed melon is grown to provide the seeds for each year's planting. A seed melon is the unifying symbol for this story.

*... And Keep
in Mind*

THE story is narrated by a sixteen-year-old boy. While he thinks of action and while he is committing the act, he lets us share his thoughts. As you read, try to understand him and the code of behavior by which he lives. By centering on the narrator, the author deliberately draws our attention from the person against whom the act is committed. The victim's code of conduct is quite different from that of the teen-age narrator. As a teen-ager, you may find yourself identifying with

the character closest to your own age. The full
force of the story and the conflict of ideals which
is the basis for it will not be felt, however, unless
you try to understand Mr. Wills' set of values as
well.

WHEN I THINK OF THE SUMMER
I was sixteen, a lot of things come crowding in to be thought
about. We had moved just the year before, and sixteen is still
young enough that the bunch makes a difference. I had a
bunch, all right, but they weren't sure of me yet. I didn't
know why. Maybe because I'd lived in town, and my father
still worked there instead of farming, like the other fathers
did. The boys I knew, even Freddy Gray and J. D., still kept
a small distance between us.

Then there was Willadean Wills. I hadn't been much interested in girls before. But I had to admit to myself that I was
interested in Willadean. She was my age, nearly as tall as I,
and up till the year before, Freddy Gray told me, she had
been good at playing Gully Keeper and Ante-Over.[1] But she
didn't play such games this year. She was tall and slender, and
Freddy Gray and J.D. and I had several discussions about
the way she walked. I maintained she was putting it on, but
J. D. claimed she couldn't help it. Freddy Gray remarked
that she hadn't walked that way last year. He said she'd
walked like any other human being. So then I said, put on or
not, I liked the way she walked, and then there was a large
silence.

It wasn't a comfortable silence, because of Mr. Wills,
Willadean's father. We were all afraid of Mr. Wills.

[1] *Gully Keeper and Ante-over:* popular tag and dodgeball games.

Mr. Wills was a big man. He had bright, fierce eyes under heavy brows and, when he looked down at you, you just withered. The idea of having him directly and immediately angry at one of us was enough to shrivel the soul. All that summer Willadean walked up and down the high road or sat on their front porch in a rocking chair, her dress flared out around her, and not one of us dared do more than say good morning to her.

Mr. Wills was the best farmer in the community. My father said he could drive a stick into the ground and grow a tree out of it. But it wasn't an easy thing with him; Mr. Wills fought the earth when he worked it. When he plowed his fields, you could hear him yelling for a mile. It was as though he dared the earth not to yield him its sustenance.

Above all, Mr. Wills could raise watermelons. Now, watermelons are curious things. Some men can send off for the best watermelon seed, they can plant it in the best ground they own, they can hoe it and tend it with the greatest of care, and they can't raise a melon bigger than your two fists. Other men, like Mr. Wills, can throw seed on the ground, scuff dirt over it, walk off and leave it and have a crop of the prettiest, biggest melons you ever saw.

Mr. Wills always planted the little field directly behind his barn to watermelons. It ran from the barn to the creek, a good piece of land with just the right sandy soil for melon raising. And it seemed as though the melons just bulged up out of the ground for him.

But they were Mr. Wills's melons; he didn't have any idea of sharing them with the boys of the neighborhood. He was fiercer about his melons than anything else; if you just happened to walk close to his melon patch, you'd see Mr. Wills standing and watching you with a glower on his face. And likely as not he'd have his gun under his arm.

Everybody expected to lose a certain quantity of their

watermelons to terrapins and a certain quantity to boys. It wasn't considered stealing to sneak into a man's melon patch and judiciously borrow a sample of his raising. You might get a load of salt in the seat of your pants if you were seen, but that was part of the game. You'd be looked down on only if you got malicious and stamped a lot of melons into the ground while you were about it. But Mr. Wills didn't think that way.

That summer I was sixteen Mr. Wills raised the greatest watermelon ever seen in the country. It grew in the very middle of his patch, three times as big as any melon anybody had ever seen. Men came from miles around to look at it. Mr. Wills wouldn't let them go into the melon patch. They had to stand around the edge.

Just like all other daredevil boys in that country, I guess, Freddy Gray and J. D. and I had talked idly about stealing that giant watermelon. But we all knew that it was just talk. Not only were we afraid of Mr. Wills and his rages but we knew that Mr. Wills sat in the hayloft window of his barn every night with his shotgun, guarding the melon. It was his seed melon. He meant to plant next year's crop out of that great one and maybe raise a whole field of them. Mr. Wills was in a frenzy of fear that somebody would steal it. Why, he would rather you stole Willadean than his melon. At least, he didn't guard Willadean with his shotgun.

Every night I could sit on our front porch and see Mr. Wills sitting up there in the window of his hayloft, looking fiercely out over his melon patch. I'd sit there by the hour and watch him, the shotgun cradled in his arm, and feel the tremors of fear and excitement chasing up and down my spine.

"Look at him," my father would say. "Scared to death somebody will steal his seed melon. Wouldn't anybody steal a man's seed melon."

"He ought to be in the house taking care of that wife of

his," my mother would say tartly. "She's been poorly all year."
You hardly ever saw Mrs. Wills. She was a wraith of a
woman, pale as a butter bean. Sometimes she would sit for an
hour or two on their porch in the cool of the day. They didn't
visit back and forth with anybody though.

"There's Willadean," my father would say mildly.

My mother would make a funny kind of sound that meant
disgust. "He cares more about that seed melon than he does
his wife," she'd say. "I wish somebody *would* steal it. Maybe
then—"

"Helen," my father would say, chiding, "you shouldn't even
think of such a thing."

About the time the great watermelon was due to come ripe,
there was a night of a full moon. J. D. and Freddy Gray and
I had decided we'd go swimming in the creek, so I left the
house when the moon rose and went to meet them. The moon
floated up into the sky, making everything almost as bright
as day, but at the same time softer and gentler than ever daylight could be. It was the kind of night when you feel as
though you can do anything in the world, even boldly asking
Willadean Wills for a date. On a night like that, you couldn't
help but feel that she'd gladly accept.

"Boy, what a moon!" J. D. said when I met them.

"Wouldn't you like to take old Willadean out on a night
like this?" Freddy Gray said.

We scoffed at him, but secretly in our hearts we knew how
he felt. We were getting old enough to think that that sort of
thing might be a lot more fun than going swimming in the
moonlight.

As I said before, I was a part of the bunch. J. D .and Freddy
Gray were my good friends. But because I was still new,
there were certain things and certain feelings where I was
left out. This was one of them; they were afraid, because I
was more of a stranger to Willadean, that she might like the

idea of dating me better than she did either of them. This was all way down under the surface, because none of us had admitted to ourselves that we wanted to be Willadean's boy friend. But far down though it was, I could feel it, and they could feel it.

"I wish I had a newspaper," I said then. "I'll bet you could read it in this moonlight."

We had reached the swimming hole in the creek, and we began shucking off our clothes. We were all excited by the moonlight, yelling at one another and rushing to be first into the water. Freddy Gray made it first, J. D. and I catapulting in right behind him. The water was cold, and the shock of it struck a chill into us. But we got rid of it by a brisk water fight and then we were all right.

We climbed out finally, to rest, and sat on the bank. That big old moon sailed serenely overhead, climbing higher into the sky, and we lay on our backs to look up at it.

"Old Man Wills won't have to worry about anybody stealing his melon tonight, anyway," Freddy Gray said. "Wouldn't anybody dare try it, bright as day like it is."

"He's not taking any chances," J. D. said. "I saw him sitting up in that hayloft when I came by, his shotgun loaded with buckshot. That melon is as safe as it would be in the First National Bank."

"Shucks," I said in a scoffing voice, "he ain't got buckshot in that gun. He's just got a load of salt, like anybody else guarding a watermelon patch."

Freddy Gray sat upright, looking at me. "Don't kid yourself, son," he said loftily. "He told my daddy that he had it loaded with double-ought buckshot."

"Why," I said, "that would kill a man."

"That's what he's got in mind," Freddy Gray said, "if anybody goes after that seed melon."

It disturbed me more than it should have. After all, I'd

never had it in mind to try for the melon, had I? "I don't
believe it," I said flatly. "He wouldn't kill anybody over a
watermelon. Even a seed melon like that one."

"Old Man Wills would," J. D. said.

Freddy Gray was still watching me. "What's got you into
such a swivet?" he said. "You weren't planning on going after
that melon yourself?"

"Well, yes," I said. "As a matter of fact, I was."

There was a moment of respectful silence. Even from me. I
hadn't known I was going to say those words. To this day I
don't know why I said them. It was all mixed up with
Willadean and the rumor of Mr. Wills having his gun loaded
with double-ought buckshot and the boys still thinking of me
as an outsider. It surged up out of me—not the idea of making
my name for years to come by such a deed, but the feeling
that there was a rightness in defying the world and Mr. Wills.

Mixed up with it all there came into my mouth the taste of
watermelon. I could taste the sweet red juices oozing over my
tongue, feel the delicate threaded redness of the heart as I
squeezed the juices out of it.

I stood up. "As a matter of fact," I said, "I'm going after it
right now."

"Wait a minute," J. D. said in alarm. "You can't do it on a
moonlight night like this. It's 200 yards from the creekbank
to that melon. He'll see you for sure."

"Yeah," Freddy Gray said, "wait until a dark night. Wait
until—"

"Anybody could steal it on a dark night," I said scornfully.
"I'm going to take it right out from under his nose. Tonight."

I began putting on my clothes. My heart was thudding in
my chest. I didn't taste watermelon any more; I tasted fear.
But it was too late to stop now. Besides, I didn't want to stop.

We dressed silently, and I led the way up the creekbank.
We came opposite the watermelon patch and ducked down

the bank. We pushed through the willows on the other side and looked toward the barn. We could see Mr. Wills very plainly. The gun was cradled in his arms, glinting from the moonlight.

"You'll never make it," J. D. said in a quiet, fateful voice. "He'll see you before you're six steps away from the creek."

"You don't think I mean to walk, do you?" I said.

I pushed myself out away from them, on my belly in the grass that grew up around the watermelon hills. I was absolutely flat, closer to the earth than I thought it was possible to get. I looked back once, to see their white faces watching me out of the willows.

I went on, stopping once in a while to look cautiously up toward the barn. He was still there, still quiet. I met a terrapin taking a bite out of a small melon. Terrapins love watermelon, better than boys do. I touched him on the shell and whispered, "Hello, brother," but he didn't acknowledge my greeting. He just drew into his shell. I went on, wishing I was equipped like a terrapin for the job, outside as well as inside.

It seemed to take forever to reach the great melon in the middle of the field. With every move, I expected Mr. Wills to see me. Fortunately the grass was high enough to cover me. At last the melon loomed up before me, deep green in the moonlight, and I gasped at the size of it. I'd never seen it so close.

I lay still for a moment, panting. I didn't have the faintest idea how to get it out of the field. Even if I'd stood up, I couldn't have lifted it by myself. A melon is the slipperiest, most cumbersome object in the world. And this was the largest I'd ever seen. It was not a long melon, but a fat round one. Besides, I didn't dare stand up.

For five minutes I didn't move. I lay there, my nostrils breathing up the smell of the earth and the musty smell of the watermelon vines, and I wondered why I was out here in the middle of all that moonlight on such a venture. There was more to it than just bravado. I was proving something to myself—and to Mr. Wills and Willadean.

I thought of a tempting way out then. I would carve my name into the deep greenness of the melon. Mr. Wills would see it the next morning when he inspected the melon, and he would know that I could have stolen it if I'd wanted to. But no—crawling to the melon wasn't the same thing as actually taking it.

I reached one hand around the melon and found the stem. I broke the tough stem off close against the smooth roundness, and I was committed. I looked toward the barn again. All quiet. I saw Mr. Wills stretch and yawn, and his teeth glistened; the moon was that bright and I was that close.

I struggled around behind the melon and shoved at it. It rolled over sluggishly, and I pushed it again. It was hard work, pushing it down the trough my body had made through the grass. Dust rose up around me, and I wanted to sneeze. My spine was crawling with the expectation of a shot. Surely he'd see that the melon was gone out of its accustomed space.

It took about a hundred years to push that melon out of the field. I say that advisedly, because I felt that much older when I finally reached the edge. With the last of my strength I shoved it into the willows and collapsed. I was still lying in the edge of the field.

"Come on," Freddy Gray said, his voice pleading. "He's—"

I couldn't move. I turned my head. He was standing up to stretch and yawn to his content, and then he sat down again. By then I was rested enough to move again. I snaked into the willows, and they grabbed me.

"You did it!" they said. "By golly, you did it!"

There was no time to bask in their admiration and respect. "Let's get it on out of here," I said. "We're not safe yet."

We struggled the melon across the creek and up the bank.

We started toward the swimming hole. It took all three of us to carry it, and it was hard to get a grip. J. D. and Freddy Gray carried the ends, while I walked behind the melon, grasping the middle. We stumbled and thrashed in our hurry, and we nearly dropped it three or four times. It was the most difficult object I'd ever tried to carry in my life.

At last we reached the swimming hole and sank down, panting. But not for long; the excitement was too strong in us. Freddy Gray reached out a hand and patted the great melon.

"By golly," he said, "there it is. All ours."

"Let's bust it and eat it before somebody comes," J. D. said.

"Wait a minute," I said. "This isn't just any old melon. This is old man Wills's seed melon, and it deserves more respect than to be busted open with a fist. I'm going to cut it."

I took out my pocketknife and looked at it dubiously. It was small, and the melon was big. We really needed a butcher knife. But when the little knife penetrated the thick green rind, the melon split of itself, perfectly down the middle. There was a ragged, silken, tearing sound, and it lay open before us.

The heart meat, glistening with sweet moisture, was grained with white sugar specks. I tugged at it with two fingers, and a great chunk of the meat came free. I put it into my mouth, closing my eyes. The melon was still warm from the day's sun. Just as in my anticipation, I felt the juice trickle into my throat, sweet and seizing. I had never tasted watermelon so delicious.

The two boys were watching me savor the first bite. I opened my eyes. "Dive in," I said graciously. "Help yourselves."

We gorged ourselves until we were heavy. Even then, we had still only eaten the heart meat, leaving untouched more than we had consumed. We gazed with sated eyes at the leftover melon, still good meat peopled with a multitude of black seeds.

"What are we going to do with it?" I said.

"There's nothing we can do," J. D. said. "I can just see us taking a piece of this melon home for the folks."

"It's eat it or leave it," Freddy Gray said.

We were depressed suddenly. It was such a waste, after all the struggle and the danger, that we could not eat every bite. I stood up, not looking at the two boys, not looking at the melon.

"Well," I said. "I guess I'd better get home."

"But what about this?" J. D. said insistently, motioning toward the melon.

I kicked half the melon, splitting it in three parts. I stamped one of the chunks under my foot. Then I set methodically to work, destroying the rest of the melon. The boys watched me silently until I picked up a chunk of rind and threw it at them. Then they swept into the destruction also, and we were laughing again. When we stopped, only the battered rinds were left, the meat muddied on the ground, the seed scattered.

We stood silent, looking at one another. "There was nothing else to do," I said, and they nodded solemnly.

But the depression went with us toward home and, when we parted, we did so with sober voices and gestures. I did not feel triumph or victory, as I had expected, though I knew that tonight's action had brought me closer to my friends than I had ever been before.

"Where have you been?" my father asked as I stepped up on the porch. He was sitting in his rocker.

"Swimming," I said.

I looked toward Mr. Wills's barn. The moon was still high and bright, but I could not see him. My breath caught in my throat when I saw him in the field, walking toward the middle. I stood stiffly, watching him. He reached the place where the melon should have been. I saw him hesitate, looking around, then he bent, and I knew he was looking at the depression in the earth where the melon had lain. He straightened, a great strangled cry tearing out of his throat. It chilled me deep down and all the way through, like the cry of a wild animal.

My father jerked himself out of the chair, startled by the sound. He turned in time to see Mr. Wills lift the shotgun over his head and hurl it from him, his voice crying out again in a terrible, surging yell of pain and anger.

"Lord, what's the matter?" my father said.

Mr. Wills was tearing up and down the melon patch, and I was puzzled by his actions. Then I saw; he was destroying every melon in the patch. He was breaking them open with his feet, silent now, concentrating on his frantic destruction. I was horrified by the awful sight, and my stomach moved sickly.

My father stood for a moment, watching him, then he jumped off the porch and ran toward Mr. Wills. I followed him. I saw Mrs. Wills and Willadean huddled together in the kitchen doorway. My father ran into the melon patch and caught Mr. Wills by the arm.

"What's come over you?" he said. "What's the matter, man?"

Mr. Wills struck his grip away. "They've stolen my seed melon," he yelled. "They took it right out from under me."

My father grabbed him with both arms. He was a brave man, for he was smaller than Mr. Wills, and Mr. Wills looked insane with anger, his teeth gripped over his lower lip, his eyes gleaming furiously. Mr. Wills shoved my father away, striking at him with his fist. My father went down into the dirt. Mr. Wills didn't seem to notice. He went back to his task of destruction, raging up and down the field, stamping melons large and small.

My father got up and began to chase him. But he didn't

have a chance. Every time he got close, Mr. Wills would sweep his great arm and knock him away again. At last Mr. Wills stopped of his own accord. He was standing on the place where the great melon had grown. His chest was heaving with great sobs of breath. He gazed about him at the destruction he had wrought, but I don't think that he saw it.

"They stole my seed melon," he said. His voice was quieter now than I had ever heard it. I had not believed such quietness was in him. "They got it away, and now it's gone."

I saw that tears stood on his cheeks, and I couldn't look at him any more. I'd never seen a grown man cry, crying in such strength.

"I had two plans for that melon," he told my father. "Mrs. Wills has been poorly all the spring, and she dearly loves the taste of melon for eating, and my melon for planting. She would eat the meat, and the next spring I would plant the seeds for the greatest melon crop in the world. Every day she would ask me if the great seed melon was ready yet."

I looked toward the house. I saw the two women, the mother and the daughter, standing there. I couldn't bear any more. I fled out of the field toward the sanctuary of my house. I ran past my mother, standing on the porch, and went into my room.

I didn't sleep that night. I heard my father come in, heard the low-voiced conversation with my mother, heard them go to bed. I lay wide-eyed and watched the moon through the window as it slid slowly down the sky and at last brought a welcome darkness into the world.

I don't know all the things I thought that night. Mostly it was about the terrible thing I had committed so lightly, out of pride and out of being sixteen years old and out of wanting to challenge the older man, the man with the beautiful daughter.

That was the worst of all, that I had done it so lightly, with so little thought of its meaning. In that country and in that time, watermelon stealing was not a crime. It was tolerated, laughed about. The men told great tales of their own watermelon-stealing days, how they'd been set on by dogs and peppered with salt-loaded shotgun shells. Watermelon raiding was a game, a ritual of defiance and rebellion by young males. I could remember my own father saying, "No melon tastes as sweet as a stolen one," and my mother laughing and agreeing.

But stealing this great seed melon from a man like Mr. Wills lay outside the safe magic of the tacit understanding between man and boy. And I knew that it was up to me, at whatever risk, to repair as well as I could the damage I had done.

When it was daylight I rose from my bed and went out into the fresh world. It would be hot later on; but now the air was dew-cool and fragrant. I had found a paper sack in the kitchen, and I carried it in my hand as I walked toward the swimming hole. I stopped there, looking down at the wanton waste we had made of the part of the melon we had not been able to eat. It looked as though Mr. Wills had been stamping here too.

I kneeled down on the ground, opened the paper sack and began picking up the black seeds. They were scattered thickly, still stringy with watermelon pulp, and soon my hands were greasy with them. I kept on doggedly, searching out every seed I could find, until at the end I had to crawl over the ground, seeking for the last ones.

They nearly filled the paper sack. I went back to the house. By the time I reached it, the sun and my father had risen. He was standing on the porch.

"What happened to you last night?" he said. "Did you get

so frightened you had to run home? It was frightening to watch him, I'll admit that."

"Father," I said, "I've got to go talk to Mr. Wills. Right now. I wish you would come with me."

He stopped, watching me. "What's the matter?" he said. "Did you steal that seed melon of his?"

"Will you come with me?" I said.

His face was dark and thoughtful. "Why do you want me?"

"Because I'm afraid he'll shoot me," I said. My voice didn't tremble much, but I couldn't keep it all out.

"Then why are you going?" he said.

"Because I've got to," I said.

My father watched me for a moment. "Yes," he said quietly, "I guess you do." He came down the steps and stood beside me. "I'll go with you," he said.

We walked the short distance between our house and his. Though it was so near, I had never been in his yard before. I felt my legs trembling as I went up the brick walk and stood at the bottom of the steps, the paper sack in my hand. I knocked on the porch floor, and Willadean came to the screen door.

I did not look at her. "I want to talk to your father."

She stared at me for a moment, then she disappeared. In a moment Mr. Wills appeared in the doorway. His face was marked by the night, his cheeks sunken, his mouth bitten in. He stared at me absentmindedly, as though I were only a speck in his thinking.

"What do you want, boy?" he said.

I felt my teeth grit against the words I had to say. I held out the paper bag toward him.

"Mr. Wills," said, "here's the seeds from your seed melon. That's all I could bring back."

I could feel my father standing quietly behind me.

Willadean was standing in the doorway, watching. I couldn't take my eyes away from Mr. Wills's face.

"Did you steal it?" he said.

"Yes, sir," I said.

He advanced to the edge of the porch. The shotgun was standing near the door, and I expected him to reach for it. Instead he came toward me, a great powerful man, and leaned down to me.

"Why did you steal it?" he said.

"I don't know," I said.

"Didn't you know it was my seed melon?"

"Yes, sir," I said. "I knew it."

He straightened up again and his eyes were beginning to gleam. I wanted to run, but I couldn't move.

"And my sick wife hungered for the taste of that melon," he said. "Not for herself, like I thought. But to invite the whole neighborhood in for a slice of it. She knew I wouldn't ever think of anything like that myself. She hungered for that."

I hung my head. "I'm sorry," I said.

He stopped still then, watching me. "So you brought me the seeds," he said softly. "That's not much, boy."

I lifted my head. "It was all I could think to do," I said. "The melon is gone. But the seeds are next year. That's why I brought them to you."

"But you ruined this year," he said.

"Yes, sir," I said. "I ruined this year."

I couldn't look at him any more. I looked at Willadean standing behind him. Her eyes were a puzzle, watching me, and I couldn't tell what she was thinking or feeling.

"I'm about as ashamed of myself last night as you are of yourself," Mr. Wills said. He frowned at me with his heavy brows. "You ruined the half of it, and I ruined the other. We're both to blame, boy. Both to blame."

It seemed there ought to be something more for me to say. I searched for it in my mind and discovered only the thought that I had found this morning in the gray light of dawning. "The seeds are next year," I said. I looked at him humbly. "I'll help you plant them, Mr. Wills. I'll work very hard."

Mr. Wills looked at my father for the first time. There was a small hard smile on his face, and his eyes didn't look as fierce as they had before.

"A man with a big farm like mine needs a son," he said. "But Willadean here was all the good Lord saw fit to give me. Sam, I do wish I had me a boy like that."

He came close to me then, put his hand on my shoulder. "We can't do anything about this year," he said. "But we'll grow next year, won't we? We'll grow it together."

"Yes, sir," I said.

I looked past him at Willadean, and her eyes were smiling too. I felt my heart give a great thump in my chest.

"And you don't have to offer the biggest melon in the world to get folks to come visiting," I blurted. "Why, I'll set on the porch with Willadean any time."

Mr. Wills and my father burst out laughing. Willadean was blushing red in the face. But somehow she didn't look mad. Flustered, I began to beat a retreat toward the gate. Then I stopped, looking back at Mr. Wills. I couldn't leave yet.

"Can I ask you one thing, Mr. Wills?" I said.

He stopped laughing, and there was no fierceness in his voice. "Anything you want to, boy," he said.

"Well, I just wanted to know," I said. "Was there double-ought buckshot in that gun?"

He reached around and picked up the gun. He unbreeched it and took out a shell. He broke the shell in his strong fingers and poured the white salt out into his palm.

"You see?" he said.

"Yes, sir," I said, taking a deep breath. "I see."
I went on then, and the next year started that very day.

Understanding
the Story

1. Why does the narrator of the story steal the melon?
2. Why are the results of his action so tragic? How does the author show this?
3. Explain the following:
   a. "There was more to it than just bravado. I was proving something to myself—and to Mr. Wills and Willadean."
   b. "I did not feel triumph or victory, as I had expected, though I knew that tonight's action had brought me closer to my friends than I had ever been before."
4. Why does the author have the narrator say, "The seeds are next year"?
5. Explain the meaning of the final sentence of the story.
6. What guide to behavior does this story provide for us?

Appreciating
the Story

1. Find evidence in the story of the author's understanding of the motives, interests, and relationships of teen-agers.
2. The title of the story has one meaning for the narrator and another for Mr. Wills. Explain the difference.
3. How does the author bring about the conflict between the narrator and Mr. Wills? How does the conflict become at once a physical conflict and a conflict of codes of behavior? Whose code is better? Defend your choice.

4. Try retelling the story from the point of view of Mr. Wills. Is this preferable to the method used by the author? Why or why not?
5. Can you find word pictures, or images, that appeal to the senses? Why has the author used these?

Papa and the Bomb

WILLIAM IVERSEN

Approaching the Story...

IF not for the seriousness of its message, "Papa and the Bomb" might appear to be a long-drawn out practical joke played on an unsuspecting teen-ager by his rather queer "old man." What starts out as a quiet family scene becomes a vision of the ideal of all mankind—world peace. There is hardly any plot—a high school student is doing his homework in the kitchen where his mother is baking a cake; Papa comes up from the cellar with a used one-pound coffee can and an idea. That idea and the discussion that follows make up the story. This seems to be rather slim material out of which to weave a powerful tale, but William Iversen does just that, largely because of the importance of the idea and the appeal of the characters who develop it.

... And Keep in Mind

WE hear a lot about the generation gap and we find it illustrated at the start of "Papa and the Bomb." As you read, note the differing views of father and son on machines and modern technology. As the discussion continues, follow the son's change in attitude—the change from doubt to faith. You will also meet a remarkable character, Papa, whose wit and wisdom are typical of a generation of parents (or grandparents) whose innate common sense made up for their lack of formal education. What is refreshing about this story is that the son appreciates Papa for what he is—a warm, wise human being. The easy, conversational style of the son (the narrator) will guide you almost effortlessly on your journey to the ideal world of Sam Pitkin, war veteran, unsuccessful businessman, father, and humanitarian.

S OMETIMES I REALLY WORRY about my old man. All my life he's been coming up with these wild ideas, so I guess I should be used to it. But I'm not. He can still surprise me.

For instance, the other night I'm sitting in the kitchen doing my geometry homework, and my mother is also in the kitchen baking a honey cake, when up he comes from the cellar with this expression on his face, and I could see he had another brainstorm.

So my mother was busy putting the cake in the oven, and I ignored him. I mean, I tried to ignore him, but he wouldn't let me. Down he sits in the other chair and starts drumming on the table with his fingers. He made me so nervous I made a blot on my paper, which means I have to start over from scratch because in the crazy class I'm in neatness counts ten per cent. But I still pretend to ignore him; only my mother

makes the mistake of looking at him, and all my efforts go
for nothing. Once he catches your eye, he feels free to talk.

"Well," he said with a big sigh. "Well, I got it."

My mother washed the mixing bowl silently, but by this
time it was too late.

"At last," he said, sighing again. "At last I got it."

There was only one thing to do now, or else this could have
gone on all night.

"What?" I asked. "What have you got now?"

"I have got," he announced solemnly, "—the bomb."

From the way he said it, you could tell he didn't mean just
any old bomb with an alarm clock attached, like some guy
tries to blow up Grand Central Station [1] with. He meant The
Bomb.

"The bomb?" my mother said. And she muttered an expression in Yiddish,[2] which roughly translated means: "This we
need like all our teeth should ache top and bottom, so they
got to be pulled out by a one-armed blacksmith."

But the point is she wasn't any more surprised than I was
to hear my father had The Bomb, because it seemed only
natural that sooner or later he would take his place as an
equal among nations. I could actually see the whole thing in
my head like a newsreel—all the different countries sitting
around the U. N. arguing—the United States, the United
Kingdom, the U.S.S.R., Ecuador, Sweden— and right in the
middle my father, with his own microphone and a little sign
reading SAM PITKIN.

Not that he would be trying to start trouble, you understand. Because even though he was in the First World War
and was promoted to the rank of corporal under combat

---

[1] *Grand Central Station:* important railroad terminal in New York
City.

[2] *Yiddish:* language derived from German, spoken by Jews in eastern
Europe.

conditions, my father has a very peaceable nature. The only time I ever heard him mention his experiences in France was once he told me about going to this famous restaurant in Paris, and when he pointed to something on the menu, the waiter set fire to a blintz. So his whole attitude would be more to talk things over quietly and see if they couldn't arrive at some kind of a deadlock. But if trouble came, he would be ready for it. I mean, since before I was born, my father has owned this Army and Navy store, and with just the stuff he's got on hand he could put six divisions in the field tomorrow.

He's got things you wouldn't dream of in that store, all surplus from World War II which he bought up by the carload—brand-new parachutes, never been opened, two thousand sets of ski-troop underwear, official Army footlockers, three hundred gallons of khaki enamel, squad tents, Signal Corps radios, battle jackets, pith helmets, file cabinets, mess trays, felt slippers from a Navy hospital, double-decker bunks from the WAC, Coast Guard searchlights with five-mile beams, two complete field kitchens in crates, mildewproof tarpaulins, cargo slings, MP whistles with white nylon nooses. Practically anything you need to fight a war my father has in his store, including rubber life rafts that hold ten men and a week's supply of water—and now we had The Bomb, also.

I mean, it wasn't beyond the realm of possibility that in all that junk he had found a machine for smashing atoms, and in fussing around with the thing in the cellar he had accidentally hit on the real goods.

So I questioned him logically.

"You got an atom bomb?" I asked.

"Better than that," he told me.

"An H-bomb?"

"More powerful."

"Where is it?"

"Here."

He held up a used coffee can of ordinary one-pound size. My mother looked at me; I looked at her, and I thought this would be the night I would have to phone my married brother and break the news that they finally came and led Pop away.

"This coffee can is a bomb?" I asked, figuring everybody should have a second chance.

He nodded emphatically. "That is correct."

"Better and more powerful than any existing weapons known to present-day science?"

"That is correct."

"I see."

Again a silence, and the air was filled with a hot puff of cake smell as my mother peeked in the oven and gently shut the door.

"So what's new at the store today?" she asked, trying to change the subject so maybe he'd snap out of it.

"What do you mean—what's new?" he said indignantly.

"You didn't tell us anything that happened."

"What could happen? I was talking to the Queen of England? A movie star came in for a pair of overalls? What?"

"That crook didn't come around for his bowling shoes yet?" my mother inquired.

My father folded his hands and sighed. "If he comes around, I'll tell you," he said.

"Six months ago he ordered them," my mother reminded him.

He sighed again, twiddling his thumbs to keep calm. "I can wait."

"A dozen pairs, all sizes!"

My mother shook her head sadly at the thought, and I really had to sympathize with how she felt, because this thing with the bowling shoes could easily turn out like it did with the red satin windbreakers. I mean, in addition to Army and

Navy supplies, my father also carries a complete line of sporting goods, and whatever he hasn't got in stock he'll order for you, with special discounts to teams.

So about two years ago, a team of about twenty guys came in and ordered windbreakers out of the club treasury they're supposed to have, and my old man had them made up to their individual measurements and got a ten-dollar deposit. So what happens, the windbreakers arrive and meantime the team has disbanded, and my old man is stuck with the merchandise.

He went around to see some of the guys' parents, and the only satisfaction he got was they promised to give their sons a good talking to so it shouldn't happen again in the future. And to make matters worse, the club president and the secretary and treasurer were now in reform school for swiping a bread truck, which will give you some idea of the type of neighborhood my father's store is in. When I go there sometimes on Saturday to help out, I first wrap up all my change like candy kisses so the coins won't jingle in my pocket, or else I would never make it alive from the subway.

I also have to take the precaution of not wearing my windbreaker, which has this team's name on the back in bright blue letters—THE ARISTOCRATS. Also, it has a big number on the left sleeve and one of the guy's names stitched over the front pocket. In my particular case it's JOE, and since my real name is Irving, I always carry a whole flock of pencils and ball pens to make the flap stand up and hide it—which is something I wish my mother would do with hers. I mean she wears this thing to the store all the time because it's easy to slip on and off, but to me it's embarrassing. For instance, I'm sitting on the stoop with this girl, Beverly, and I look up and see my mother coming up the block in number 7, ROCKY.

Well, with the bowling shoes it could work out the same way, which is why my mother always asks did the man come for them. I mean, all we need is a dozen pairs of bowling shoes to add to our wardrobe of twenty red windbreakers. Even with hard wear I'm going to be buried as number 13—SWIFTY.

So, by this time my mother was rinsing out a few things in the sink, my father was scratching his back against the chair, and I started once again to draw an isosceles triangle. But once again he interrupts me, suddenly aggravated because my mother reminded him about the bowling shoes.

"Go ahead," he says to me, "—go ahead, study hard, be an accountant."

"I'm not studying to be an accountant," I told him, even though he knows it perfectly well. "I'm only trying to do my geometry homework."

But he wouldn't even listen.

"Draw straight lines," he went on. "Perfectly straight, with a ruler."

"Well, what's wrong with that?" I asked. "You want me to pass, don't you?"

This was purely a rhetorical question, because anything below an eighty average he throws a fit all over the place that I'm not taking advantage of the education he's got to sweat to provide.

"With a ruler," he repeated. "It's inhuman."

"What's inhuman?"

"Never mind, never mind, he said with a sigh. "Just remember—there are no straight lines in nature."

"So what's that got to do with anything?"

"Everything—it's got everything to do with everything. It's unnatural to have a straight line. A straight line is strictly for a machine."

That's what I mean about my old man; you can't figure him. Now he is irritated by straight lines. So much so, he tells me they're strictly for machines, which is about the worst thing my father can say about anything, because the thing that bothers him most in life is any kind of machine whatsoever— even an automatic can opener you hang on the wall drives him wild. He hates machines.

"Look," I told him. "If it makes you any happier, I'll draw crooked lines; all right? Freehand."

He blew his cheeks out, looking at me, thinking.

"It's not a question of my happiness," he said. "It's the happiness of the whole world I'm talking about."

"So all right then; I'll throw away my ruler and everybody will be happy."

"Don't be funny."

"I'm not being funny. I'm merely carrying your argument to its logical conclusions."

"I'm not arguing," he argued. "I'm telling you something . . . The whole trouble with the world today is caused by too many straight lines."

"By what?"

"By too many straight lines," he insisted. "By rulers, by measuring to the billionth of an inch, by taking pulses and blood pressures."

"What are you talking about?" I groaned. I mean, I was actually in pain by this time. "What's wrong with taking pulses and blood pressure?"

"It leads to the fallacy."

"What fallacy?"

"That by taking the pulse you can know all about how it is with the heart."

"Nobody thinks that—no doctor believes such a thing!"

"Maybe not in theory, but in practice he does. A man goes to him with a pain in the chest; the doctor listens and takes his pulse. The man could be dying from sorrow, but if the pulse is regular, there's nothing wrong with him. . . . Go home, take it easy, have a couple of pills before meals!"

"Sure," I agreed. "Sure, because as far as the doctor can tell there's nothing physically wrong!"

"Maybe not physically, but could he count the feelings? Could he tell from hearing the drum beat what kind of music the orchestra is playing?"

"Of course he couldn't. That's not the doctor's business!"

"It's everybody's business!"

"Papa's right," my mother said, standing behind him with a handful of wrung-out clothes and making big eyes and nods to agree with anything, just to keep peace before bedtime.

"Listen to Papa; Papa knows. If a man is feeling sad, everybody should try to cheer him up."

"That's right," I said, willing to let the whole matter drop. "But with the medical field what it is today, the ordinary doctor hasn't got time to make jokes with everybody who comes in his office!"

"Time!" my father shouted, slapping the table so everything jumped. "Clocks! More measurements! Without clocks a doctor would have time!"

And then I had to listen to him go on and on about clocks and watches, and how they're killing everybody—especially my Uncle Max, who's a big wheel in men's socks.

"All day long in the office with five minutes for this, and five minutes for that, like life is a lot of hard-boiled eggs! I go in to see him for five minutes, and there he sits behind the desk, gray in the face from trying to keep up with the clock! With such a complexion, even in person he looks like he's on TV!"

My mother hung up the clothes in the bathroom, put out the milk bottles, and still he's raving—without arguments any more; just sitting there saying, "Tick-tock, tick-tock," and waiting for somebody to disagree with him. It was already twenty minutes after ten, and no homework done.

"Look," I said finally. "Look, Pop—let's not discuss it any more tonight, huh? All I meant was if somebody is unhappy, you can't expect an ordinary doctor is going to cure him. This needs a psychologist."

"A psychologist!"

He threw up his hands like he was shooting for a basket with ten seconds left to play.

"After all," I said, "you started this whole thing because I was trying to draw a straight line with a ruler. But whether you like rulers or you want to abolish clocks is beside the point, because the whole world happens to feel otherwise, and without these things we would have no civilization like we know it today!"

He smacked his head with his hand and waved his arm around the room. "This is civilization?"

"Yes!" I replied emphatically, because I could see my mother felt bad that he was picking on her kitchen. "Yes, and if you hadn't sat here and ate a big meal tonight with two helpings of food which was shipped by trains that run by clocks, and was cooked in machine-made pots with gas that engineers with rulers figured out how to send through pipes all the way from Texas, you wouldn't be sneering at civilization! You'd be walking up and down complaining, 'Where's my dinner?'"

He was amazed at the sharpness of this line of reasoning, but still he tried to squirm out.

"A man's got to eat!" he protested, like I was trying to take the bread out of his mouth.

"So you haven't missed any meals yet," I told him. "What are you complaining?"

"I'm not complaining, but civilization isn't just a matter of three meals a day. Civilization is what happens afterward—it's what a man does when the stomach is full."

"Like falling asleep in the easy chair," I said, punching

home my final points. "Like going down the cellar to shake
the furnace and inventing a bomb to destroy our entire material culture—is that being civilized?"

"Wait!" he said, holding up his hand. And I could tell from
the gleam in his eye that this was what he had been leading
up to all along. "Allow me to explain something."

"Sure," I said, knowing the worst was yet to come.

"If you don't mind, that is." I shrugged.

"All right, then," he said, settling down for a long, windy
night of it. "Try to listen to what I have to say for a change.
Just for a change."

He picked up the coffee can, slowly, so I wouldn't miss anything, like a magician getting ready for a trick.

"Now," he began, squinting his eyes thoughtfully. "First of
all."

My mother looked at me with a dark glare, like Now-see-
what-you-did-with-your-big-mouth.

"This bomb," my father went on, holding the coffee can on
the tips of his fingers for all to admire—"this bomb is not for
destruction. This bomb could be the saving of the whole
human race."

"Good," I said. "I'm glad to hear it."

"In addition, it solves the one big problem that all the
greatest scientific brains couldn't solve so easy."

"What problem is that?"

"The problem of how to deliver it. All the time you read in
papers that the one thing that is constantly stumping the
experts is how to deliver the bomb. This bomb you can deliver
by the millions. It's small, it's portable, it's light."

"And the price is right," I agreed, but he didn't notice.

"Besides," he said, smiling dreamily to himself, "who
would suspect a coffee can? A coffee can could get through
the Iron Curtain, and nobody the wiser."

"And then what happens?" I asked, trying to nudge him along so I could maybe get started sometime before three.

He looked surprised.

"What happens? It blows up."

"Not in here!" my mother said, frowning. "Out in the street with that thing!"

"Don't worry," he told her. "It wouldn't hurt anything—no noise, no smoke, no damage. That's the beauty of it."

"What have you got there?" I asked.

He took the lid off the can, and my mother backed away just in case. I looked inside and saw my face reflected in the tin bottom.

"It's empty," I told my mother.

"It's loaded," my father insisted. "Look again—can't you see?"

"See what?"

"The possibilities. It's full of tremendous possibilities."

"Possibilities for what?"

"For bringing peace to the world," he said, and his voice was almost a whisper as he leaned across the table. "You could put something inside."

Suddenly, in the bright kitchen light, his face was like a painting. It wasn't a pretty face, but it was kind and very tired, and in it I could see a thousand ancestors looking across the table at me—people I never even heard of, going back for hundreds of years, and always hoping and always trying to figure out some way to make a dream come true. I couldn't joke about his bomb any more.

"I see what you mean," I told him. "What would you put in it?"

"Something—a message. I don't know."

He sat looking down at the linoleum, holding the empty can like a beggar, thinking.

"You could write something on a piece of paper," he said,

"—some words that everybody could understand—something about please, for God's sake, let's cut out this crazy nonsense and live together like human beings. About giving kids a chance to grow up and make a better world without this constant wrangling. About forgetting all about rulers and clocks, and inches and minutes, so we could have instead miles and years that the heart could fill with things that matter, and no more of these big ideas and fancy theories that come from the mind alone . . . that always end up behind barbed wire with guns in their hands, marching in straight lines like machines. . . . Let's get together, you could say. . . . Let's have some peace and quiet . . . and if you can't do something decent or think of anything good to say . . . then just shut up and take it easy."

It wasn't anything new that he said—anything that would change the world overnight. My English teacher would have flunked him for not being fully prepared, but to hear him tell it, you could almost believe it was practical—that such a note in a coffee can could make a difference in history.

My mother sat there listening, holding a potholder in one hand, like she expected his thoughts were going to be too hot for her to handle. She sighed. "Ah, the trouble," she said, "the trouble. If they blow everything up, what? With the cities in ruins, who could live there?"

"It isn't the cities so much," my father said. "It's more the neighborhoods—the neighborhoods and towns where people live their lives. I could feel sorry for a factory, maybe, or a bridge or a skyscraper, but what would be worse to me is all the four-room apartments, the two-family houses and corner grocery stores—somebody's little house in the suburbs he's working fifteen years to pay off. And the parks and the libraries and the playgrounds, with the swings hanging empty and the sparrows dead, and lying on the ground a wheel from a baby carriage."

Half of me sat looking at my father, seeing the terrible things he mentioned, and the other half of me stood outside looking at the three of us sitting around the kitchen table, knowing it was getting later by the minute, and unless we were bombed before nine, I still had to do my homework. . . . Meantime, we sat there breathing.

"Write the message," my mother said quietly. "Write what you feel, Sam, and put it in there."

He looked into the can, staring deep down inside, like it had no bottom.

"I couldn't write," he said. "Only Shakespeare could write such a thing, or the men who wrote the Bible."

My mother turned to me.

"Maybe Irving . . ." she said, holding out the potholder like she wasn't sure, and my father slowly nodded.

"Maybe Irving," he agreed. "Maybe Irving, if he studies hard and passes all the tests, not just in school but in the streets and in life—maybe Irving will some day be such a poet, such a prophet with words, that he could write it down in all languages so everybody could read and understand and remember."

Which is just another concrete example of what I mean about my father—one minute he's sneering that I'm going to be an accountant, and the next minute he's making a poet out of me. And not just for birthday cards or get-well- quick, but to write some whole big thing etched in brass that's going to reform the entire human race. I mean, it's all I can do to squeak through English and make a synopsis of *The Return of the Native*,[3] and he's got me composing these tremendous limericks like Henry Wadsworth-Longfellow.[4]

[3] *The Return of the Native:* novel by Thomas Hardy (1840–1928), British novelist and poet.

[4] *Henry Wadsworth Longfellow:* popular American poet (1807–1882).

But he was serious, my father. He put the can back on the table, and his eyes said, "Fill it." And with that, the weight seemed to go from his shoulders.

"The cake smells done," he told my mother with a big yawn and a stretch. And when she brought it out, he could hardly give it five minutes to cool before he had a piece.

We had a piece also to join him, and with his he drank about a quart of milk. After that, he gets up from the table satisfied, and while my mother washes the plates, he's already in there brushing his teeth so it sounds like somebody scrubbing down the walls. Then my mother kisses my ear good night, and next I hear the alarm clock winding, followed by two minutes of silence before the snoring.

And there I am, alone with this coffee can.

Originally, I had only three problems to think about—one with the isosceles triangle, one with a rhomboid, and another to show how to construct a tangent to a circle from a given point without using the center. But now, at eleven-fifteen, I had in addition my father's bomb. I mean, he could go to bed and forget it, but there it was, right in front of me, and I couldn't get it out of my mind.

It just sat there looking so empty I couldn't think of anything else. Like in that poem, *The Ancient Mariner*,[5] by Coleridge, where the albatross hangs from the guy's neck; that's how that coffee can got to be with me— a burden, a thing I couldn't shake off. In a whole half-hour of solid staring at it, I got nowhere with the problem of what a person could say in so many exact words that would have the effect my father wanted. In fact, I gradually came to the conclusion that there weren't any exact words, but only wishes and feelings.

I don't know; I may have been just sleepy, but when I

[5] *The Ancient Mariner:* long narrative poem by the British poet, Samuel Taylor Coleridge (1772–1834).

opened the can after a while, it wasn't empty any more. It was filled to the top, and not just with possibilities, but with all the feelings my father had put into it. Sitting there in the quiet kitchen, I could see added to them the hopes and prayers of everybody lucky enough to still be able to hope and pray, myself included, and the first thing I knew that can was really loaded. Then I put the lid back on, shutting in the reflection of my face smiling in the tin bottom.

That's what I mean about my old man—he is contagious. He may be a little nuts; he might make foolish mistakes in business; but he's got such a bad case of humanity, it's catching. Just to hear him go, night after night, getting mad at things like rulers and machines and straight lines—just to hear him snoring in the other room even—gives you the feeling that no matter what happens, mankind is somehow going to come out on top. This is the bomb my father has—the most powerful weapon on earth, and he doesn't even know he's got it.

But that wasn't what made me smile. I smiled because I suddenly remembered that I could let my homework go until the next day. Every Friday morning, between physical training and geometry, through some odd freak in the schedule I have a study period.

Understanding the Story

1. What kind of person is Papa? How is this revealed to us by the author?
2. Explain these bits of Papa's wisdom:
   a. "The man could be dying from sorrow, but if the pulse is regular, there is nothing wrong with him."
   b. "Civilization is what a man does when the stomach is full."
3. What opposing points of view do Papa and

his son have about civilization? How does
Papa get his son to come around to his point
of view?

4. What is Papa's "bomb?" What is his prescription for peace? What terrible alternative does he describe?

5. Explain the significance of Irving's comment about the can: ". . . when I opened the can after a while, it wasn't empty any more."

6. What does Irving mean when he says about his father: ". . . he's got such a bad case of humanity, it's catching."

7. Describe the family life of the Pitkins using the details the author gives us. Describe the relationships that seem to exist among them.

*Appreciating
the Story*

1. How does the narrator's conversational style contribute to the effectiveness of the story?

2. How does the dialogue effectively use the folk idiom?

3. Find as many humorous incidents and comments as you can.

4. How is an element of suspense injected into the story? How does it add to the effect of the author's message?

5. Why does Papa say his "bomb" is more powerful than an H-bomb? Explain the apparent contradiction in Papa's bomb.

6. Is Papa an idealist or a realist? Explain your answer.

7. What elements in his story add to our understanding of Irving's character? In what ways is he a typical tenth-year high school student? In what ways is he unusual?

Reviewing
the
Unit

*For Comparative
Study*

1. Both stories use objects that mean much more than they really are. In one, it's a watermelon. In another, it's a coffee can. What does each really come to mean ?
2. Compare the Wills family and the Pitkin family. In what ways are they similar? In what ways are they different?
3. Compare Mr. Wills and Papa. Each uses different means to gain his ends. Which do you prefer? Why?
4. Would Irving do what the narrator does in "The Taste of Melon"?
5. Contrast the conflicts between the older and the younger generation in each of the stories. How does the younger generation come around to the view of the older in each case?
6. In each story, there is criticism of the code of behavior or the beliefs of our society. How does each author present the criticism? What view does he want us to take?

*Building Your
Vocabulary*

Match the nouns taken from stories in this unit with the word or words that give their meaning.

Column A

1. brainstorm   a. coating on damp paper
2. bravado   b. mistaken idea
3. deadlock   c. amount above what is used
4. fallacy   d. sudden inspiration
5. mildew   e. place of protection
6. ritual   f. trembling
7. sanctuary   g. pretended courage
8. surplus   h. standstill
9. sustenance   i. ceremony
10. tremor   j. means of livelihood

For Creative
Writing

Use each of the following as the opening sentence for a short story.

1. This I believe.
2. My ideal person is . . .
3. I admired what he did.
4. I was proud of myself.
5. I have faith in . . .
6. The world I want to live in . . .
7. I stood up for my rights.
8. One on God's side is a majority.
9. Must justice be blind?
10. To thine own self be true.

EXPLORING
HIDDEN
DEPTHS

NEARLY two hundred years ago, Robert Burns, the Scottish poet, wrote:

> Man's inhumanity to man
> Makes countless thousands mourn.

The words are as true today as they were then. During your entire lifetime, there has not been a single day of peace in the world. Men have been fighting and killing one another in some part of the globe. In many countries, even where there is no war, millions of men have been used by their fellow men to gain wealth and power. Even the minimal goal of toleration—live and let live—has not been achieved. The higher goals of mutual understanding, mutual appreciation, and cooperation for the common good seem as far away as ever.

"Love thy neighbor as thyself" appears in both the Old and the New Testaments, but as an ideal, it is constantly being violated. The list of man's hates is almost endless, yet we know that man is not born with hate. He learns it; he is taught to hate. He learns to hate anyone different: a person of a different religion, color, nationality, or social class. The same mankind that is moved by all the noble ideals we just read about can be capable of cruelty and thoughtless inhumanity.

The stories in this unit are concerned with prejudice, suspicion, cruelty, and blind obedience to heartless custom. By studying their terrible results, we may realize that there is an alternative. The Golden Rule must be made to prevail. The same Robert Burns who disapproved of man's inhumanity to man also predicted that "it's coming yet, for a' that, that man to man, the world o'er shall brothers be for a' that."

A Kind of
Murder

HUGH PENTECOST

*Approaching
the Story...*

WHO has not at some time played a practical joke
on someone? Most often, we tried only to embar-
rass our victim. But how can anyone truly know
the difference between a harmless prank and a
cruel trick? In "A Kind of Murder," the butt of
this kind of foolish behavior is a teacher—tradi-
tionally fair game for certain kinds of students
who find safety in the numbers of their classmates and seek to increase their own importance
by belittling others. The setting for this story is
a private school—a military academy. In the middle of the term, one of the teachers on the staff
dies suddenly. A new teacher arrives on the
scene. The results of his reception by the students
constitute the plot of this tale of humiliation and
regret.

*...And Keep
in Mind*

HUGH PENTECOST has chosen to play the role of
narrator of this story. To do this, he must go back
to the time when he was fifteen and a student at
the academy. As you read, note how he gains our
sympathy for the new teacher. Note how this
merely heightens the effect of the actions of the
students. Pentecost himself emerges as an im-

mensely human person, yet he is torn by conflicting loyalties. Try to understand why he acts as
he does. Ask yourself whether you would have
done the same thing in his place. Are you like
the narrator or can you truly consider yourself
better than he is? If you can't, then perhaps this
story will have a deeper meaning for you. It just
might cause you to think before you act as the
students do in "A Kind of Murder."

YOU MIGHT SAY
this is the story of a murder—although nobody was killed. I
don't know what has become of Mr. Silas Warren, but I have
lived for many years with the burden on my conscience of
having been responsible for the existence of a walking dead
man.

I was fifteen years old during the brief span of days that I
knew Mr. Silas Warren. It was toward the end of the winter
term at Morgan Military Academy. Mr. Etsweiler, the chemistry and physics teacher at Morgan, had died of a heart at-
tack one afternoon while he was helping to coach the hockey
team on the lake. Mr. Henry Huntingdon Hadley, the headmaster, had gone to New York to find a replacement. That
replacement was Mr. Silas Warren.

I may have been one of the first people to see Mr. Warren
at the Academy. I had been excused from afternoon study
period because of a heavy cold, and allowed to take my books
to my room to work there. I saw Mr. Warren come walking
across the quadrangle toward Mr. Hadley's office, which was
located on the ground floor under the hall where my room
was.

Mr. Warren didn't look like a man who was coming to stay long. He carried one small, flimsy suitcase spattered with travel labels. Although it was a bitter March day he wore a thin, summer-weight topcoat. He stopped beside a kind of brown lump in the snow. That brown lump was Teddy, the school dog.

Teddy was an ancient collie. They said that in the old days you could throw a stick for Teddy to retrieve until you, not he, dropped from exhaustion. Now the old, gray-muzzled dog was pretty much ignored by everyone except the chef, who fed him scraps from the dining room after the noon meal. Teddy would be at the kitchen door, promptly on time, and then find a comfortable spot to lie down. He'd stay there until someone forced him to move.

Mr. Warren stopped by Teddy, bent down, and scratched the dog's head. The old, burr-clotted tail thumped wearily in the snow. Mr. Warren straightened up and looked around. He had narrow, stooped shoulders. His eyes were pale blue, and they had a kind of frightened look in them. *He's scared*, I thought; *coming to a new place in the middle of a term, he's scared.*

I guess most of the other fellows didn't see Mr. Warren until he turned up at supper time at the head of one of the tables in the dining room. We marched into the dining room and stood behind our chairs waiting for the cadet major to give the order to be seated. The order was delayed. Mr. Henry Huntingdon Hadley, known as Old Beaver because of his snowy white beard, made an announcement.

"Mr. Warren has joined our teaching staff to fill the vacancy created by the unfortunate demise of Mr. Etsweiler." Old Beaver had false teeth and his s's whistled musically. "I trust you will give him a cordial welcome."

"Be seated," the cadet major snapped.

We sat. Old Beaver said grace. Then we all began to talk.

I was at Mr. Warren's right. He had a genial, want-to-be-liked
smile.

"And your name is?" he asked me in a pleasant but flat
voice.

"Pentecost, sir."

He leaned toward me. "How's that?" he asked.

"Pentecost, sir."

Sammy Callahan sat across from me on Mr. Warren's left.
Sammy was a fine athlete and a terrible practical joker. I saw
a gleam of interest in his eyes. As Mr. Warren turned toward
him Sammy spoke in an ordinary conversational tone. "Why
don't you go take a jump in the lake, sir?"

Mr. Warren smiled. "Yes, I guess you're right," he said.

Sammy grinned at me. There was no doubt about it—Mr.
Warren was quite deaf!

It was a strange kind of secret Sammy and I had. We didn't
really know what to do with it, but we found out that night.
Old Beaver was not a man to start anyone in gradually. It
would have been Mr. Etsweiler's turn to take the night study
hour, so that hour was passed on to Mr. Warren.

He sat on the little platform at the head of the study hall—
smiling and smiling. I think there must have been terror in
his heart then. I think he may even have been praying.

Everyone seemed unusually busy studying, but we were
all waiting for the test. The test always came for a new master the first time he had night study hour. There would be a
minor disturbance and we'd find out promptly whether this
man could maintain discipline, or not. It came after about five
minutes—a loud, artificial belch.

Mr. Warren smiled and smiled. He hadn't heard it.

Belches sprang up all over the room. Then somebody threw
a handful of torn paper in the air. Mr. Warren's smile froze.

"Now, now boys," he said.

More belches. More torn paper.

"Boys!" Mr. Warren cried out, like someone in pain.

Then Old Beaver appeared, his eyes glittering behind rimless spectacles. There was something I never understood about Old Beaver. Ordinarily his shoes squeaked. You could hear him coming from quite a distance away—squeak-squeak, squeak-squeak. But somehow, when he chose, he could approach as noiselessly as a cat, without any squeak at all. And there he was.

The study hall was quiet as a tomb. But the silence was frighteningly loud, and the place was littered with paper.

"There will be ten demerit marks against every student in this room," Old Beaver said in his icy voice. "I want every scrap of paper picked up instantly."

Several of us scrambled down on our hands and knees. Mr. Warren smiled at the headmaster.

"Consider the lilies of the field," Mr. Warren said. "They toil not, neither do they spin. Yet I tell you that Solomon in all his glory—"

"Silence!" Old Beaver hissed, with all the menace of a poised cobra. He turned to Mr. Warren. "I'll take the balance of this period, Mr. Warren. I suggest you go to your room and prepare yourself for tomorrow's curriculum."

I didn't have any classes with Mr. Warren the next day, but all you heard as you passed in the corridors from one class period to the next were tales of the jokes and disorders in the physics and chemistry courses. Somehow nobody thought it was wrong to take advantage of Mr. Warren.

The climax came very quickly. In the winter, if you weren't out for the hockey or winter sports teams, you had to exercise in the gym. There were the parallel bars, and the rings, and the tumbling mats. And there was boxing.

The boxing teacher was Major Durand, the military commandant. I know now that he was a sadist. Major Durand was filled with contempt for everyone but Major Durand. I saw the look on his face when Mr. Warren appeared.

Mr. Warren had been assigned to help in the gym. He was something to see—just skin and bones. He had on a pair of ordinary black socks and, I suspect, the only pair of shoes he owned—black oxfords. He'd borrowed a pair of shorts that could have been wrapped twice around his skinny waist. Above that was a much mended short-sleeved undershirt. He looked around, hopeless, amiable.

"Mr. Warren!" Major Durand said. "I'd like you to help me demonstrate. Put on these gloves if you will." He tossed a pair of boxing gloves at Mr. Warren, who stared at them stupidly. One of the boys helped him tie the laces.

"Now, Mr. Warren," Durand said. The Major danced and bobbed and weaved, and shot out his gloves in short vicious jabs at the air. "You will hold your gloves up to your face, sir. When you're ready you'll say 'Hit!'—and I shall hit you."

I'd seen Major Durand do this with a boy he didn't like. You held up the gloves and you covered your face and then, with your throat dry and aching, you said "Hit!"—and Major Durand's left or right would smash through your guard and pulverize your nose or mouth. It was sheer strength I know now, not skill.

Mr. Warren held up his gloves, and he looked like an actor in an old Mack Sennett comedy [1] —the absurd clothes, the sickly smile.

Durand danced in front of him. "Whenever you say, Mr. Warren. Now watch this, boys. The feint—and the jab."

"Hit!" said Mr. Warren, his voice suddenly falsetto.

Pow! Major Durand's left jab smashed through the guard of Mr. Warren's nose. There was a sudden geyser of blood.

---

[1] *Mack Sennett comedy:* movie produced by Mack Sennett (1884–1960), stressing broad slapstick comedy.

"Again, Mr. Warren!" the Major commanded, his eyes glittering.

"I think I'd better retire to repair the damage," Mr. Warren said. His undershirt was spattered with blood and he had produced a soiled handkerchief which he held to his nose. He hurried out of the gym at a sort of shambling gallop.

That night the payoff came in study hall. Mr. Warren was called on this time to substitute for Old Beaver, who had taken over for him the night before. Sammy Callahan staged it. Suddenly handkerchiefs were waved from all parts of the room—handkerchiefs stained red. Red ink, of course.

"Hit!" somebody shouted. "Hit, hit!" Nearly all the boys were bobbing, weaving, jabbing.

Mr. Warren, pale as a ghost, cotton visibly stuffed in one nostril, stared at us like a dead man.

Then there was Old Beaver again.

Somehow the word was out at breakfast the next morning. Mr. Warren was leaving. He didn't show at the breakfast table. I felt a little squeamish about it. He hadn't been given a chance. Maybe he wasn't such a bad guy.

It was during the morning classroom period that we heard it. It was a warm day for March and the ice was breaking up on the lake. The scream was piercing and terrified. Somebody went to the window. The scream came again.

"Somebody's fallen through the ice!"

The whole school—a hundred and fifty boys and masters—hurried down to the shore of the lake. The sun was so bright that all we could see was a dark shape flopping out there, pulling itself up on the ice and then disappearing under water as the ice broke. Each time the figure rose there was a wailing scream.

Then the identification. "It's Teddy!" someone shouted.

The school dog. He'd walked out there and the ice had caved in on him. The screams were growing weaker. A couple of us made for the edge of the ice. Old Beaver and Major Durand confronted us.

"I'm sorry, boys," Old Beaver said. "It's a tragic thing to have to stand here and watch the old dog drown. But no one— no one connected with the school—is to try to get to him. I'm responsible for your safety. That's an order."

We stood there, sick with it. Old Teddy must have seen us because for a moment there seemed to be new hope in his strangled wailing.

Then I saw Mr. Warren. He was by the boathouse, his old suitcase in his hand. He looked out at the dog, and so help me there were tears in Mr. Warren's eyes. Then, very calmly, he put down his bag, took off his thin topcoat and suit jacket. He righted one of the overturned boats on the shore and pulled it to the edge of the lake.

"Mr. Warren! You heard my order!" Old Beaver shouted at him.

Mr. Warren turned to the headmaster, smiling. "You seem to forget, sir, I am no longer connected with Morgan Military Academy, and therefore not subject to your orders."

"Stop him!" Major Durand ordered.

But before anyone could reach him, Mr. Warren had slid the flat-bottomed rowboat out onto the ice. He crept along on the ice himself, clinging to the boat, pushing it across the shiny surface toward Teddy. I heard Mr. Warren's thin, flat voice.

"Hold on, old man! I'm coming."

The ice gave way under him, but he clung to the boat and scrambled up—and on.

"Hold on, old man!"

It seemed to take forever. Just before what must have been the last, despairing shriek from the half-frozen dog, Mr. Warren reached him. How he found the strength to lift the watersoaked collie into the boat, I don't know; but he managed, and then he came back toward us, creeping along the cracking ice, pushing the boat to shore.

The chef wrapped Teddy in blankets, put him behind the stove in the kitchen, and gave him a dose of warm milk and cooking brandy. Mr. Warren was hustled to the infirmary. Did I say that when he reached the shore with Teddy the whole school cheered him?

Old Beaver, for all his tyranny, must have been a pretty decent guy. He announced that night that Mr. Warren was not leaving after all. He trusted that, after Mr. Warren's display of valor, the boys would show him the respect he deserved.

I went to see Mr. Warren in the infirmary that first evening. He looked pretty done in, but he also looked happier than I'd ever seen him.

"What you did took an awful lot of courage," I told him. "Everybody thinks it was really a swell thing to do."

Mr. Warren smiled at me—a thoughtful kind of a smile. "Courage is a matter of definition," he said. "It doesn't take courage to stand up and let yourself get punched in the nose, boy. It takes courage to walk way. As for Teddy—somebody had to go after him. There wasn't anyone who could but me, so courage or not, I went. You'd have gone if Mr. Hadley hadn't issued orders." He sighed. "I'm glad to get a second chance here. Very glad."

Somehow I got the notion it was a last chance—the very last chance he'd ever have.

It was a week before Mr. Warren had the night study hall again. It was a kind of test. For perhaps fifteen minutes nothing happened and then I heard Sammy give his fine, artificial belch. I looked up at Mr. Warren. He was smiling happily. He hadn't heard. A delighted giggle ran around the room.

I was on my feet. "If there's one more sound in this room

I'm going after Old Beaver," I said. "And after that I'll personally take on every guy in this school if necessary, to knock sense into him!"

The room quieted. I was on the student council and I was also captain of the boxing team. The rest of the study period was continued in an orderly fashion. When it was over and we were headed for our rooms, Mr. Warren flagged me down.

"I don't know quite what was going on, Pentecost," he said, "but I gather you saved the day for me. Thank you. Thank you very much. Perhaps when the boys get to know me a little better they'll come to realize—" He made a helpless little gesture with his bony hands.

"I'm sure they will, sir," I said. "I'm sure of it."

"They're not cruel," Mr. Warren said. "It's just high spirits, I know."

Sammy Callahan was waiting for me in my room. "What are you, some kind of a do-gooder?" he said.

"Give the guy a chance," I said. "He proved he has guts when it's needed. But he's helpless there in the study hall."

Sammy gave me a sour grin. "You and he should get along fine," he said. "And you'll need to. The guys aren't going to be chummy with a do-gooder like you."

It was a week before Mr. Warren's turn to run the study hour came around again. In that time I'd found that Sammy was right. I was being given the cold shoulder. Major Durand, who must have hated Mr. Warren for stealing the heroic spotlight from him, was giving me a hard time. One of the guys I knew well came to me.

"You're making a mistake," he told me. "He's a grown man and you're just a kid. If he can't take care of himself it's not your headache."

I don't like telling the next part of it, but it happened.

When Mr. Warren's night came again, the study hall was quiet enough for a while. Then came a belch. I looked up at

Mr. Warren. He was smiling. Then someone waved one of those fake bloody handkerchiefs. Then, so help me, somebody let out a baying howl—like Teddy in the lake.

Mr. Warren knew what was happening now. He looked down at me, and there was an agonizing, wordless plea for help in his eyes. I—well, I looked away. I was fifteen. I didn't want to be called a do-gooder. I didn't want to be snubbed. Mr. Warren *was* a grown man and he should have been able to take care of himself. The boys weren't cruel: they were just high spirited—hadn't Mr. Warren himself said so?

I looked up from behind a book. Mr. Warren was standing, looking out over the room. His stooped, skinny shoulders were squared away. Two great tears ran down his pale cheeks. His last chance was played out.

Then he turned and walked out of the study hall.

No one ever saw him again. He must have gone straight to his room, thrown his meager belongings into the battered old suitcase, and taken off on foot into the night.

You see what I mean when I say it was a kind of murder? And I was the murderer.

***Understanding
the Story***

1. Explain the meaning of the title.
2. Describe Mr. Warren's character. How are we made aware of it?
3. What do the students at the academy first learn about Mr. Warren? How do they use their knowledge?
4. Explain Mr. Warren's definition of courage.
5. "They're not cruel," Mr. Warren said. "It's just high spirits, I know." Do you agree or disagree with Mr. Warren? Why?
6. What are Pentecost's conflicting motives? Which motive wins out?

7. Why does Pentecost consider himself a murderer?

Appreciating
the Story

1. The opening paragraph is effective. What purposes does it achieve?
2. How does the author arouse our sympathy for Mr. Warren?
3. Why does the author include the episode of Mr. Warren's heroism?
4. What does the way he tells the story reveal about the character of Pentecost?
5. The author might have ended the story after Mr. Warren saved Teddy. Would this ending have been preferable to the actual one? Why or why not?
6. What is gained by leaving Mr. Warren's fate unknown?
7. What does the author intend us to learn from the story? Does his way of telling the story help or hinder him in achieving this intention? Explain your answer.

The Trouble

J. F. POWERS

*Approaching
the Story . . .*

SEVERAL years ago, a well-known educator
warned that "we are allowing social dynamite to
accumulate in our large cities." His prophecy has
been borne out by rioting across the country,
from Los Angeles to Detroit to Newark. These
riots have been racial in character, and the big-
city slum has been their setting.

The story you are about to read is set in a riot
between blacks and whites in a large city. Written in the 1940's, it anticipates the violence that
has broken out in recent years. The tragedy of
racial conflict is made universal, although in the
story, we see only its effect on one Negro family.
The events are related by a young boy. Everything is seen through his eyes—the action, the
other characters, the effects of "the trouble" on
everyone. Movement in the story is slow. The
author wants us to experience the full effect of
the agony this one family, a small piece of mankind, is suffering. The purpose of the story is to
arouse our feelings against the injustice of blind
hate. Decide for yourself if it is successful.

*... And Keep
in Mind*

THIS is a story in which much has to be inferred
by the reader. Although the language is simple,
you must read closely to discover the setting of
the story, the nature of "the trouble," the feelings
of the people involved, and the point of view of
the person who is recounting the events. The
author makes you work hard, but as you do, you
come to feel that you are living through the experience with the young narrator. What does he
think about whites? How does he react to the
events involving Mama? How does he act toward
the people on the scene? When does he (and
you) come to understand the full extent of the
tragedy? The answers to these questions will
affect you deeply. You will not be able to avoid
asking yourself, "What can *I* do to stop this kind
of 'trouble'?"

WE WATCHED
at the window all that afternoon.

Old Gramma came out of her room and said, Now you
kids get away from there this very minute, and we would until she went back to her room. We could hear her old rocking-
chair creak when she got up or sat down and so we always
ran away from the window before she came into the room to
see if we were minding her good or looking out. Except once
she went back to her room and didn't sit down, or maybe she
did and got up easy so the chair didn't creak, or maybe we
got our signals mixed, because she caught us all there and

shooed us away and pulled down the green shade. The next time we were very sure she wasn't foxing us before we went to the window and lifted the shade just enough to peek out.

It was like waiting for rats as big as cats to run out from under a tenement so you could pick them off with a .22. Rats are about the biggest live game you can find in ordinary times and you see more of them than white folks in our neighborhood—in ordinary times. But the rats we waited for today were white ones and they were doing most of the shooting themselves. Sometimes some coloreds would come by with guns, but not often; they mostly had clubs. This morning we'd seen the whites catch up with a shot-in-the-leg colored and throw bricks and stones at his black head till it got all red and he was dead. I could still see the wet places in the alley. That's why we kept looking out the window. We wanted to see some whites get killed for a change, but we didn't much think we would, and I guess what really expected to see was nothing, or maybe them killing another colored.

There was a rumpus downstairs in front and I could hear a mess of people tramping up the stairs. They kept on coming after the second floor and my sister Carrie, my twin, said maybe they were whites come to get *us* because we saw what they did to the shot-in-the-leg colored in the alley. I was scared for a minute, I admit, but when I heard their voices plainer I knew they were coloreds and it was all right, only I didn't see why there were so many of them.

Then I got scared again, only different now, empty scared all over, when they came down the hall on our floor, not stopping at anybody else's door. And then there they were, banging on our door, of all the doors in the building. They tried to come right on in, but the door was locked.

Old Gramma was the one locked it and she said she'd clean house if one of us kids so much as looked at the knob even. She threw the key down her neck somewhere and I went and told her that was our door the people were pounding on and where was the key. She reached down her neck and there was the key all right. But she didn't act much like she intended to open the door. She just stood there staring at it like it was somebody alive, saying the litany to the Blessed Virgin: *Mère du Christ, priez pour nous, Secours des chrétiens, priez.*[1] Then all the sudden she was crying, tears were blurry in her old yellow eyes, and she put the key in the lock, her veiny hands shaking, and unlocked the door.

They had Mama in their arms. I forgot all about Old Gramma, but I guess she passed out. Anyway, she was on the floor and a couple of men were picking her up and a couple of women were saying, Put her here, put her there. I wasn't worried as much about Old Gramma as I was about Mama.

A bone, God it made me sick, had poked through the flesh of Mama's arm, all bloody like a sharp stick, and something terrible was wrong with her chest. I couldn't look any more and Carrie was screaming. That started me crying. Tears got in the way, but still I could see the baby, one-and-a-half, and brother George, four-and-a-half, and they had their eyes wide open at what they saw and weren't crying a bit, too young to know what the hell.

They put Old Gramma in her room on the cot and closed the door on her and some old woman friend of hers that kept dipping a handkerchief in cold water and laying it on Old Gramma's head. They put Mama on the bed in the room where everybody was standing around and talking lower and lower until pretty soon they were just whispering.

Somebody came in with a doctor, a colored one, and he had a little black bag like they have in the movies. I don't think our family ever had a doctor come to see us before. Maybe before I was born Mama and Daddy did. I heard the

[1] *Mère du Christ:* Mother of Christ, pray for us; Help of Christians, pray.

doctor tell Mr. Purvine, that works in the same mill Daddy does, only the night shift, that he ought to set the bone, but honest to God he thought he might as well wait as he didn't want to hurt Mama if it wasn't going to make any difference.

He wasn't nearly as brisk now with his little black bag as he had been when he came in. He touched Mama's forehead a couple of times and it didn't feel good to him, I guess, because he looked tired after he did it. He held his hand on her wrist of the good arm, but I couldn't tell what this meant from his face. It mustn't have been any worse than the forehead, or maybe his face had nothing to do with what he thought and I was imagining all this from seeing the shape Mama was in. Finally he said, I'll try, and began calling for hot water and other things and pretty soon Mama was all bandaged up white.

The doctor stepped away from Mama and over to some men and women, six or seven of them now—a lot more had gone—and asked them what had happened. He didn't ask all the questions I wanted to ask—I guess he already knew some of the answers—but I did find out Mama was on a streetcar coming home from the plant—Mama works now and we're saving for a cranberry farm—when the riot broke out in that section. Mr. Purvine said he called the mill and told Daddy to come home. But Mr. Purvine said he wasn't going to work tonight himself, the way the riot was spreading and the way the coloreds were getting the worst of it.

As usual, said a man with glasses on, the Negroes ought to organize and fight the thing to a finish. The doctor frowned at that. Mr. Purvine said he didn't know. But one woman and another man said that was the right idea.

If we must die, said the man with glasses on, let it not be like hogs hunted and penned in an inglorious spot! The doctor said, Yes, we all know that, but the man with glasses on went on, because the others were listening to him, and I was glad

he did, because I was listening to him too: We must meet the
common foe; though far outnumbered, let us still be brave,
and for their thousand blows deal one death-blow! What
though before us lies the open grave? Like men we'll face
the murderous, cowardly pack, pressed to the wall, dying,
but—fighting back!

They all thought it was fine and a woman said that was
poetry and I thought if that is what it is I know what I want
to be now, a poetryman. I asked the man with glasses on if
that was his poetry, though I did not think it was for some
reason, and the men and women all looked at me like they
were surprised to see me there and like I ought not hear such
things, except the man with glasses on, and he said, No, son,
it was not his poetry, he wished it was, but it was Claude
McKay's,[2] a Negro, and I could find it in the public library.
I decided I would go to the public library when the riot was
over and it was the first time in my life I ever thought of the
public library the way I did then.

They all left about this time, except the doctor and the
old woman friend of Old Gramma's. She came out of Old
Gramma's room, and when the door opened I saw Old
Gramma lying on the cot wtih her eyes closed. The old
woman asked me if I could work a can opener and I said, Yes,
I can, and she handed me a can of vegetable soup from the
shelf. She got a meal together and us kids sat down to eat.
Not Carrie, though. She sat in our good chair with her legs
under her and her eyes closed. Mama was sleeping and the
doctor rolled up the shade at the window and looked out
while we ate. I mean brother George and the baby. I couldn't
eat. I just drank my glass of water. The old woman said, Here,
here, I hadn't ought to let good food go to waste and was

[2] *Claude McKay:* American poet, author of *Songs of Jamaica* (1912)
and *Harlem Shadows* (1922).

that any way to act at the table and I wasn't the first boy in the world to lose his mother.

I wondered was she crazy and I yelled I wasn't going to lose my mother and I looked to see and I was right. Mama was just sleeping and the doctor was there in case she needed him and everything was taken care of and—everything. The doctor didn't even turn away from the window when I yelled at the old woman and I thought at least he'd say I'd wake my mother up shouting that way, or maybe that I was right and the old woman was wrong. I got up from the table and stood by the doctor at the window. He only stayed there a minute more then and went over to feel Mama's wrist again. He did not touch her forehead this time.

Old Gramma came out of her room and said to me, Was that you raising so much cain in here, boy? I said, Yes, it was, and just when I was going to tell her what the old woman said about losing Mama I couldn't. I didn't want to hear it out loud again. I din't even want to think it in my mind. Old Gramma went over and gazed down at Mama. She turned away quickly and told the old woman, Please, I'll just have a cup of hot water, that's all, I'm so upset. Then she went over to the doctor by the window and whispered something to him and he whispered something back and it must've been only one or two words, because he was looking out the window the next moment.

Old Gramma said she'd be back in a minute and went out the door and slip-slapping down the hall. I went to the window; the evening sun was going down, and I saw Old Gramma come out the back entrance of our building. She crossed the alley and went in the back door of the grocery-store.

A lot of racket cut loose about a block up the alley. It was still empty, though. Old Gramma came out of the grocery-store with something in a brown bag. She stopped in the mid-

dle of the alley and seemed to be watching the orange evening sun going down behind the buildings. The sun got in her
hair and somehow under her skin kind of and it did a wonderful thing to her. She looked so young for a moment that I saw
Mama in her, both of them beautiful New Orleans ladies.

The racket cut loose again, nearer now, and a pack of men
came running down the alley, about three dozen whites
chasing two coloreds. One of the whites was blowing a bugle
—*tan tivvy tan tivvy tan tivvy*—like the white folks do when
they go fox-hunting in the movies or Virginia. I looked down,
quick, to see if Old Gramma had enough sense to come inside and I guess she did because she wasn't there. The two
coloreds ran between two buildings, the whites ran after them
and then the alley was quiet again. Old Gramma stepped
out and I watched her stoop and pick up the brown bag that
she had dropped before.

Another big noise made her drop it again. A whole smear
of men swarmed out of the used-car lot and came galloping
down the alley like wild buffaloes. Old Gramma scooted inside our building and the brown bag stayed in the alley. This
time I couldn't believe my eyes, I saw what I thought I'd
never see, I saw what us kids had been waiting to see ever
since the riot broke out—a white man fixing to get himself
nice and killed. A white man running—running, God Almighty, from about a million coloreds. And he was the one
with the tan-tivvy bugle too. I hoped the coloreds would do
the job up right.

The closer the white man came the worse it got for him,
because the alley comes to a dead end when it hits our building. All at once, I don't know why, I was praying for that fool
white man with the bugle to get away. But I didn't think he
had a Chinaman's chance, the way he was going now, and
maybe that's what made me pray for him.

Then he did a smart thing. He whipped the bugle over his

shoulder like you do with a horseshoe for good luck and it
hit the first colored behind him smack in the head, knocking
him out, and that slowed up the others. The white man
turned into the junkyard behind the furniture warehouse and
the Victory Ballroom. Another smart thing, if he used his
head. The space between the warehouse and the Victory is
just wide enough for a man to run through. It's a long piece
to the street, but if he made it there he'd be safe probably.

The long passageway must've looked too narrow to him,
though, because the fool came rushing around the garage
next to our building. For a moment he was the only one in
the alley. The coloreds had followed him through the junkyard and probably got themselves all tangled up in garbage
cans and rusty bed springs and ashpiles. But the white man
was a goner just the same. In a minute they'd be coming for
him for real. He'd have to run the length of the alley again to
get away and the coloreds have got the best legs.

Then Old Gramma opened our back door and saved him.

I was very glad for the white man until suddenly I remembered poor Mama all broken to pieces on the bed and then I
was sorry Old Gramma did it. The next moment I was glad
again that she did. I understood now I did not care one way
or the other about the white man. Now I was thinking of
Mama—not of myself. I did not see what difference it could
make to Mama if the white man lived or died. It only had
something to do with us and him.

Then I got hold of a very strange idea. I told myself the
trouble is somebody gets cheated or insulted or killed and
everybody else tries to make it come out even by cheating
and insulting or killing the cheaters and insulters and killers.
Only they never do. I did not think they ever would. I told
myself that I had a very big idea there and when the riot was
over I would go to the public library and sit in the reading
room and think about it. Or I would speak to Old Gramma

204 EXPLORING HIDDEN DEPTHS

about it, because it seemed like she had the same big idea and like she had had it a long time too.

The doctor was standing by me at the window all the time. He said nothing about what Old Gramma did, and now he stepped away from the window and so did I. I guess he felt the same way I did about the white man and that's why he stepped away from the window. The big idea again. He was afraid the coloreds down below would yell up at us, did we see the white man pass by. The coloreds were crazy mad all right. One of them had the white man's bugle and he banged on our door with it. I was worried Old Gramma had forgot to lock it and they might walk right in and that would be the end of the white man and the big idea.

But Old Gramma pulled another fast one. She ran out into the alley and pointed her yellow finger in about three wrong directions. In a second the alley was quiet and empty, except for Old Gramma. She walked slowly over against our building, where somebody had kicked the brown bag, and picked it up.

Old Gramma brought the white man right into our room, told him to sit down and poured herself a cup of hot water. She sipped it and said the white man could leave whenever he wanted to, but it might be better to wait a bit. The white man said he was much obliged, he hated to give us any trouble, and Oh, oh, is somebody sick over there, when he saw Mama, and that he'd just been passing by when a hundred neg—when he was attacked.

Old Gramma sipped her hot water. The doctor turned away from the window and said, Here they come again, took another look, and said, No, they're going back. He went over to Mama and held her wrist. I couldn't tell anything about her from his face. She was sleeping just the same. The doctor asked the white man, still standing, to sit down. Carrie only opened her eyes once and closed them. She hadn't changed her position in the good chair. Brother George and the baby stood in a corner with their eyes on the white man. The baby's legs buckled then—she'd only been walking about a week—and she collapsed softly to the floor. She worked her way up again without taking her eyes off the white man. He even looked funny and out of place to me in our room. I guess the man for the rent and Father Egan were the only white people come to see us since I could remember and now it was only the man for the rent since Father Egan died.

The doctor asked the white man did he work or own a business in this neighborhood. The white man said, No, glancing down at his feet, no, he just happened to be passing by when he was suddenly attacked like he said before. The doctor told Old Gramma she might wash Mama's face and neck again with warm water.

There was noise again in the alley, windows breaking and fences being pushed over. The doctor said, You could leave now, to the white man, it's a white mob this time, you'd be safe.

No, the white man said, I should say not, I wouldn't be seen with them, they're as bad as the others almost.

It is quite possible, the doctor said.

Old Gramma asked the white man if he would like a cup of tea.

Tea? No, he said, I don't drink tea, I didn't know you drank it.

I didn't know you knew her, the doctor said, looking at Old Gramma and the white man.

You colored folks, I mean, the white man said, Americans, I mean. Me, I don't drink tea, always considered it an English drink and bad for the kidneys.

The doctor did not answer. Old Gramma brought him a cup of tea.

And then Daddy came in. He ran over to Mama and fell

down on his knees like he was dead, like seeing Mama with her arm broke and her chest so pushed in killed him on the spot. He lifted his face from the bed and kissed Mama on the lips; and then, Daddy, I could see, was crying, the strongest man in the world was crying with tears in his dark eyes and coming down the side of his big hard face. Mama called him her John Henry [3] sometimes and there he was, her John Henry, the strongest man, black or white, in the whole damn world, crying.

He put his head down on the bed again. Nobody in the room moved until the baby toddled over to Daddy and patted him on the ear like she wanted to play the games those two make up with her little hands and his big ears and eyes and nose. But Daddy didn't move or say anything, if he even knew she was there, and the baby got a blank look in her eyes and walked away from Daddy and sat down, *plump*, on the floor across the room, staring at Daddy and the white man, back and forth, Daddy and the white man.

Daddy got up after a while and walked very slowly across the room and got himself a drink of water at the sink. For the first time he noticed the white man in the room. Who's he, he said, who's he? None of us said anything. Who the hell's he? Daddy wanted to know, thunder in his throat like there always is when he's extra mad or happy.

The doctor said the white man was Mr. Gorman and went over to Daddy and told him something in a low voice.

Innocent! What's he doing in this neighborhood then? Daddy said, loud as before. What's an *innocent* white man doing in this neighborhood now, answer me that! He looked at all of us in the room and none of us that knew what the white man was doing in this neighborhood wanted to explain

[3] *John Henry:* railroad builder, hero of a cycle of Negro ballads and tall tales, noted for his strength.

to Daddy. Old Gramma and the doctor and me, none of us
that knew, would tell.

I was just passing by, the white man said, as they can tell
you.

The scared way he said it almost made me laugh. Was this
a white man, I asked myself. Alongside Daddy's voice the
white man's sounded plain foolish and weak, a little old pink
tug squeaking at a big brown ocean liner about the right of
way. Daddy seemed to forget all about him and began asking
the doctor a lot of questions about Mama in a hoarse whisper
I couldn't hear very well. Daddy's face got harder and harder
and it didn't look like he'd ever crack a smile or shed a tear
or anything soft again. Just hard, it got, hard as four spikes.

Old Gramma came and stood by Daddy's side and said
she had called the priest when she was downstairs a while
ago getting some candles. She was worried that the candles
weren't blessed ones. She opened the brown bag then and
that's what was inside, two white candles. I didn't know
grocerystores carried them.

Old Gramma went to her room and took down the picture
of the Sacred Heart all bleeding and put it on the little table
by Mama's bed and set the candles in sticks on each side of
it. She lit the candles and it made the Sacred Heart, punc-
tured by the wreath of thorns, look bloodier than ever and
made me think of that song, To Jesus' Heart All Burning, the
kids sing at Our Saviour's on Sundays.

The white man went up to the doctor and said, I'm a Catholic too. But the doctor didn't say anything back, only nodded.
He probably wasn't one himself, I thought, not many of the
race are. Our family wouldn't be if Old Gramma and Mama
didn't come from New Orleans, where Catholics are thicker
than flies or Baptists.

Daddy got up from the table and said to the white man,
So help me God, mister, I'll kill you in this room if my wife

dies! The baby started crying and the doctor went to Daddy's side and turned him away from the white man and it wasn't hard to do because now Daddy was kind of limp and didn't look like he remembered anything about the white man or what he said he'd do to him if Mama . . . or anything.

I'll bet the priest won't show up, Daddy said.

The priest will come, Old Gramma said, the priest will always come when you need him, just wait. Her old lips were praying in French.

I hoped he would come like Old Gramma said, but I wasn't so sure. Some of the priests weren't much different from anybody else. They knew how to keep their necks in. Daddy said to Mama once if you only wanted to hear about social justice you could turn on the radio or go to the nearest stadium on the Fourth of July and there'd be an old white man in a new black suit saying it was a good thing and everybody ought to get some and if they'd just kick in more they might and anyway they'd be saved. One came to Our Saviour's last year and Father Egan said this is our new assistant and the next Sunday our new assistant was gone—poor health. But Daddy said he was transferred to a church in a white neighborhood because he couldn't stand to save black souls. Father Egan would've come a-flying, riot or no riot, but he was dead now and we didn't know much about the one that took his place.

Then he came, by God, the priest from Our Saviour's came to our room while the riot was going on. Old Gramma got all excited and said over and over she knew the priest would come. He was kind of young and skinny and pale, even for a white man, and he said, I'm Father Crowe, to everybody in the room and looked around to see who was who.

The doctor introduced himself and said Old Gramma was Old Gramma, Daddy was Daddy, we were the children, that was Mr. Gorman, who just was passing by, and over there was poor Mama. He missed Old Gramma's old woman friend;

I guess he didn't know what to call her. The priest went over and took a look at Mama and nodded to the doctor and they went into Old Gramma's room together. The priest had a little black bag too and he took it with him. I suppose he was getting ready to give Mama Extreme Unction.[4] I didn't think they would wake her up for Confession or Holy Communion, she was so weak and needed the rest.

Daddy got up mad as a bull from the table and said, Remember what I said, mister, to the white man.

But why me, the white man asked, just because I'm white?

Daddy looked over at Mama on the bed and said, Yeah, just because you're white, yeah, that's why . . . Old Gramma took Daddy by the arm and steered him over to the table again and he sat down.

The priest and the doctor came out of Old Gramma's room and right away the priest faced the white man, like they'd been talking about him in Old Gramma's room, and asked him why he didn't go home. The white man said he'd heard some shouting in the alley a while ago that didn't sound so good to him and he didn't think it was safe yet and that was why.

I see, the priest said.

I'm a Catholic too, Father, the white man said.

That's the trouble, the priest said.

The priest took some cotton from his little black bag, dipped his fingers in holy oil and made the sign of the cross on Mama's eyes, nose, ears, mouth, and hands, rubbing the oil off with the cotton, and said prayers in Latin all the time he was doing it.

I want you all to kneel down now, the priest said, and we'll say the rosary. But we mustn't say it too loud because she is sleeping.

[4] *Extreme Unction:* a Roman Catholic sacrament in which a priest anoints a dying person, praying for his salvation.

We all knelt down except the baby and Carrie. Carrie said she'd never kneel down to God again. Now Carrie, Old Gramma said, almost crying. She told Carrie it was for poor Mama and wouldn't Carrie kneel down if it was for poor Mama?

No! Carrie said, it must be a white God too! Then she began crying and she did kneel down after all.

Even the white man knelt down and the doctor and the old woman friend of Old Gramma's, a solid Baptist if I ever saw one, and we all said the rosary of the five sorrowful mysteries.[5]

Afterwards the white man said to the priest, Do you mind if I leave when you do, Father? The priest didn't answer and the white man said, I think I'll be leaving now, Father. I wonder if you'd be going my way?

The priest finally said, All right, all right, come along, you won't be the first one to hide behind a Roman collar.

The white man said, I'm sure I don't know what you mean by that, Father. The priest didn't hear him, I guess, or want to explain, because he went over to Mama's bed.

The priest knelt once more by Mama and said a prayer in Latin out loud and made the sign of the cross over Mama! *In nomine Patris et Filii et Spiritus Sancti.*[6] He looked closer at Mama and motioned to the doctor. The doctor stepped over to the bed, felt Mama's wrist, put his head to her chest, where it wasn't pushed in, and stood up slowly.

Daddy and all of us had been watching the doctor when the priest motioned him over and now Daddy got up from the table, kicking the chair over he got up so fast, and ran to the bed. He sank, shaking all over, to his knees, and I believe he

---

[5] *Rosary of the five sorrowful mysteries:* Roman Catholic devotion stressing meditation on the death of Jesus.

[6] *In nomine . . . :* In the name of the Father and of the Son and of the Holy Ghost.

must've been crying again, although I thought he never would again and his head was down and I couldn't see for sure.

I began to get an awful bulging pain in my stomach. The doctor left the bed and grabbed the white man by the arm and was taking him to the door when Daddy jumped up, like he knew where they were going, and said, Wait a minute, mister!

The doctor and the white man stopped at the door. Daddy walked draggily over to them and stood in front of the white man, took a deep breath, and said in the stillest kind of whisper, I wouldn't touch you. That was all. He moved slowly back to Mama's bed and his big shoulders were sagged down like I never saw them before.

Old Gramma said *Jésus!* and stumbled down on her knees by Mama. Then the awful bulging pain in my stomach exploded and I knew that Mama wasn't just sleeping now and I couldn't breathe for a long while and then when I finally could I was crying like the baby and Brother George and so was Carrie.

Understanding the Story

1. What is the meaning of the title of the story?
2. What do we slowly come to realize about the narrator? How is this knowledge imparted to us?
3. What is the setting of the story? How do you know?
4. What do we learn about the neighborhood, the family, and the family life of the narrator?
5. What is the attitude of the child toward whites? Of the white man toward the child's family? Of his father toward the white man? Of "the man with the glasses on"?

6. What do you imagine is the narrator's "very big idea"?

7. How does the narrator come to realize what is happening?

8. What inference can you draw from the observation of the narrator: "I guess the man for the rent and Father Egan were the only white people come to see us since I could remember. . . ."

*Appreciating
the Story*

1. How does having "the trouble" narrated through the eyes of a young child add to the effectiveness of the story?

2. How does the author succeed in translating the idea of social injustice into realistic and understandable terms?

3. Is the author merely reporting the thoughts of the boy who acts as narrator, or does he include his own point of view about the events of the story? Support your answer with references to the story.

4. What is gained by the vagueness of the description of the exact nature of "the trouble"?

5. How is the full extent of the tragedy that befalls the family as a result of the riot brought home to the reader?

6. How do the actions of Old Gramma, the white man, and Carrie contribute to the effectiveness of the story? Is each of them necessary to the story? Why?

The Lottery

SHIRLEY JACKSON

*Approaching
the Story . . .*

To most of us, a lottery is a game of chance in which people try to win a prize. Shirley Jackson has used the device of the lottery to weave a tale of terror. We hardly suspect this, however, when we read the innocent opening sentence: "The morning of June 27th was clear and sunny, with the fresh warmth of a full-summer day; the flowers were blossoming profusely and the grass was richly green." The author focuses on the ritual of the lottery. It begins to take on an almost religious quality. We begin to wonder whether the lottery is necessary to insure the survival of those who take part in it. We learn that the lottery had its origins in the "long ago" before any of the people now in it can remember. It has become "tradition."

"There's *always* been a lottery," the oldest man reminds the others. You will realize that the very vagueness of its beginnings, the strictness with which it is carried out, and the apparent inevitability of its result succeed in making us set aside our disbelief that such a thing could really happen.

*. . . And Keep
in Mind*

You won't be able to avoid the question, "What really is coming off here?" Others, too, demand to be answered. Why is the lottery being held? How is it possible for such a lottery to take place? What is the author trying to prove? As you read, note the ,slow and terrifying buildup to the unforgettable climax. Note how the author transforms the warmth of a summer day into a nightmare of horror. What are these seemingly pleasant townspeople *really* like? Why do they react to the lottery as they do? You will find that the answers to these questions, as stated or suggested in the story, will take you on a journey to the hidden recesses of inhumanity within us. And while the author offers no comment on the horrible proceedings, can we not provide our own and draw our own conclusions?

T HE MORNING OF June 27th was clear and sunny, with the fresh warmth of a full-summer day; the flowers were blossoming profusely and the grass was richly green. The people of the village began to gather in the square, between the post office and the bank, around ten o'clock; in some towns there were so many people that the lottery took two days and had to be started on June 26th, but in this village, where there were only about three hundred people, the whole lottery took less than two hours, so it could begin at ten o'clock in the morning and still be through in time to allow the villagers to get home for noon dinner.

The children assembled first, of course. School was recently over for the summer, and the feeling of liberty sat uneasily on most of them; they tended to gather together quietly for a while before they broke into boisterous play, and their talk was still of the classroom and the teacher, of books and reprimands. Bobby Martin had already stuffed his pockets full of stones, and the other boys soon followed his example, selecting the smoothest and roundest stones; Bobby and Harry Jones and Dickie Delacroix—the villagers pronounced this name "Dellacroy"—eventually made a great pile of stones in one corner of the square and guarded it against the raids of the other boys. The girls stood aside, talking among themselves, looking over their shoulders at the boys, and the very small children rolled in the dust or clung to the hands of their older brothers or sisters.

Soon the men began to gather, surveying their own children, speaking of planting and rain, tractors and taxes. They stood together, away from the pile of stones in the corner, and their jokes were quiet and they smiled rather than laughed. The women, wearing faded house dresses and sweaters, came shortly after their menfolk. They greeted one another and exchanged bits of gossip as they went to join their husbands. Soon the women, standing by their husbands, began to call to their children, and the children came reluctantly, having to be called four or five times. Bobby Martin ducked under his mother's grasping hand and ran, laughing, back to the pile of stones. His father spoke up sharply, and Bobby came quickly and took his place between his father and his oldest brother.

The lottery was conducted—as were the square dances, the teen-age club, the Halloween program—by Mr. Summers, who had time and energy to devote to civic activities. He was a round-faced, jovial man and he ran the coal business, and people were sorry for him, because he had no children and his wife was a scold. When he arrived in the square, carrying the black wooden box, there was a murmur of conversation among the villagers, and he waved and called, "Little late

today folks." The postmaster, Mr. Graves, followed him,
carrying a three-legged stool, and the stool was put in the
center of the square and Mr. Summers set the black box down
on it. The villagers kept their distance, leaving a space between themselves and the stool, and when Mr. Summers
said, "Some of you fellows want to give me a hand?" there
was a hesitation before two men, Mr. Martin and his oldest
son, Baxter, came forward to hold the box steady on the
stool while Mr. Summers stirred up the papers inside it.

The original paraphernalia for the lottery had been lost
long ago, and the black box now resting on the stool had been
put into use even before Old Man Warner, the oldest man
in town, was born. Mr. Summers spoke frequently to the villagers about making a new box, but no one liked to upset
even as much tradition as was represented by the black box.
There was a story that the present box had been made with
some pieces of the box that had preceded it, the one that
had been constructed when the first people settled down to
make a village here. Every year, after the lottery, Mr.
Summers began talking again about a new box, but every
year the subject was allowed to fade off without anything's
being done. The black box grew shabbier each year; by now
it was no longer completely black but splintered badly along
one side to show the original wood color, and in some places
faded or stained.

Mr. Martin and his oldest son, Baxter, held the black box
securely on the stool until Mr. Summers had stirred the papers thoroughly with his hand. Because so much of the ritual
had been forgotten or discarded, Mr. Summers had been successful in having slips of paper substituted for the chips of
wood that had been used for generations. Chips of wood, Mr.
Summers had argued, had been all very well when the village
was tiny, but now that the population was more than three
hundred and likely to keep on growing, it was necessary to

use something that would fit more easily into the black box. The night before the lottery, Mr. Summers and Mr. Graves made up the slips of paper and put them in the box, and it was then taken to the safe of Mr. Summers' coal company and locked up until Mr. Summers was ready to take it to the square next morning. The rest of the year, the box was put away, sometimes one place, sometimes another; it had spent one year in Mr. Graves's barn and another year underfoot in the post office, and sometimes it was set on a shelf in the Martin grocery and left there.

There was a great deal of fussing to be done before Mr. Summers declared the lottery open. There were the lists to make up—of heads of families, heads of households in each family, members of each household in each family. There was the proper swearing-in of Mr. Summers by the post-master, as the official of the lottery; at one time, some people remembered, there had been a recital of some sort, performed by the official of the lottery, a perfunctory, tuneless chant that had been rattled off duly each year; some people be-lieved that the official of the lottery used to stand just so when he said or sang it, others believed that he was supposed to walk among the people, but years and years ago this part of the ritual had been allowed to lapse. There had been, also, a ritual salute, which the official of the lottery had had to use in addressing each person who came up to draw from the box, but this also had changed with time, until now it was felt necessary only for the official to speak to each person ap-proaching. Mr. Summers was very good at all this; in his clean white shirt and blue jeans, with one hand resting carelessly on the black box, he seemed very proper and important as he talked interminably to Mr. Graves and the Martins.

Just as Mr. Summers finally left off talking and turned to the assembled villagers, Mrs. Hutchinson came hurriedly along the path to the square, her sweater thrown over her shoulders, and slid into place in the back of the crowd. "Clean forgot what day it was," she said to Mrs. Delacroix, who stood next to her, and they both laughed softly. "Thought my old man was out back stacking wood," Mrs. Hutchinson went on, "and then I looked out the window and the kids was gone, and then I remembered it was the twenty-seventh and came a-running." She dried her hands on her apron, and Mrs. Delacroix said, "You're in time, though. They're still talking away up there."

Mrs. Hutchinson craned her neck to see through the crowd and found her husband and children standing near the front. She tapped Mrs. Delacroix on the arm as a farewell and began to make her way through the crowd. The people separated good-humoredly to let her through; two or three people said, in voices just loud enough to be heard across the crowd, "Here comes your Missus, Hutchinson," and "Bill, she made it after all." Mrs. Hutchinson reached her husband, and Mr. Summers, who had been waiting, said cheerfully, "Thought we were going to have to get on without you, Tessie." Mrs. Hutchinson said, grinning, "Wouldn't have me leave m'dishes in the sink, now, would you, Joe?" and soft laughter ran through the crowd as the people stirred back into position after Mrs. Hutchinson's arrival.

"Well, now," Mr. Summers said soberly, "guess we better get started, get this over with, so's we can go back to work. Anybody ain't here?"

"Dunbar," several people said. "Dunbar, Dunbar."

Mr. Summers consulted his list. "Clyde Dunbar," he said. "That's right. He's broke his leg, hasn't he? Who's drawing for him?"

"Me, I guess," a woman said, and Mr. Summers turned to look at her. "Wife draws for her husband," Mr. Summers said. "Don't you have a grown boy to do it for you, Janey?" Although Mr. Summers and everyone else in the village knew the answer perfectly well, it was the business of the official of the lottery to ask such questions formally. Mr. Summers waited with an expression of polite interest while Mrs. Dunbar answered.

"Horace's not but sixteen yet," Mrs. Dunbar said regretfully. "Guess I gotta fill in for the old man this year."

"Right," Mr. Summers said. He made a note on the list he was holding. Then he asked, "Watson boy drawing this year?"

A tall boy in the crowd raised his hand. "Here," he said. "I'm drawing for m'mother and me." He blinked his eyes nervously and ducked his head as several voices in the crowd said things like "Good fellow, Jack," and "Glad to see your mother's got a man to do it."

"Well," Mr. Summers said, "guess that's everyone. Old Man Warner make it?"

"Here," a voice said, and Mr. Summers nodded.

A sudden hush fell on the crowd as Mr. Summers cleared his throat and looked at the list. "All ready?" he called. "Now, I'll read the names—heads of families first—and the men come up and take a paper out of the box. Keep the paper folded in your hand without looking at it until everyone has had a turn. Everything clear?"

The people had done it so many times that they only half listened to the directions; most of them were quiet, wetting their lips, not looking around. Then Mr. Summers raised one hand high and said, "Adams." A man disengaged himself from the crowd and came forward. "Hi, Steve," Mr. Summers said, and Mr. Adams said, "Hi Joe." They grinned at one another humorlessly and nervously. Then Mr. Adams reached into the black box and took out a folded paper. He held it firmly by one corner as he turned and went hastily back to his place in the crowd, where he stood a little apart from his family, not looking down at his hand.

"Allen," Mr. Summers said. "Anderson. . . . Bentham."

"Seems like there's no time at all between lotteries any more," Mrs. Delacroix said to Mrs. Graves in the back row. "Seems like we got through with the last one only last week."

"Time sure goes fast," Mrs Graves said.

"Clark. . . . Delacroix."

"There goes my old man," Mrs. Delacroix said. She held her breath while her husband went forward.

"Dunbar," Mr. Summers said, and Mrs. Dunbar went steadily to the box while one of the women said, "Go on, Janey," and another said, "There she goes."

"We're next," Mrs. Graves said. She watched while Mr. Graves came around from the side of the box, greeted Mr. Summers gravely, and selected a slip of paper from the box. By now, all through the crowd there were men holding the small folded papers in their large hands, turning them over and over nervously. Mrs. Dunbar and her two sons stood together, Mrs. Dunbar holding the slip of paper.

"Harburt. . . . Hutchinson."

"Get up there, Bill," Mrs. Hutchinson said, and the people near her laughed.

"Jones."

"They do say," Mr. Adams said to Old Man Warner, who stood next to him, "that over in the north village they're talking of giving up the lottery."

Old Man Warner snorted. "Pack of crazy fools," he said. "Listening to the young folks, nothing's good enough for *them*. Next thing you know, they'll be wanting to go back to living in caves, nobody work any more, live *that* way for a while. Used to be a saying about 'Lottery in June, corn be heavy soon.' First thing you know, we'd all be eating stewed chickweed and acorns. There's *always* been a lottery," he added petulantly. "Bad enough to see young Joe Summers up there joking with everybody."

"Some places have already quit lotteries," Mrs. Adams said.

"Nothing but trouble in *that*," Old Man Warner said stoutly. "Pack of young fools."

"Martin." And Bobby Martin watched his father go forward. "Overdyke.... Percy."

"I wish they'd hurry," Mrs. Dunbar said to her older son. "I wish they'd hurry."

"They're almost through," her son said.

"You get ready to run tell Dad," Mrs. Dunbar said.

Mr. Summers called his own name and then stepped forward precisely and selected a slip from the box. Then he called, "Warner."

"Seventy-seventh year I been in the lottery," Old Man Warner said as he went through the crowd. "Seventy-seventh time."

"Watson." The tall boy came awkwardly through the crowd. Someone said, "Don't be nervous, Jack," and Mr. Summers said, "Take your time, son."

"Zanini."

After that, there was a long pause, a breathless pause, until Mr. Summers, holding his slip of paper in the air, said, "All right, fellows." For a minute, no one moved, and then all the slips of paper were opened. Suddenly, all the women began to speak at once, saying, "Who is it?," "Who's got it?," "Is it the Dunbars?" "Is it the Watsons?" Then the voices began to say, "It's Hutchinson. It's Bill." "Bill Hutchinson's got it."

"Go tell your father," Mrs. Dunbar said to her older son.

People began to look around to see the Hutchinsons. Bill Hutchinson was standing quiet, staring down at the paper in his hand. Suddenly, Tessie Hutchinson shouted to Mr. Summers, "You didn't give him time enough to take any paper he wanted. I saw you. It wasn't fair!"

"Be a good sport, Tessie," Mrs. Delacroix called, and Mrs. Graves said, "All of us took the same chance."

"Shut up, Tessie," Bill Hutchinson said.

"Well, everyone," Mr. Summers said, "that was done pretty fast, and now we've got to be hurrying a little more to get done in time." He consulted his next list. "Bill," he said, "you draw for the Hutchinson family. You got any other households in the Hutchinsons?"

"There's Don and Eva," Mrs. Hutchinson yelled. "Make *them* take their chance!"

"Daughters draw with their husbands' families, Tessie," Mr. Summers said gently. "You know that as well as anyone else."

"It wasn't *fair*," Tessie said.

"I guess not, Joe," Bill Hutchinson said regretfully. "My daughter draws with her husband's family, that's only fair. And I've got no other family except the kids."

"Then, as far as drawing for families is concerned, it's you," Mr. Summers said in explanation, "and as far as drawing for households is concerned, that's you, too. Right?"

"Right," Bill Hutchinson said.

"How many kids, Bill?" Mr. Summers asked formally.

"Three," Bill Hutchinson said. "There's Bill, Jr., and Nancy, and little Dave. And Tessie and me."

"All right, then," Mr. Summers said. "Harry, you got their tickets back?"

Mr. Graves nodded and held up the slips of paper. "Put them in the box, then," Mr. Summers directed. "Take Bill's and put it in."

"I think we ought to start over," Mrs. Hutchinson said, as quietly as she could. "I tell you it wasn't *fair*. You didn't give him time enough to choose. *Every*body saw that."

Mr. Graves had selected the five slips and put them in the box, and he dropped all the papers but those onto the ground, where the breeze caught them and lifted them off.

"Listen, everybody," Mrs. Hutchinson was saying to the people around her.

"Ready, Bill?" Mr. Summers asked, and Bill Hutchinson, with one quick glance around at his wife and children, nodded.

"Remember," Mr. Summers said, "take the slips and keep them folded until each person has taken one. Harry, you help little Dave." Mr. Graves took the hand of the little boy, who came willingly with him up to the box. "Take a paper out of the box, Davy," Mr. Summers said. Davy put his hand into the box and laughed. "Take just *one* paper," Mr. Summers said. "Harry, you hold it for him." Mr. Graves took the child's hand and removed the folded paper from the tight fist and held it while little Dave stood next to him and looked up at him wonderingly.

"Nancy next," Mr. Summers said. Nancy was twelve, and her school friends breathed heavily as she went forward, switching her skirt, and took a slip daintily from the box. "Bill, Jr.," Mr. Summers said, and Billy, his face red and his feet over-large, nearly knocked the box over as he got a paper out. "Tessie," Mr. Summers said. She hesitated for a minute, looking around defiantly, and then set her lips and went up to the box. She snatched a paper out and held it behind her.

"Bill," Mr. Summers said, and Bill Hutchinson reached into the box and felt around, bringing his hand out at last with the slip of paper in it.

The crowd was quiet. A girl whispered, "I hope it's not Nancy," and the sound of the whisper reached the edges of the crowd.

"It's not the way it used to be," Old Man Warner said clearly. "People ain't the way they used to be."

"All right," Mr. Summers said. "Open the papers. Harry, you open little Dave's."

Mr. Graves opened the slip of paper and there was a general sigh through the crowd as he held it up and everyone could see that it was blank. Nancy and Bill, Jr., opened theirs at the same time, and both beamed and laughed, turning around to the crowd and holding their slips of paper above their heads.

"Tessie," Mr. Summers said. There was a pause, and then Mr. Summers looked at Bill Hutchinson, and Bill unfolded his paper and showed it. It was blank.

"It's Tessie," Mr. Summers said, and his voice was hushed. "Show us her paper, Bill."

Bill Hutchinson went over to his wife and forced the slip of paper out of her hand. It had a black spot on it, the black spot Mr. Summers had made the night before with the heavy pencil in the coal-company office. Bill Hutchinson held it up, and there was a stir in the crowd.

"All right, folks," Mr. Summers said. "Let's finish quickly."

Although the villagers had forgotten the ritual and lost the original black box, they still remembered to use stones. The pile of stones the boys had made earlier was ready; there were stones on the ground with the blowing scraps of paper that had come out of the box. Mrs. Delacroix selected a stone so large she had to pick it up with both hands and turned to Mrs. Dunbar. "Come on," she said. "Hurry up."

Mrs. Dunbar had small stones in both hands, and she said, gasping for breath, "I can't run at all. You'll have to go ahead and I'll catch up with you."

The children had stones already, and someone gave little Davy Hutchinson a few pebbles.

Tessie Hutchinson was in the center of a cleared space by now, and she held her hands out desperately as the villagers moved in on her. "It isn't fair," she said. A stone hit her on the side of the head.

Old Man Warner was saying, "Come on, come on, everyone." Steve Adams was in the front of the crowd of villagers, with Mrs. Graves beside him.

"It isn't fair, it isn't right," Mrs. Hutchinson screamed, and then they were upon her.

Understanding the Story

1. Why is the lottery being held? Give several points of view on this question as expressed by several characters in the story.
2. How does the author carefully prepare for the ending of the story?
3. Of what importance is the black box? Why is emphasis placed on strict adherence to rules?
4. What is the role of Old Man Warner?
5. What do you think is the purpose of the author in writing "The Lottery"?
6. Do you agree with Mrs. Hutchinson that the lottery isn't fair? Justify your opinion.

Appreciating the Story

1. Trace the change from matter-of-factness to terror in the mood of the story. How does the author slowly build up to the terrifying climax?
2. When do you first become aware of the nature of the lottery? How does the author make you aware?
3. What is the significance of the saying quoted by Old Man Warner, "Lottery in June, corn be heavy soon"? (You may find it helpful to do some research on *The Golden Bough* by Sir James Frazer.)
4. How does the author give the story a timeless quality?

5. Who is responsible for the tragedy this lottery
   represents? Explain your answer.
6. Would the ending have been less effective if
   Mr. Hutchinson were the victim? If one of the
   Hutchinson children were the victim? Justify
   your opinion.

Reviewing the Unit

For Comparative Study

1. Each of the stories has a victim. What is the cause of the tragedy that befalls each? How could the tragedies have been avoided?
2. What do the victims of the tragedies in these stories have in common? How does this add to the effectiveness of the stories?
3. There is no single guilty person in any of the stories. Groups of people are responsible for the human tragedies in each story. Explain how this is so.
4. Each of these stories criticizes relationships between human beings. Which story is most effective in making these criticisms? Why?
5. What hopeful signs, if any, are there in these stories that relationships between human beings can be improved? How would you take advantage of these?
6. Two of the stories are told in the first person, "A Kind of Murder" and "The Trouble". "The Lottery" is told by the author. Which method of narration appeals to you most? Why?

Building Your Vocabulary

Match the adjectives taken from "A Kind of Murder" with the words they describe in the story.

Column A	Column B
1. absurd	a. clothes
2. agonizing	b. demise
3. cordial	c. gallop
4. despairing	d. jab
5. flimsy	e. plea
6. genial	f. shriek
7. icy	g. smile
8. shambling	h. suitcase
9. unfortunate	i. voice
10. vicious	j. welcome

For Creative Writing

Use one of the following as a title for an original short story.

1. I Put My Foot in My Mouth
2. Forgive and Forget
3. A Confession
4. A Joke Gone Sour
5. Too Late . . .
6. Turn Back the Clock?
7. My Own Worst Enemy
8. A Prejudice
9. An Injury
10. Safe or Sorry?

PURSUING THE GOAL OF HAPPINESS

THE Declaration of Independence states that all men "are endowed by their Creator with certain inalienable rights; that among these are life, liberty, and the pursuit of happiness." The wording indicates that all of us have the right to look for happiness, but that happiness itself is not a right to which we are entitled at birth. Not only do all of us seek happiness, but apparently each of us has a different idea of the happiness he is pursuing.

The stories in this unit all have as their theme the meaning of happiness. They are presented in the hope that they will help you form your own idea of this goal. The characters in the stories of this unit, as well as the locales, are quite varied. You will meet a young boy in pre-Communist China, an Italian-American family from Brooklyn, and two sisters who have long been separated. They all have a different ideal of happiness.

All the stories present evidence on two aspects of the pursuit of happiness. They all have something to say about the relationship between money or material wealth and happiness. They all have something to say as well about individ-

ual responsibility in the pursuit of happiness. As
you read the stories in this unit, try to define
happiness for yourself and plan a way to seek it.
Ends and means are closely related.

Li Chang's
Million

HENRY GREGOR FELSEN

*Approaching
the Story ...*

MANY of us, in our search for happiness are unaware of the search of others for happiness. Can
we be truly content while the lives of so many
of our fellow humans are filled with misery? "Li
Chang's Million" poses this question in terms of
two people—an American pilot and a young Chinese boy.

This story takes place in Peking before it became the capital of Communist China. Not only
is Peking "the most Chinese of all China's large
cities," but it is certainly the most beautiful city
in China, with its many palaces and temples. Few
Americans visit it now, and one wonders what
has happened to all the Li Changs in the twenty-
odd years since the events of this story.

The million dollars referred to in the title of
the story really represents in the Chinese currency of that time an amount equal to about two
hundred American dollars, because of the wide-
spread inflation in the country.

*... And Keep
in Mind*

THE pilot in this story is in a position to change
the life of a boy whose name he does not even

know. As you read, determine, from what the
pilot tells us, what kind of man he is. Is he right
in his belief that he can buy happiness for the
young Chinese boy? Would making millionaires
of the Li Changs of this world both soothe our
consciences and bring happiness to them? In a
broader sense, is happiness ours to hand out, or
is it something each one of us must create for
himself?

Li Chang is not just one exploited child. He
represents all the children of this world who are
deprived of their childhood because they have to
work at an early age. The boy in this story is
Chinese. But he might be African, Latin American—or perhaps American.

I DON'T KNOW
what comes to your mind when you think about China.
Maybe you picture the way it looks on the map, or the wide
dusty plains, or the great barren mountain ranges that have
not yet been fully explored. Perhaps you think of the great
swarms of people in the cities, or pigtails, or the rickshas, or
the temples, or the rivers that teem with houseboats . . . I
always think of little Li Chang.

I am Li Chang's American friend, but he doesn't know
that. We never spoke, or even smiled, but I am his friend. I
am sure he doesn't remember me, just as I am certain I will
never forget him. Actually, I don't even know his name. I
call him Li Chang because he must have a name, and I want
to think of him as more than a small, anonymous boy in the
great bazaar in Peiping—a boy whose life I planned to change.

I had flown in to Peiping on a marine transport plane, and I was staying at the Grand Hotel de Pekin while the mechanics worked over a balky port motor. We wanted perfection out of that motor before we started back across the Pacifiic.

On the night I met Li Chang, I was bored with sightseeing, although Peiping is the most Chinese of all China's large cities, and is as Oriental as a Midwest county seat is American. I was tired of the grandeur of the Forbidden City, and fed up with the crush and noise of the Chinese City outside the Tartar wall.[1] I decided to shop—always a stimulating and strenuous activity in China.

I left the hotel and chose a ricksha from the clamoring mob of boys that swept over me as soon as I went down the front steps. I told my boy to take me to the bazaar, and settled back for the smooth ride.

As I was pulled to the bazaar, I felt that if I was not actually sitting on top of the world, I was only one step down. I had drawn my pay before flying to China, and had four hundred dollars in my pocket. Four hundred dollars American, but no less than two million dollars in the North China currency.

If there is a more wonderful feeling in this world than being in a strange, Oriental city, halfway around the world from home, with two million dollars in your pocket, I cannot imagine what it would be. True, it was two million in an inflated currency. Dinner cost two thousand dollars, gloves twenty-five thousand, a hotel room eighteen thousand a night, and a good camera went at three hundred thousand. But there is magic in the name and thought of a million dollars; no matter what the currency and despite inflation, my two million represented a small fortune. There were thousands of Chinese in Peiping who would have worked for me night and day for five years for that two million in gaudy bills.

[1] *Tartar wall:* a wall surrounding one of the parts of Peking.

It was a short ride to the bazaar, and when we arrived, I gave my boy the standard hundred dollars for the distance, ignored his cries for more and went toward the archway that was the entrance to the bazaar.

As I went in, I was surrounded by the inevitable crowd of beggars holding out their hands and asking for money in voices that ranged from the most piteous cries to cheerful shouts. The healthy-looking little beggar boys, bold as flies, crowded closest, impudently shouting, "*i mao ch'ien!*" (One dime money). Others shouted in English, the usual cry being, "No momma, no poppa, no chow [2] for t'ree day!" And one lad was crying, "No momma, no poppa, no flight pay!"

I waved them away, shouting the only Chinese expression of disapproval I knew—*pu hao*. I had been in China long enough to pass to the second stage of feeling about it. The first stage was one of shock and pity at the appalling poverty. The second, which I with my two million dollars enjoyed at the moment, was one of calloused indifference. I accepted starvation and misery as part of the scene, and thought no more about it. To me, all Chinese looked alike, and were either trying to beg or sell. As I walked into the bazaar, I don't think I even regarded them as human, but as a noisy, annoying, faceless mass. Two million dollars in one's pocket and a good meal in one's stomach can do that.

I wandered around the stalls for about two hours. I examined fur gloves and leather boots, Chinese musical instruments, kimonos, cameras, intricately carved canes, silverware and silks. Whether or not I intended to make a purchase, I haggled loudly and vehemently, in the fashion Chinese approve in a buyer, feeling all the while the wonderful sense of opulence and power the money in my pocket gave to me.

I enjoyed every moment of my slow progress, drinking in the strange Oriental atmosphere, listening to the shrill, sing-

[2] *Chow:* slang for food.

song talk, examining curious carvings and handicraft, and getting a particular satisfaction out of my blustering arguments over prices, which delighted the ever-present crowd of onlookers.

In the course of this aimless wandering, I suddenly turned down a small alley that was darker and quieter than the others. The lights overhead were less numerous, and noises fewer and softer. I was about to turn back to the clamor of the main line of stalls when my attention was caught by a shop at the very end of this little alley. There were furs exhibited in the window, and having heard that expensive furs could be had cheaply in Peiping, I went to investigate.

As I walked into the shop, a stout Chinese in a long black gown, and wearing a round black skullcap, rose to greet me. With several other men in the shop, he had been drinking tea at a small table. I indicated that I wished to examine the furs and he showed me a rack of finished coats.

I looked at the coats with a negligent—I will even say sneering air. I knew that a look of interest in any garment would cause its price to leap, and for that reason I handled the furs as though they were the shoddiest coats I had ever seen.

I looked at one a trifle longer than the others, and the bland Chinese who stood at my elbow spoke for the first time. "*Ting hao*," he said. "Very good."

"*Pu hao*," I grunted in reply. "*Ting pu hao.*"

I was positive the old rascal could speak excellent English. Most of the Chinese merchants can, but they do better business with Americans if they pretend they know no English. "It's very badly made," I said, touching the coat.

"Very well made," the Chinese insisted, slipping his hands into the sleeves of his gown. "Most excellent workmanship."

I examined the garment carelessly. "Very bad," I said,

just for the sake of argument. "See how badly it is sewn. It would be laughed at in America."

I looked up with a smirk still on my lips, hoping to discomfit the man. But he had moved, and when I looked up, I gazed into a pair of hurt, sad eyes.

Sitting across the room, behind a counter, unnoticed by me until this moment, sat a boy who looked to be no more than six or seven years of age. While the old men had been sitting around drinking tea, he had been working—and had not stopped until I had by word and action indicated my low opinion of the way the coat had been sewn.

For a moment I was completely off balance. I let the coat fall from my hand, and felt a sudden rush of shame. For the boy sat on a high stool, and before him on the counter were two squares of fur that he was sewing by hand. I walked over to him. With a small needle, he was making a line of stitches as tiny and even as could be done on any machine. It was his work I had criticized.

"Sorry, Junior," I said lightly. "I didn't mean to run down your work."

The boy looked at me in silence. He had the most hurt expression on his face I had ever caused anyone. I looked into his inky-black eyes, and noticed there were shadows under them. I noticed how his smooth little face already showed signs of the tired, resigned expression it was growing into. I noticed how his head and shoulders were already bent, and how, even when he rested, his back did not straighten. We stared at one another for a long minute—this child whose work I had sneered at and I—and then one of the men spoke to him and he bowed his head and his small fingers took up their slow, painstaking stitching again.

I turned and walked out of the shop. It was late, and the bazaar was closing. The long lines of stalls were boarded up and their owners were shuffling home. The lights were going out, and the beggars, sleeping on the sidewalk, hardly roused themselves to ask sleepily for alms as I went past. I hailed a dozing ricksha boy and rode back to the hotel. All I could see was the poverty and misery. The mystery, the romance, the spell of the Orient had been smashed by the hurt look of a child.

I went up to my room and went to bed, but I couldn't sleep. I kept thinking of the boy and feeling him on my conscience. At an age when he should have been thinking of toys, and at an hour when he should have been in bed, he was sitting behind a counter on a high stool, stitching carefully and slowly, while the long hours and hard work stole the brightness from his eyes and the youth from his body.

I felt ashamed of the way I had acted, and I wanted him to know. I wanted to go back and tell him that it was all right, that his workmanship was the best I had ever seen, and not to feel bad. I wanted to tell him that he ought not to be working, but playing—I thought of him in terms of the children of his age I knew in the States, and how he should be playing as they were, and not bending over the monotonous stitching night after night. I wanted to do anything I could to help him, and suddenly it came to me.

I was so excited I rolled out of bed and paced the floor. It was too late tonight, but the next day, as soon as the bazaar opened, I would do it. I took my wallet, opened it, and counted out half the money. Tomorrow, although he did not know it, the little boy, little . . . Li Chang, I called him suddenly, Little Li Chang would be a millionaire.

I almost shouted in my joy at that moment. I laughed, felt tears in my eyes, and thought about the look on Li Chang's face when I walked in and gave him a present of a million dollars. I didn't know what that million dollars could do for him. It wasn't a fortune. But it might be enough to rescue him from his dreary fate with that needle. It might buy him a few precious years of carefree childhood before it was gone and he had to work again. Perhaps he could afford to become a boy again. I would ask the men. I would try to buy whatever happiness I could for the little boy I had hurt that night.

I went to sleep with a light heart, impatient for the morning.

I was awakened before dawn by a hand shaking me. It was the pilot of our plane, and he was completely dressed in flying clothes. "Come on, sleepy," he grinned, "get your clothes on. The mechs have fixed the motor, and we have to be in the air at 0500. We're flying down to Tsingtao [3] to pick up a colonel, and then back to Hawaii."

"But I can't leave now," I protested. "I have something important to do. I can't . . ."

The pilot looked at his watch. "A truck is calling for us in half an hour. You can buy that souvenir next trip. We'll be making this run again next month."

As we circled over Peiping, gaining altitude, I looked down on that great walled city and wondered if Li Chang were awake. In a few hours he would be returning to those tiny, never-ending stitches. Perhaps, because of my actions the night before, he would be beaten or treated harshly. If he remembered me at all, it would be as the cause of further sorrow. And I was a thousand feet above him, with his million dollars in my pocket. Next month, the pilot had said. Next trip, Li Chang would have his money.

We flew away from Peiping and from China. When we reached Hawaii, I was ordered back to the States. I have not returned to China since, and I doubt if I shall ever go again. And Li Chang's million went very quickly in this country.

I don't know what you think about when the talk gets around to what's wrong with China. Maybe you think about

[3] *Tsingtao:* seaport in eastern China.

the lack of communications, or ancestor worship, or politics and civil war, I think of little Li Chang.

Understanding the Story

1. What important information does the narrator give us about himself? How does he describe his attitude toward the Chinese? How did that attitude develop?
2. Contrast the pilot's feeling of wealth with the poverty of the people who greet him at the bazaar.
3. How does the pilot's attitude change on his way back from the tailor shop? Why?
4. Why does the pilot keep "thinking of the boy and feeling him on his conscience"?
5. Explain the meaning of these thoughts of the pilot:
   a. "I didn't know what that million dollars could do for him ... It might buy him a few precious years of carefree childhood before it was gone ..."
   b. "I would try to buy whatever happiness I could for the little boy I had hurt that night."

Appreciating the Story

1. What is the purpose of the first paragraph of the story? How does it arouse our interest?
2. What does the second paragraph add? How does it increase suspense?
3. What idea of the pilot's character do you get from his telling of the story? Why does it seem to be an honest portrait?
4. What might have been the results for Li Chang if he had received the money the pilot

intended for him? Would the money have
solved his problem? Explain your views.

5. How does the final paragraph unify the story?
   What does the first sentence of the final paragraph refer to?

The Song
Caruso Sang

PATRICK McCALLUM

*Approaching
the Story ...*

Two generations ago, when the events of this
story take place, there was a great influx of immigrants from Southern Europe. They, like every
group that came before them to our shores,
brought skills and talents that enriched the life
of the United States. Italians brought with them
their love of music, especially opera.

This love of music is at the heart of "The Song
Caruso Sang." Enrico Caruso was considered the
greatest tenor of his day. For nearly twenty
years, he was the idol of opera lovers at the Met-
ropolitan Opera. His records are collectors' items
and are played and admired by music lovers to
this day. One of these records is the prized possession of the Esposito family, and how it affects
their lives is the subject of this story.

As You Read

THE story is related by George Washington Esposito, fourteen, the youngest member of his
family. Through his words, we are invited into
the parlor of the family to take part in their Sunday evening custom—listening to the Caruso record. What does the record mean to the family?
Find out why its possession comes to be a threat
to the family's happiness. With whom do you

agree—Dick, Enrico, and Giovanni—or Papa and George? Your answer will reveal a good deal about your own idea of happiness, because the author succeeds in making the story of this one family rich in meaning for all of us. The song Caruso sang can bring happiness to those who will but listen.

W ELL, IT'S ALL OVER NOW and everything is okay again, although not very long ago it looked like the whole Esposito family was going to break right up. That would have been pretty bad, because we're a big family—Mamma and Papa and six kids, counting Beppe, who is married now and last year made me an uncle.

My name is George Washington Esposito because I was born the day Papa became an American citizen. He was so proud that he named me after our first president. I sort of think he hoped some day I might be a president, too. But that was fourteen years ago, and so far there's been no sign of my heading in that direction.

What I want to tell you about is the record, and what happened to it and to the Espositos because of it. I know it sounds crazy when I tell you all the things that a recording of *Celeste Aida* [1] by Enrico Caruso did to us, but it's the truth, all of it.

As long as I can remember anything at all, I remember the Sunday evenings in our parlor, even when I was little and we lived on the East Side of Manhattan. It's gone on the same right here in Brooklyn, too.

The whole family was always together then—Papa and

[1] *Celeste Aida:* "Heavenly Aida," famous aria of Verdi's opera, *Aida.*

Mamma, of course, and Angelina, Beppe (now with Rosa and little Peppino), Enrico, Giovanni, Mary Alice, and me, George Washington. We last two are the only Espositos who have real American names, though Mamma calls us "Maria" and "Giorgio."

Let me tell you it was a roomful, especially when the Pezzullos from next door came over. You can imagine how we squeezed together on the horsehair sofa and filled all the chairs, the straight-backed ones with the round knobs that pressed against our spines when we sat up straight as we ought to in them, as well as the ones from the kitchen; and still some of us had to sit on the floor. But we didn't mind. What did it matter where you sat when you were listening to beautiful music? That's something to be enjoyed anywhere.

You see, Papa had this job at Sheeler's, the big music store just off Times Square. It wasn't much of a job in those days, but even if he was a janitor, it paid enough for him to take care of his family, and he could be near music. Before he came to America, Papa played the violoncello in the string quartet at the Ristorante Ricco, one of the best places to eat in Naples in case you ever go there. But after the first big war, when times got bad, Papa wrote to Uncle Guido in America, and Uncle Guido said to come over, so he and Mamma and Beppe came to New York. That was clear back in 1920.

I was telling you about Papa's job. As I said, he didn't mind being a janitor, because it meant he was where he could hear music all day. Mr. Sheeler took a liking to Papa and let him bring records home over the weekend, so we could all hear the wonderful music that Papa listened to every day at the store as he swept and mopped the floors.

So that's the way the Sunday evenings began. We had a phonograph, a second hand one that Papa got at the store real cheap; not the latest model, of course, but it had a clear tone, and that's what counts. It was my job to wind it up between records, but that's as much as Papa would let any of us do; he always changed the records himself. In all the years he brought records home only one was broken and two scratched. That's pretty good, I'd say.

We all love music. From the very beginning, even back in Italy before my oldest brother, Beppe, was born, the Esposito house had music in it. And after Mamma and Papa got to America and could afford it, there was a piano, and Angelina and Beppe took lessons. Later there was a violin for Giovanni; and Mamma, who had done some singing herself before she got married, taught Enrico to sing, because he had the best voice, and maybe just a little because his name was Enrico. As for me, I'm learning to play the piccolo in the school band.

There was more than music to our Sundays in the parlor. There was the being together, and for me that was best of all. During the week we were all running in and out of the house to and from school and work; only at supper could we be together, and then only for a little while, because Angelina had her night classes at business college, and Beppe and Giovanni were turning out for basketball at the YMCA, and Enrico practiced his singing in the bedroom with the door closed, and Mary Alice and I had our homework. So it was really only Sunday in the evening that we could gather in the parlor with lights dim and listen while Papa played the operas of Verdi and the symphonies of Beethoven.

For over an hour we would listen. Then Papa would say, "That's all tonight," and start to close down the top of the phonograph.

"But the record, Papa!" Everyone in the room chimed in. "We want to hear the record!"

Papa would look mystified, as though he didn't know what we were talking about. "The record, what record?"

"The Caruso record, Papa!" we would come back at him, everyone grinning. "You know which one we mean!"

"Ah!" He would nod as though just barely remembering. "The Caruso record." He would smile then. "Well, *bambini*,[2] if you insist." He would shake his head. "But I do not understand why you want every time this same record."

Papa knew his part in the game. He would pick up the record, the one I mentioned before, *Celeste Aïda,* from the table, where he had placed it, knowing that we would demand to hear it.

To me, it is the best recording Caruso ever made of that lovely aria of Verdi's. Maybe it's because I've heard it almost every Sunday since I can remember; maybe it's because this is the only one of its kind, since no other copies were made, and it is ours.

Well, here is how it came to be: you see, long ago Papa had known Caruso in Naples, because sometimes the great tenor would come to Ricco's for a late supper when he was singing at the San Carlo.[3] He even sang with the quartet when he felt like it—just got up in the middle of supper and sang. It was really something to hear, Papa says.

Papa had written Caruso that he and Mamma and Beppe would soon be in New York. The great man had made him promise to write if ever the Espositos came to America. He was not one to forget his old friends. If he had been, there wouldn't have been the record nor the thing that happened to us because of it.

I've heard so many times the story of Papa's meeting in New York with the man my brother Enrico was named after that now I almost feel I was there, myself, that day when Papa, following Caruso's instructions, went to the recording

[2] *Bambini:* children, Italian.
[3] *San Carlo:* famous opera house in Naples.

studio where the famous tenor was making an album of opera selections.

It was while he was singing into the big, flower-shaped horn of the recording machine that Papa entered the studio, having been permitted with the card that Caruso had sent him.

The aria was nearly over, the high clear notes of that difficult solo going onto the soft wax disc so easily. *Ay! Mamma mia!* There was a voice straight out of heaven!

He turned away from the horn as he let go of the last note, and it was then he saw Papa through the glass and waved and smiled, crying out, "*Eh, Pasqualino, cumme stai?*" [4] and even before Papa could answer that he was fine, Caruso came rushing out of the studio and embraced him joyfully. "Come!" he said in Italian—this was before Papa knew any English. "We shall hear the record and then have some lunch. A feast it shall be! A feast to welcome my old friend to his new home!" Then he laughed and embraced Papa again.

They sat down to listen to the record.

The last note of *Celeste Aida* faded away. There was a pause, then "*Eh, Pasqualino, cumme stai?*" came out of the loud-speaker as clearly as the aria just finished.

Papa said Caruso turned speechlessly and pointed his finger at Papa and then at himself in astonishment.

The engineers in the recording room had funny looks on their faces as they hurried out. "I'm afraid you'll have to do it over, Mr. Caruso," one of them said, "it'd be pretty hard to cut out that last part without ruining the music; there isn't enough of a pause between the last note of the singing and the words you spoke afterward."

Caruso shrugged his shoulders. "Okay," he said and grinned. "Then we do it over." He got up and started into the

[4] *Eh, Pasqualino, cumme stai?*: dialect for "Hey, little Pasquale, how are you?"

studio again. "I will not be long, Pasqualino," he promised. "Then we do eat."

Papa says his heart seemed to quiver and his voice would hardly come as he stopped the singer. "Enrico," he said, "what is to become of the one you just made?"

Caruso went through the motions of breaking an invisible record over his knee, grinning as he did so.

Papa nodded gravely, his voice trembling as he continued. "Enrico, may I have it?" he asked, almost in a whisper.

The tenor did not seem to understand. "You want that record, Pasqualino?" he asked. "But why? It is no good. I can make you a better one right now."

"No, no, my friend!" Papa begged. "Please, I want only that one, the one where you speak to me and call my name."

Caruso laughed and slapped Papa on the back. "Ah, now I see!" he said. "Of course you may have it! One *Celeste Aida* just for you!" And he added, "With my special autograph!"

So, nearly every Sunday since, we have heard the golden voice of Enrico Caruso singing *Celeste Aida*, then felt proud and happy as we heard this greatest tenor af all time call out joyfully to our own father, "*Eh, Pasqualino, cumme stai?*" as if he were right in our parlor with us.

You can understand now why we all thought so much of the record. It was more than just a recording of *Celeste Aida* by Enrico Caruso. Yet, I don't think I could tell you all the things it was to us. Like red wine on the table, the smell of garlic in the kitchen, early Mass on Sunday, and the sound of Neopolitan Italian being spoken, it was just part of our lives; we never knew any different. It isn't easy to explain things like that. . . .

Well, the years passed and we all grew older. The big boys began to shave and the girls to round out their figures. Beppe got married, and Angelina got a secretarial position, a good one with an import-export firm because she knew both English and Italian and was a good secretary besides.

The Sunday evenings continued through all these changes in our lives. By now Papa had a better job at Sheeler's; he didn't have to borrow records either. We saved our money through the years and bought our own. One Christmas we all put together, my brothers and sisters and I, and bought Papa and Mamma a new radio-phonograph, the best there is; they were so surprised and happy that they both cried when they saw it under the tree.

Papa's record by Caruso, though, was still the prize possession of the Espositos, and it never seemed to get scratched or worn. Of course, no one touched it but Papa, and he was very careful, playing it only once a week, and always with a new needle.

It was after that first Sunday when my sister Angelina brought Dick Mantini, her boss, home to supper and our concert afterward, that things began to change. Dick's just a young guy, but he's got a swell position in this export outfit, and Angelina is his secretary. He sure got a funny look on his face when we began our act of "The record, Papa! Let us hear the record!" Then Angelina explained what it was all about, and Dick smiled politely as Papa carefully lowered the needle onto the whirling disc.

I never saw anyone spring to life as quickly as Dick when he realized that "*Eh, Pasqualino, cumme stai?*" was on the record.

"That's terrific!" Dick exclaimed. "There's a real collector's item, I'd say. Ought to be worth a lot of money." The parlor got real quiet when he asked Papa, "Have you ever tried to sell it?"

Papa didn't seem to understand. "Sell? What do you mean, sell?"

"Why, there are people who would pay you a lot of money

for that record, Mr. Esposito; I couldn't say how much, but plenty, I'll bet. The singing alone, this being the only copy, would be worth a lot." He shook his head in amazement. "And with that business at the end, you could make a small fortune on it."

The room became awfully quiet, a different quiet from when we were listening to the music.

"Well," Papa sighed, "it's not for sale. It is mine, given by my friend Enrico Caruso. I will sell first my right arm."

Beppe, on the horsehair sofa with Rosa and Peppino, started to speak. "But, Papa," he began—only, when Papa looked in his direction he didn't finish what he started to say.

There was an atmosphere of uneasiness in the parlor that night and I had a feeling that Dick's idea would not just fade away by itself. . . .

The following Sunday, Beppe got up after we had heard the record and made a little speech. "Papa," he began, and everyone in the parlor knew what he was going to say.

"This week I have been thinking, and I have talked with Dick and with Enrico and Giovanni."

Papa sat up stiff but didn't say anything. Mamma looked as if she'd rather be out in the kitchen making *lasagne*.

"Papa," Beppe went on, "for a long time now you've dreamed of owning a little piece of land out in Jersey, where you could have a garden and grow some grapes and fruit trees. You and Mamma have worked hard, and now it is time you took life easy. You owe it to yourselves."

Papa still did not speak. Beppe looked around him like maybe he wished Enrico or Giovanni was doing the talking.

"Well, Papa," he continued, after a pause that was nearly a sigh, "we think you ought to sell the record. Dick says he knows a man who is interested in such things and probably would give you plenty of money for it. Maybe a thousand dollars, even."

We all blinked our eyes at Beppe's words. A thousand dollars! For a record? Even if it is by Caruso? Not possible! Yet I'd never seen Beppe with a more serious expression on his face. Believe me, he wasn't kidding.

Papa spoke at last. "My record is not for sale," he said quietly but firmly. "I said before, I say again, not for a thousand or five thousand. We talk about it no more." He got up and left the parlor.

Beppe and Rosa and the baby went home, and the rest of us went to bed. I thought the talk of the record was finished and, without knowing why, I was kind of relieved. Still, letting myself dream for a minute, it would be nice to have a little farm in New Jersey. We often talked about it and dreamed of our own grapes and a few apple and cherry trees. But to sell the record? Somehow, even the little farm we wanted so much didn't seem worth that sacrifice.

It was the next day, just as I was sure the matter was closed, that Beppe came to the house all excited; while we were eating supper it was.

Beppe's eyes were bright as he told Papa about the new idea. "You wouldn't even have to sell the record, Papa!" he said breathlessly. "I talked to Dick about it again today. He says he thinks you could just sell the rights to it; you'd only have to let one of the big companies borrow the record and make a copy of it. You might get even more money than from a private collector. Think of it, Papa!" He leaned clear across the table and looked into Papa's face, waiting for him to say something.

Papa kept right on eating his supper and after what seemed a long, long time, said, "I will think." But there was not even a trace of a smile on his face when he said it.

"Can I find out how to get in touch with the right party at the recording company, just in case?" Beppe asked, still leaning across the table.

Papa took another sip of wine, then nodded slowly. I could tell he wanted to forget the whole business.

Speaking of forgetting, I'd be just as glad to forget that next couple of weeks after Papa said okay to Beppe. For the first time in my memory we didn't even have the music in the parlor. You see, except for Papa and Mamma, nobody was speaking to anybody.

After Papa had agreed to Beppe's suggestion, my oldest brother contacted someone who was interested in the record and wanted to hear it. "The way they talk," Beppe explained, "I think they might give even more than a thousand for the record."

Papa finally agreed that the people from the recording company could hear the Caruso record, but they'd have to come to our house to do so; he wouldn't let the record out of the house.

It was then the unhappiness began. All my brothers and sisters, and with shame I must include myself, began thinking of the different ways we could spend the money, even before we had any idea how much it would be. Only Papa and Mamma said nothing. They were like two lost children who didn't know which way to turn; they would sit and listen to Angelina and Enrico and Giovanni and Mary Alice and me, and Beppe when he came from his house, quarreling about the money.

Giovanni wanted us to have a car, a big, new one. We'd never had a car, but he could think of all the reasons why we really needed one.

Angelina said that it would be nice to have a home out on Long Island and commute to work on the train.

Enrico thought we should all take a trip back to Italy, and he could study voice there.

Beppe and Rosa still held out for the farm in New Jersey,

as it would be a good place to bring the baby on sunny weekends.

I don't think Mary Alice and I knew what we wanted, because we changed our minds every day. All of us were guilty of stretching the amount we thought we'd get for the record to cover whatever it was we wanted. . . .

The man from the recording company was coming on Sunday evening to listen to the record and decide whether or not it was what his company wanted. By that Sunday our house was not a place to be in if you were in a good mood and wanted to stay that way. Once, when I looked into Mamma's face I could tell she'd been crying, and Papa, who was always cheerful, never smiled any more.

Mamma had insisted that everybody come to dinner that Sunday, just like always, even if we were all mad at each other.

"Such faces," Papa said with a sigh as we all sat down at the table. "Only Peppino looks happy."

The little boy laughed when he heard his name. The rest of us looked down at our plates, just as we had when we were little and Papa scolded us for fighting.

"It is over two weeks now," Papa went on, "that the boss of Angelina tells us maybe we can get much money for our record. I feel this is not good, but as to give only the use of the record does not really seem bad I say nothing."

Papa sighed and shook his head sadly. "But, *si*, it is bad, very bad. I know this now. Ever since we think to sell I watch this family, and I see it is no more a family. Before, it is happy, and this house is filled with love and much laughing. Now there are only angry faces and fighting. Always before this time I hurry home from my work at night; now I stay away."

I could hear Mamma beginning to sniffle at the other end of the table.

"Why is this?" Papa continued. "It is because of a record, a record by my dear friend Enrico Caruso which for many years brings much joy to the Espositos." His voice sounded strange, not Papa's voice at all. "Now the thing that for many years is happiness for Pasqualino Esposito is unhappiness. I ask myself can I buy with money this happiness once again, and I find the only answer is *No*."

You could almost hear the silence in the room. Finally Giovanni spoke. "But, Papa," he reminded, "you'd still have your record and the little farm in Jersey with the apples and grapes. . . .

"Apples and grapes I can buy at the fruit stand of Pezzullo," Papa interrupted. "A family I cannot buy in any place." He left the room.

Mamma got up, too, and looked at us as though to say something, but then she turned without saying it and followed Papa into the parlor and closed the door.

Beppe was the first to speak after they had gone. "Papa's right," he said. "It's all my fault."

"Your fault?" Giovanni asked.

Beppe nodded. "I insisted that Papa consider selling after he'd said he didn't want to. If only I'd—"

"Don't be stupid, Beppe!" Giovanni interrupted. "You were right to insist. You were just thinking of the good of the family. Once this is all over and the record is sold, Papa will see it is right. As you said just now, he'll have his record and the money, too."

"But the family?" Beppe asked. "Didn't you hear Papa and see his face just now? And Mamma, too? That's what made me realize it. We stand a chance of losing more than we could ever gain in dollars."

They argued on, everybody pitching in, until finally Beppe banged his fist on the table and said, "We're not going to sell the record, so what's the use of arguing?"

The others stopped talking, although Giovanni did remind Beppe that in any case it was too late to call up Mr. Kamp, the man from the recording company, and tell him not to bother to come.

I found myself awfully glad about what Beppe had said. I knew now that the last thing I wanted was for us to sell the Caruso record. If it went out of our house, then something awfully important would be gone out of our family, perhaps forever. . . .

The recording company representative, Mr. Kamp, a bald-headed little man, came on the dot of seven-thirty, just as he was supposed to. We all went into the parlor and sat down. Mr. Kamp sat alone on the horsehair sofa. The room was deadly quiet, like just before a thunderstorm.

Papa picked up the record from its place among the others on the table and put it on the turntable. It began to turn, and he lowered the needle carefully into the outside groove. His hand was shaking noticeably.

We all looked at each other in surprise. It wasn't *Celeste Aida* at all! In confusion, Papa had put on *Vesti la Giubba,*[5] instead. Both records, the big, thick kind they used to make before I was born, looked exactly alike.

Papa asked Mr. Kamp's pardon for the mistake and took *Celeste Aida* from the table and put it on the machine.

The little man from the recording company leaned forward and stared at the floor as he listened to the record. When it was finished he merely nodded and asked to hear it again.

Papa sat by the phonograph looking intently at each of us as Caruso sang of his love for Aida. Following Papa's gaze, I saw Angelina and Beppe and Enrico and Giovanni and Mary Alice all with the same worried expression, one just

[5] *Vesti la Guibba:* "Put on the mask," famous aria in Leoncavallo's opera, *I Pagliacci.*

like the next. They were not like my brothers and sisters at all, nor was this the happy time of those other Sundays.

"Best *Celeste Aida* ever recorded by Caruso, I'm convinced," Mr. Kamp said in a businesslike tone after hearing it the second time. He was the authority on Caruso for his company, he told us, and had heard all the great tenor's records, "but none quite like this." He was smiling for the first time. "That little personal touch at the end would make it a record seller, too," he told us, and laughed as though he thought he'd said something funny.

He got up off the sofa and, jamming his hands down into his pockets, paced across the parlor twice, his bald head almost glowing. He seemed very excited. "Mr. Esposito," he said in an even more businesslike tone than before, "my company will pay you five thousand dollars for all rights to the use of this recording if it's what we want, and I do not hesitate to assure you that it is." He began to explain the details.

There were little gasps all over the room. Five thousand dollars! We had never really dreamed of so much!

Papa nodded, but looked as though he weren't even listening.

It was then that Beppe stood up and told Mr. Kamp the record was not for sale.

"Sorry you had to come out to Brooklyn for nothing." Beppe apologized. "We just this afternoon decided not to sell the record or the rights to it."

Both Papa and Mamma just sat looking at Beppe as though they couldn't believe what they were hearing.

Enrico and Giovanni didn't just sit there, though. They both began talking at once, each having forgotten that it would be better for the whole family, as they'd agreed, if we didn't sell our record. I began to tremble, and wanted to speak but couldn't.

Mr. Kamp stood up, too, as Beppe, his arms folded across his chest, stood facing Enrico and Giovanni defiantly, shaking his head. "If I might get a word in here," the record-company representative said, "I would like to tell you I have been authorized to go as high as six thousand if necessary."

"Six thousand!" Enrico and Giovanni shouted together. Angelina and Mary Alice looked as though they might weaken, but Beppe stood his ground.

I'll never be able to explain, not even to myself, just how it happened, but, with a sob of "No! No!" I grabbed the record from off the table and threw it onto the floor, breaking it into a thousand pieces.

Everything in the room stopped dead-still where it was. Giovanni's hands hovered above Beppe's shoulders, where they were about to grab and shake him good. Papa's face had an expression of sorrow and joy and relief all at once as he took my hand. Mamma broke the silence sobbing and saying over and over in Italian, "Good son!" The others just stood staring at me in disbelief.

Mr. Kamp finally grabbed his hat and left, muttering to himself, "Crazy as loons, all of them!"

I ran into the kitchen, no longer able to control my sobs. The others followed, all except Beppe, and they were crying and hugging me and saying I had done the right thing, that it was the only way to bring them to their senses. Papa, his arm around my shoulder, assured me, "This is a family again, and nothing else matters."

Understanding the Story

1. What do we learn about the narrator? What does he reveal of the family life of the Espositos?

2. What does the Caruso record mean to the family? How do you know?

3. What effect does the possible sale of the record have upon the Esposito family? What does the way he would spend the money reveal about each member of the family?
4. Papa says: "I ask myself can I buy with money this happiness once again, and I find the only answer is No." Do you agree or disagree with Papa? Why?
5. "If it went out of our house, then something awfully important would be gone out of our family, perhaps forever." Define the *something* referred to.
6. Why does Mama say "Good son!" to George?

Appreciating the Story

1. Why is a record an especially suitable object for the author's purpose?
2. Does our finding out in the very first sentence, that everything turns out well take away from enjoyment of the story? Explain your opinion.
3. What is gained by having the youngest member of the family tell the story in the first person? What might have been the effect if the narrator had been Papa? Beppe?
4. What would have been gained or lost by having the story end at the point where the record is sold for the offered $6000?
5. What is the moral of the story? Is it forced on the plot or is it a natural outcome of the action? Explain your answer.

The Richer,
The Poorer

DOROTHY WEST

*Approaching
the Story . . .*

In "The Richer, The Poorer," Dorothy West
raises the universal question: *How* should we
pursue happiness? Her method is to contrast different ways that two sisters use to achieve the
same goal. Lottie and Bess become, thanks to her
treatment of them, concrete examples of what
might have been vague, abstract symbols of two
opposing attitudes toward life. On one hand, one
sister believes in preparing today for tomorrow.
On the other, the second sister believes in living
"each day as if there were no other." All of us
have had to act, at one time or another, in ac-
cordance with one or the other of these two basic
approaches to living. Should I do my housework
first or watch that television program? Should I
spend my allowance or save it for a time I might
need it more? This story will shed some surprising light on these questions.

*. . . And Keep
in Mind*

As you read the story, make clear in your own
mind the rules that guide Lottie and Bess in their
lives. Ask yourself: What are the dangers in
each? Must the pursuit of happiness be all of one

and none of the other? Must it be all work or all play? If not, why are there so many people we know who resemble either Lottie or Bess? More important than taking sides with either character is for you to work out your own attitude toward life. Should you accept Lottie's or Bess's, or should you work out your own plan in your search for happiness? This story is short and pointed. It raises many important issues. You may agree with the author's approach; you may disagree with it. But "The Richer, The Poorer" will set you to thinking about the way to achieve the purpose of your life.

O VER THE YEARS Lottie had urged Bess to prepare for her old age. Over the years Bess had lived each day as if there were no other. Now they were both past sixty, the time for summing up. Lottie had a bank account that had never grown lean. Bess had the clothes on her back, and the rest of her worldly possessions in a battered suitcase.

Lottie had hated being a child, hearing her parents' skimping and scraping. Bess had never seemed to notice. All she ever wanted was to go outside and play. She learned to skate on borrowed skates. She rode a borrowed bicycle. Lottie couldn't wait to grow up and buy herself the best of everything.

As soon as anyone would hire her, Lottie put herself to work. She minded babies, she ran errands for the old.

She never touched a penny of her money, though her child's mouth watered for ice cream and candy. But she could not bear to share with Bess, who never had anything to share with her. When the dimes began to add up to dollars, she lost her taste for sweets.

By the time she was twelve, she was clerking after school in a small variety store. Saturdays she worked as long as she was wanted. She decided to keep her money for clothes. When she entered high school, she would wear a wardrobe that neither she nor anyone else would be able to match.

But her freshman year found her unable to indulge so frivolous a whim, particularly when her admiring instructors advised her to think seriously of college. No one in her family had ever gone to college, and certainly Bess would never get there. She would show them all what she could do, if she put her mind to it.

She began to bank her money, and her bankbook became her most private and precious possession.

In her third year high she found a job in a small but expanding restaurant, where she cashiered from the busy hour until closing. In her last year high the business increased so rapidly that Lottie was faced with the choice of staying in school or working fulltime.

She made her choice easily. A job in hand was worth two in the future.

Bess had a beau in the school band, who had no other ambition except to play a horn. Lottie expected to be settled with a home and family while Bess was still waiting for Harry to earn enough to buy a marriage license.

That Bess married Harry straight out of high school was not surprising. That Lottie never married at all was not really surprising either. Two or three times she was halfway persuaded, but to give up a job that paid well for a homemaking job that paid nothing was a risk she was incapable of taking.

Bess's married life was nothing for Lottie to envy. She and

Harry lived like gypsies, Harry playing in second-rate bands all over the country, even getting himself and Bess stranded in Europe. They were often in rags and never in riches.

Bess grieved because she had no child, not having sense enough to know she was better off without one. Lottie was certainly better off without nieces and nephews to feel sorry for. Very likely Bess would have dumped them on her doorstep.

That Lottie had a doorstep they might have been left on was only because her boss, having bought a second house, offered Lottie his first house at a price so low and terms so reasonable that it would have been like losing money to refuse.

She shut off the rooms she didn't use, letting them go to rack and ruin. Since she ate her meals out, she had no food at home, and did not encourage callers, who always expected a cup of tea.

Her way of life was mean and miserly, but she did not know it. She thought she lived frugally in her middle years so that she could live in comfort and ease when she most needed peace of mind.

The years, after forty, began to race. Suddenly Lottie was sixty, and retired from her job by her boss's son, who had no sentimental feeling about keeping her on until she was ready to quit.

She made several attempts to find other employment, but her dowdy appearance made her look old and inefficient. For the first time in her life Lottie would gladly have worked for nothing, to have some place to go, something to do with her day.

Harry died abroad, in a third-rate hotel, with Bess weeping as hard as if he had left her a fortune. He had left her nothing but his horn. There wasn't even money for her passage home.

Lottie, trapped by the blood tie, knew she would not only

have to send for her sister, but take her in when she returned. It didn't seem fair that Bess should reap the harvest of Lottie's lifetime of self-denial.

It took Lottie a week to get a bedroom ready, a week of hard work and hard cash. There was everything to do, everything to replace or paint. When she was through the room looked so fresh and new that Lottie felt she deserved it more than Bess.

She would let Bess have her room, but the mattress was so lumpy, the carpet so worn, the curtains so threadbare that Lottie's conscience pricked her. She supposed she would have to redo that room, too, and went about doing it with an eagerness that she mistook for haste.

When she was through upstairs, she was shocked to see how dismal downstairs looked by comparison. She tried to ignore it, but with nowhere to go to escape it, the contrast grew more intolerable.

She worked her way from kitchen to parlor, persuading herself she was only putting the rooms to right to give herself something to do. At night she slept like a child after a long and happy day of playing house. She was having more fun than she had ever had in her life. She was living each hour for itself.

There was only a day now before Bess would arrive. Passing her gleaming mirrors, at first with vague awareness, then with painful clarity, Lottie saw herself as others saw her, and could not stand the sight.

She went on a spending spree from the specialty shops to beauty salon, emerging transformed into a woman who believed in miracles.

She was in the kitchen basting a turkey when Bess rang the bell. Her heart raced, and she wondered if the heat from the oven was responsible.

She went to the door, and Bess stood before her. Stiffly

she suffered Bess's embrace, her heart racing harder, her eyes suddenly smarting from the onrush of cold air.

"Oh, Lottie, it's good to see you," Bess said, but saying nothing about Lottie's splendid appearance. Upstairs Bess, putting down her shabby suitcase, said, "I'll sleep like a rock tonight," without a word of praise for her lovely room. At the lavish table, top-heavy with turkey, Bess said, "I'll take light and dark both," with no marveling at the size of the bird, or that there was turkey for two elderly women, one of them too poor to buy her own bread.

With the glow of good food in her stomach, Bess began to spin stories. They were rich with places and people, most of them lowly, all of them magnificent. Her face reflected her telling, the joys and sorrows of her remembering, and above all, the love she lived by that enhanced the poorest place, the humblest person.

Then it was that Lottie knew why Bess had made no mention of her finery, or the shining room, or the twelve-pound turkey. She had not even seen them. Tomorrow she would see the room as it really looked, and Lottie as she really looked, and the warmed-over turkey in its second-day glory. Tonight she saw only what she had come seeking, a place in her sister's home and heart.

She said, "That's enough about me. How have the years used you?"

"It was me who didn't use them," said Lottie wistfully. "I saved for them. I forgot the best of them would go without my ever spending a day or a dollar enjoying them. That's my life story in those few words, a life never lived.

"Now it's too near the end to try."

Bess said, "To know how much there is to know is the beginning of learning to live. Don't count the years that are left us. At our time of life it's the days that count. You've too much catching up to do to waste a minute of a waking hour feeling sorry for yourself."

Lottie grinned, a real wide open grin, "Well, to tell the truth I felt sorry for you. Maybe if I had any sense I'd feel sorry for myself, after all. I know I'm too old to kick up my heels, but I'm going to let you show me how. If I land on my head, I guess it won't matter. I feel giddy already, and I like it."

Understanding
the Story

1. Compare the two sisters, Lottie and Bess. How do their personalities differ? How do their attitudes towards life differ?
2. Explain the following statements in the story:
   a. "The years, after forty, began to race."
   b. "Now they were both past sixty, the time for summing up."
   c. "How have the years used you?
      " 'It was me who didn't use them,' said Lottie . . ."
   d. "To know how much there is to know is the beginning of learning to live."
3. Who gains more from Bess's return—Bess or Lottie? Justify your answer.
4. Explain the title. Who is "the richer"? Why? Who is "the poorer"? Why?
5. With whose idea of happiness do you agree—Lottie's or Bess's? Why? Or what idea of happiness do you have that combines elements of both?

Appreciating
the Story

1. An aphorism is a brief statement of a truth or a feeling. Find several examples of excellent aphorisms in the story.

2. How is the author able to condense an account of the lives of two persons into a short short story?

3. Half the story deals with the first sixty years of the lives of the two sisters. The other half deals only with their reunion. How might this emphasis on the reunion be justified?

4. What problems does the author face in attempting to relate the lives of two persons almost at the same time? How does she overcome them?

5. To what extent does the author's purpose in writing the story go against our accepted values? What dangers are there in following Bess's way of life?

Reviewing the Unit

For Comparative Study

1. In what important way are the pilot, Dick Mantini, and Lottie similar? Explain.
2. How might Bess have reacted to Mr. Kamp's proposition in "The Song Caruso Sang"? What might Lottie have done? Explain.
3. Explain the contrast in these statements:
   "I would try to buy whatever happiness I could for the little boy I had hurt that night." (the pilot in "Li Chang's Million")
   "I ask myself can I buy with money this happiness once again, and I find the only answer is No." (Papa in "The Song Caruso Sang")
   With which view do you agree? Why?
4. Suppose the following were the endings to the stories in this unit:
   a. Li Chang gets the million from the pilot.
   b. Bess has no sister to come back to.
   c. Beppe breaks the wrong record and the family still has the valuable Caruso record.
   What effect would these endings have had on the characters involved?
5. Form your own definition of happiness from a reading of these stories. How would you go about achieving it?
6. "Who is a rich man? He that is happy with his portion." Do you agree or disagree with this statement? Why?

Building Your Vocabulary

Write a brief paragraph about life in old China in which you use the following words that appear in "Li Chang's Million."

ancestor worship
bazaar
chow
houseboats
kimono
Oriental
pigtails
rickshas
skull cap
Tartar

For Creative Writing

Use one of the following as the ending for a short story.

1. I had used up my three wishes.
2. Man, that was happiness.
3. That was my happiest moment.
4. I got what I wanted, but I certainly had to work for it.
5. It only took a little courage.
6. Was it a happy New Year?
7. It had been another Blue Monday, or had it?
8. In spite of everything that happened, I still wasn't happy.
9. That's how I achieved my dream.
10. I had what I wanted more than anything else.

About the Authors

ASIMOV, ISAAC (1920–   ) has had three careers: as teacher (he has a doctorate from Columbia); as popularizer of science for the general public (*The Intelligent Man's Guide to Science*, 1960); and as the author of science fiction novels and short stories. His *Fantastic Voyage* was successfully made into a movie. The collection of science fiction stories, *The Martian Way, and Other Stories*, 1955, is highly recommended.

BENCHLEY, NATHANIEL (1915–   ), the eldest son of the late, famed writer-actor, Robert Benchley, has worked as a city reporter for the *New York Herald Tribune* and with *Newsweek's* drama desk. Since 1946, he has devoted himself chiefly to the writing of fiction. His stories have appeared in such magazines as *Life, Holiday, New Yorker,* and others and were collected in *A Firm Word or Two*, 1965. He has written a biography of his father and several novels among which are *The Off-Islanders* (made into the film, "The Russians Are Coming") and *Sail a Crooked Ship*.

CULVER, MONTY has taught fiction-writing at the University of Pittsburgh. Also a fine short story writer, his stories have appeared in *Atlantic* (his story "Black Water Blues" was included in *Best Short Stories of 1951: The O'Henry Awards*), *Esquire, and The Saturday Evening Post* where "The Chance of a Lifetime" was first published.

DEAL, BORDEN (1922–   ), a native of Mississippi, has lived in Mexico and Alabama. In the past years (his first story was published in 1948), he has published over one hundred short stories, five novels, and has written for movies, television, radio and the stage. He won a Guggenheim Fellowship in

1957. His works have been translated into more than twelve languages. His stories have been honored by inclusion in *Best Short Stories of 1949* and *Best Short Stories of 1962*.

FELSEN, HENRY GREGOR (1916–   ) is the author of more than thirty books, many of which have achieved great popularity with teen-agers. *Hot Rod* and *Street Rod* are two of his most popular novels. He served in the Marine Corps during World War II. His *Letters to a Son in Uniform* was syndicated nationally in newspapers in 1966. He has also written for television.

GUEST, ANNA has written stories for teen-age readers in such magazines as *Seventeen* where "Beauty Is Truth" first appeared.

HUGHES, LANGSTON (1902–1967) was one of the foremost Negro men of letters. He was an outstanding poet who took his forms and materials from Negro folk sources and who used blues and jazz rhythms effectively. He has written plays and novels and an autobiography. The best introduction to his work is *The Langston Hughes Reader*, 1958. His collections of short stories include the *Simple* volumes, *Simple Speaks His Mind*, 1950, and *Simple Stakes a Claim*, 1957. Other collections are *Laughing to Keep from Crying*, 1952, and *Something in Common and Other Stories*, 1963.

IVERSEN, WILLIAM had a turn at acting in summer stock, motion pictures, radio, and television before seriously taking up writing. After producing radio shows for the Voice of America, he published his first story in 1950, and in 1954, he stated "I took a permanent leave-of-absence from all good sense and became a full-time freelance writer." His stories and articles have appeared in such national publications as *McCall's, Holiday, Cosmopolitan, Redbook,* and *Good Housekeeping*.

JACKSON, SHIRLEY (1919–1965) was a Californian who came east to live in Vermont. Her death at 45 removed from the literary scene one of America's finest writers of intellectual horror stories. It was said that, because she wrote so frequently about ghosts and witches and magic, she used a broomstick for a pen. She wrote two humorous books of her family life, *Life Among the Savages*, 1953, and *Raising Demons*, 1957. *The Lottery or the Adventures of James Harris*, 1949, is a collection of her eerie and gruesome fantasies. *The Magic of Shirley Jackson*, edited by Stanley Edgar Hyman, 1966, is an excellent introduction to her work.

LAVIN, MARY (1912–   ) was born in Boston and raised and educated in Ireland. A member of the Irish Academy of Letters, she has won Guggenheim Fellowships twice. Her stories are frequently included in the annual collection of *Best American Short Stories*. Her first collection of stories, *Tales from Bectine Bridge*, 1942, won the James Tait Black Memorial Prize for the best fiction in the United Kingdom. *Selected Stories*, 1959, and *The Great Wave and Other Stories*, 1961, are two collections of her fine stories.

MC CALLUM, PATRICK is a short-story writer for popular magazines. "The Song Caruso Sang" first appeared in *American Magazine*.

MC CULLERS, CARSON (1917–1967) was born in Georgia, and, after "finishing high school very early," came to New York to study at Columbia and New York University. Her novels, *The Heart Is a Lonely Hunter*, 1940, (recently made into a motion picture) and *Reflections in a Golden Eye*, 1941, (also a recent movie) established her as a novelist and won her an award, 1943, from the American Academy of Arts and Letters. *The Member of the Wedding* was turned into a play which won the New York Drama Critics Award for the best American play of the year, 1950. The best introduction to her work is *The Ballad of the Sad Cafe; the Novels and Stories of Carson McCullers*, 1951.

PENTECOST, HUGH is the pseudonym of Judson Philips. Born in Massachusetts, he has been a writer since his graduation from Columbia University in 1925. He has written over two dozen mystery novels and many short stories and novelettes. His stories have appeared in many magazines, among them *Cosmopolitan* and *Ellery Queen's Mystery Magazine* to which he is a frequent contributor. He is the founder and executive producer of The Sharon Playhouse in Sharon, Connecticut, which has, as one of its purposes, the encouragement of young talent in all of the creative arts.

POWERS, J. F. (1917–   ) His short story, "Lions, Harts, Leaping Does" was selected for the *O. Henry Prize Stories of 1944*. His first collection of short stories, *Prince of Darkness and Other Stories*, 1947, established him as a major writer and *The Presence of Grace*, 1957, his second collection, confirmed this. His first novel, *Morte d' Urban*, won the National Book Award for 1963. His work has appeared in the *Best of the Best American Short Stories, 1915–1950*.

SUCKOW, RUTH (1892–1960) was born in and wrote about Iowa. Her carefuly crafted stories are realistic studies of the people of that state, particularly of German immigrants and their Americanization. Her short stories are collected in *Iowa Interiors*, 1926; *Children and Other People*, 1931; and *Some Others and Myself*, 1952, which contains seven stories and a memoir.

WEST, DOROTHY (1910–   ) attended the Columbia University School of Journalism. She edited the Negro quarterly magazines *Challenge* and *New Challenge* which published the early work of several well-known Negro writers. Her short stories have been nationally syndicated. Her novel, *The Living Is Easy*, was published in 1948.

Acknowledgments

For permission to use copyrighted material, grateful acknowledgment is made to:

Carson McCullers:

"Sucker" by Carson McCullers, Copyright © 1963 by Carson Mc-Cullers. Reprinted by permission of Robert Lantz/Candide-Donadio Literary Agency, Inc. First published in the *Saturday Evening Post*.

Holt, Rinehart and Winston, Inc.:

"A Start in Life" from *Iowa Interiors* by Ruth Suckow. Copyright © 1926 by Alfred A. Knopf, Inc. Copyright © 1954 by Ruth Suckow. Reprinted by permisison of Holt, Rinehart and Winston, Inc.

Harold Ober Asosciates Inc.:

"One Friday Morning" by Langston Hughes. Reprinted by permission of Harold Ober Associates, Inc. Copyright © 1941 by Langston Hughes. Reprinted by permission of Harold Ober Associates, Inc. Copyright © 1941 by Langston Hughes.

McGraw Hill Book Company, Inc.:

"A Firm Word or Two" by Nathaniel Benchley from *A Firm Word or Two* by Nathaniel Benchley. Copyright © 1965 by Nathaniel Benchley. McGraw-Hill Book Company. Used by permission. This selection appeared in *The New Yorker*, January 31, 1959.

McIntosh and Otis, Inc.:

"The Chance of A Lifetime" by Monty Culver. Copyright © 1966 by the Curtis Publishing Company. Appeared originally in *The Saturday Evening Post*. Reprinted by permission of McIntosh and Otis, Inc.

The Devin-Adair Company:

"The Story of the Widow's Son" by Mary Lavin, taken from *44 Irish Short Stories* edited by Devin A. Garrity. Copyright © 1955 by the Devin-Adair Company, New York. Reprinted by permission of the publisher.

Isaac Asimov:

"The Fun They Had" by Isaac Asimov. Copyright © 1967 by Quinn Publishing Co., Inc. Reprinted by permission of the author.

Paul R. Reynolds:

"The Song Caruso Sang" by Patrick McCallum. Copyright © 1956 by the author. "A Taste of Melon" by Bordon Deal. Copyright © 1962 by The Curtis Publishing Company. Reprinted by permission of Paul R. Reynolds.

Ashley Famous Agency, Inc.:
"Papa and the Bomb" by William Iversen. Copyright © 1954 by William Iversen. *Redbook Magazine.* Reprinted by permission of Ashley Famous Agency, Inc.

Brandt & Brandt:
"A Kind of Murder" by Hugh Pentecost. First published in *Ellery Queen Mystery Magazine.* © 1962 by Davis Publications, Inc.; Reprinted by permission of Brandt & Brandt.

Doubleday & Company, Inc.:
"The Trouble" copyright © 1944 by J. F. Powers. Reprinted by permission of Doubleday & Company, Inc.

Farrar, Straus & Giroux, Inc.:
"The Lottery" by Shirley Jackson, from *The Lottery* by Shirley Jackson, copyright © 1948, 1949 by Shirley Jackson. First published in *The New Yorker.*

Henry Gregor Felson:
"Li Chang's Million" by Henry Gregor Felsen © by Henry Gregor Felsen. First published in *Woman's Day.*

Dorothy West:
"The Richer, The Poorer" by Dorothy West. Reprinted by permission of the author.

The editor regrets that he has been unable to locate the author of the following story in spite of exhaustive effort:
"Beauty Is Truth" by Anna Guest.
If she or her heirs is located subsequent to publication, she is hereby entitled to due compensation.